SENTINEL OF THE SAHYADRIS

(Memories and Reflections)

E S MODAK

Originals
(an imprint of Low Price Publications)
Delhi-110052

Distributed By
D.K. Publishers Distributors (P) Ltd.
4834/24, Ansari Road, Darya Ganj,
New Delhi-110002
Phones: 3278584, 3278368, 3261465,
e-mail: dkpd@del3.vsnl.net.in
visit us at: www.dkpd.com

First Published 2001
ISBN 81-7536-224-3

Published By
Originals
(an imprint of Low Price Publications)
A-6, Nimri Commercial Centre,
Near Ashok Vihar Phase-IV,
Delhi-110052
Phones: 7401672, 7452453
e-mail: lpp@nde.vsnl.net.in
visit us at: www.lppindia.com

Printed At:
D K Fine Art Press P Ltd.
Delhi-110052

Contents

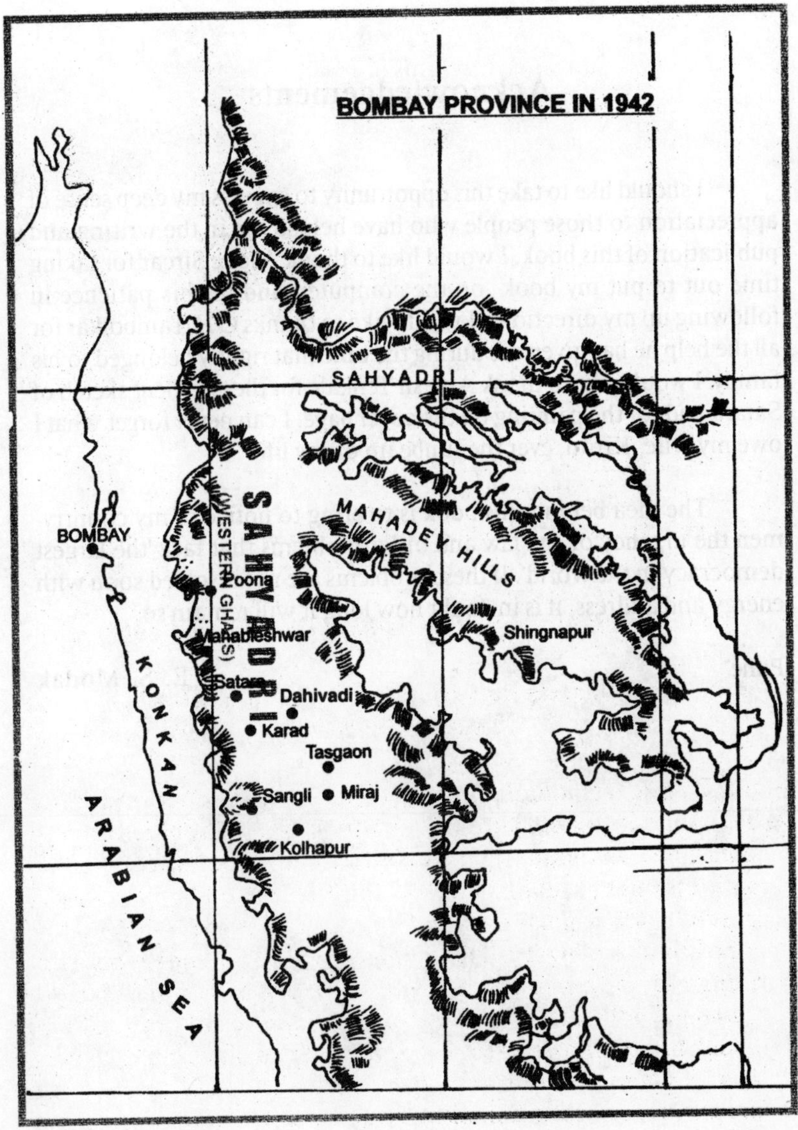

BOMBAY PROVINCE IN 1942

Acknowledgements

I should like to take this opportunity to express my deep sense of appreciation to those people who have helped me in the writing and publication of this book. I would like to thank Asoke Sircar for taking time out to put my book on the computer, and for his patience in following up my directions. I would like to thanks C H Tambolkar for all the help he has given me during the time that rightly belonged to his family. I would like to thank Antesh Tenkale for the excellent sketch of Satara and for the painting on the cover page. I can never forget what I owe my wife, Kiron, ever the sunbeam of my life.

The idea behind this book is to bring to notice of my country-men the urgency of the law and order problems that face 'the largest democracy in the world'. If these problems are not resolved soon with energy and address, it is in doubt how long it will remain so.

Pune

E. S. Modak

PROLOGUE

In the book of Ecclesiastes, or the Preacher, it is written: "To everything there is a season, and a time to every purpose under the Heaven:

A time to be born and a time to die:
A time to plant and a time to pluck up that which is planted:
A time to kill, and a time to heal, a time to break down, and a time to build up:
A time to weep, and a time to laugh:
A time to embrace, and a time to refrain from embracing:
A time to gain and a time to lose:
A time to rend and a time to sew:
A time to keep silence and a time to speak.........

I am persuaded that the time has come for me to speak about the things that have happened to me. In the matter of Kashmir, in particular, I have kept my silence too long. In the interest of truth and fair play and, in the interest of the nation, I must describe and comment on certain incidents that took place there during my tenure as the Inspector General of Police, J & K - incidents that may be far removed from the present time, but which, I do believe, have a direct bearing on what has happened since I left, and what is happening there today.

I have to say a word here about my frequent use of the dialogue in my narrative of events. My reader has every right to ask how I can possibly reproduce the actual words - especially after the lapse of so many years - during which I have not become any younger.

It is said of Thomas Wolfe, the novelist, that he had the capacity of total recall from the age of four. I read his first novel 'Look Homeward Angel' many years ago. Besides his ability to remember the past, he wrote it in soaring lyrical prose.

I do not lay claim to that kind of talent, but do aver that, very often, scenes, people, conversation, even from the remote past, leap before my eyes in vivid technicolor, and with stereophonic sound.

My words may not be exact, but the essence of what was said and done is true, as much as such things can be true. This is especially so, when they strike an emotional chord at the very centre of your being.

As for as my style of writing, such as it is, I have no gift for lyrical prose. I have, however, tried my best to write with lucidity, simplicity and, I hope, with euphony. How far I have succeeded is for my readers to judge.

CHAPTER I

IN THE SHADE OF THE SAHYADRIS

On the fifteenth of December of 1942 before noon, I took over charge as the Assistant Superintendent of Police (ASP), Eastern Division, Satara. I had completed my training as a probationer ASP in the previous year and a half at the Police Training School in Nasik. After selection by competitive examination, I joined as a probationer ASP from day one, not as a cadet. Even on the parade ground, the head drill instructor addressed you as 'Sir', though he made you run like mad in field signals, and dacoit operations. I would continue as a probationer for a year, after which I would be confirmed as an ASP provided I was found fit. Since the training was pretty thorough, an officer was hardly ever found unfit.

On that morning, I wore my Review Order (or first) uniform, and went to report to the District Superintendent of Police (DSP), a couple of rooms away from mine, on the upper floor of the solid stone building that was the DSP's office. Later, I was to find that there were few such stone buildings for the Police in the Province. The DSP was a man called Yates. He had a ruddy complexion, like most of the Europeans east of the Suez, and with flaxen hair and almost white eyebrows - he had an uncanny resemblance to the actor, Spencer Tracy. They had told me at the PTS that he was a very strict man; he was certainly strict with the ASPs, but I found out that he was not so strict with the lower subordinates. My personal clerk, Shaikh, had been his personal clerk before. He told me that once, travelling with the DSP in his car, the latter had complained about his wife's 'angular' behaviour and outlook. I had a taste of it myself, on arrival, as I had stayed with the Yates's for a few days; I got out of their house as fast as I could.

After the exchange of a few pleasantries, Yates said, " You have come to a very difficult district, make no mistake. Normally, we have more than our fair share of murders, dacoities, and what have you.

But now there is this added problem of sabotage. The Congress say they are peaceful, but the chaps who have gone underground here are definitely not. They are on the warpath: a train has been looted near Karad, an Inspection bungalow at Tasgaon was burnt, a post office was looted in Shirala and telegraph wires have been cut in half a dozen places."

"Don't we have any information about these people," I asked diffidently. "I mean the Congress workers...?"

"The regular Congress workers were arrested in August," the DSP snapped. "Do you think we would be so slack as to overlook them? No, these are all new people, young fellows by the looks of it. Apropos of that, I have some work cut out for you." He pressed the bell and asked the orderly to call somebody. A young man was ushered in. He was in his thirties, wore off-white pyjamas with a brown coat and an imitation fur cap.

"This is Babalal Tamboli, an informer of mine," Yates said. "He is a good chap and has given this list of saboteurs along with their addresses.". He handed over a piece of paper. " I want you to search them and their houses for any weapons, guns, revolvers, ammunition, etc. Get cracking, *Ek dum*."

I got up to go. "May I talk to this man for a little while in my room, Sir?" I asked.

Yates glared at me balefully. "What for?', he barked. " I have given you a job to do. Do it". I saluted and left.

I thought that these men all be residing in Satara. They could hardly be found in their houses during the daytime. How was I then to get cracking *ek dum*? I sent for my Reader sub-inspector, Yeravdekar. He was an elderly man with a quizzical expression on his face. I gave him the list and repeated what the DSP had said.

"I think I shall have to make the searches tonight, don't you think, Yeravdekar"? . I asked. "Should I go and tell the DSP that?"

He laughed,. "Excuse me, Sir, " he said. "Let me read aloud the names and addresses. First, Y.B.Chavan, Karad, which is 30 miles from Satara; Second, Nana Patil, Yede- Machindra - that is a village in Karad *taluka*; third, Vasant Patil, Padmala, Tasgaon *taluka* - 80 miles from here; fourth, G D Lad, Kundal, Sangli State - you'll have to take permission of the DSP, Sangli; Fifth, Baburao Charankar, Shirala - that's in Western Division. Some more..." It will take you at least four days to make the searches," he said.

"Anyway, shouldn't I tell the DSP about Shirala, that it is not in my jurisdiction?" I said.

Yeravdekar shook his head slowly. "I wouldn't advise that, Sir. The DSP knows that Shirala is in the Western Division., You have police powers anywhere in the district and he can send you anywhere. It's a test. Your first test, if I may say so."

"You may well say so," I said. "I am a greenhorn, am I not?"

"In this district you won't remain one for long. Go to the police stations concerned first and take the help of the local officers," he said, in answer to my unspoken question. "They know all the ropes, and the DSP expects you to do that."

I 'raided' the house of Yeshwantrao Balwantrao Chavan in Karad. (Later Chief Minister of Maharashtra, Defence Home and Finance Minister and Deputy Prime Minister of India). The house consisted of a one-room tin shed. He wore a dhoti but no shirt, and stood in a corner while we made the search. We found no incriminating evidence, no revolver, ammunition, or even pamphlets. I did not feel that there were any grounds for arresting him, merely on the say-so of Babalal Tamboli whom I was not allowed to question. I believe that that night he went underground.

I found nobody and no pistols, guns or ammunition in any of the other searches. As for the search at Kundal, I had to obtain the permission of the DSP of Sangli, a retired inspector from the Bombay police. He insisted on my taking an officer from Sangli with me before entering' his 'territory'.

This was my first introduction to *the Patri Sarkar*- the Government of the Bastinado - and my initiation into police work in Satara. Satara could not be said to be an unfamiliar place to me. I was born in Satara. My father began his service in Satara as a Deputy Collector and I had now begun my service there as an ASP. My grandfather (his father) had lived in Satara for some years after his retirement, and we, as children, used to stay with him on our way to and from Belgaum, where my father was also posted.

Nestling in the lap of the Sahyadris (which the British called the Western Ghats), Satara was once the capital of the Maratha Empire. Its old Fort, Ajinkya (Azam) Tara, lies to the south of the town, and at the end of one of the main Sahyadri spurs, jutting out on the Yenna Valley. The landscape of Satara district consists of the main Sahyadri Range on the west and southwest, and the Shikarpur- Shingnapur section of the Mahadev Hills on the east. The latter was just thirteen miles from Gondavle (Dahiwadi Police Station) where I often camped. The Sahyadri scarp, with its peaks and saddles, separates the Konkan from Satara district, while the Mahadev Range, a major offshoot of the Sahyadris, runs eastwards with several minor ranges going east and southeast. The entire landscape was peppered with forts, some built by the petty chiefs who owned the surrounding land, some by the Bijapur kings, and yet others by Shivaji and succeeding Maratha rulers.

I was not interested in the landscape or the forts, either from the scenic or historic point of view at the time, but I had, perforce, to climb them from Makrangad in the west to Mahimangad in the east, to Machindragad in the south in search of dacoits and saboteurs. True, the forts were mostly in ruins, but each of them had a room or two in habitable condition, and near them, a small tank or well with potable water - collected from the Monsoon rains, perhaps. Moreover, though I did not catch a single felon in any of them, some of them showed signs of recent occupation, and with scant information available, one could not take the risk of overlooking anything. The regular paths up to the main gates had been obliterated, and we had to force our way through fallen rocks, boulders and brambles. This was no easy task at best of times, slippery and dangerous in the rains.

It may not be out of place to give here a brief outline of the history and origin of my family name. In his book titled: ‘ Modak Kulavrittant’ (the history and the genealogy of the Modak clan), K H Khare has described how the Modaks, who originally had names like Desai, Mahajan, Oak, were Chitpavan Brahmins who had settled in a village called Panchnadi in the Dapoli *Taluka* of the Konkan. Most of them came down to Satara, Pune and Ahmednagar in search of jobs. I remember how my grandfather (at that time in Satara) would tell us that his ancestor came through the Ambenali (Fitzgerald) Ghat to

Satara, and thence went to Pune; how, along with the others, he took up the lowly job of a scrivener in the *daftars* (offices) of the Peshwas, copying out their voluminous records. The script used in writing was *Modi* - not a form of shorthand, but a flowing script in which you could write very fast, each line from left to right, without lifting the hand even once. I used to know it because it was required learning at the PTS in Nasik; many of the old records in the police stations were in *Modi.* My grandfather said there were several theories about the origin of the surname, but he found this one the most plausible - that it was given to the scribes who became adept in writing in *Modi.*

Khare's book includes the genealogy of the Modaks who became Christians up to and including the name of my older son, Ravindra. The Christian branch does not have any claim to purity of the chitpavan blood, as it was much diluted on the distaff side, but it does lay claim to the name, whatever be its origin.

Yates was soon transferred and a man called James Hobson became the DSP. He was a short, squat man with pale blue eyes and thick glasses. He told me, himself, that he had been an ordinary Tommy in the First World War. The regular officer ranks had been 'decimated' owing to the heavy bombardment on the front, and towards the end of the War, many British NCO's, emergency recruits and the like had been given commissioned ranks. These men had to be provided jobs after the war, and the overseas dominions became handy recruiting grounds - particularly, India. The cleverer and the more educated ones found places in the ICS, the others in the IPS, Forest Department and Customs. Hobson must have polished his grammar after joining the police, but he did not appreciate any help from his subordinates, the 'natives' (Indians). Yeravdekar told me that he had once corrected a draft of Hobson's, which had made the latter furious. Hobson gave him such a bad remark on his confidential record that he lost his promotion for ever. If my reader thinks that no man could be as mean as all that, I could assure him that Hobson was mean enough to do anything. I came to acquire a surfeit of personal experience of him. Unknown to me, it seems that when my father was District Magistrate of Thana, Hobson was his DSP. My father had made an adverse remark about his work, I saw this remark many years later when I was IG. Hobson had long since gone, but his confidential record was in the dormant file register, and my steno showed it to me as a curiosity. Hobson bided his time and took his revenge on me. So did Sir Charles Bristow, Adviser., Home, whom I had never seen. These two officers, at least, did not believe in the maxim that the sins of the fathers should not be visited on the children.

All ASP's had to undergo a certain routine as laid down in the Police Manual. An ASP had to inspect all the police stations and outposts in his charge. These inspections included inspections of poisons' shops and shops making fireworks. One of the items in these inspections, which I thought very important, was to interview all the policemen, examine their work and knowledge of crime and criminals, as well as law, and ask them about their grievances and complaints. I have always believed that the last was the most important. The only opportunity that a policeman had was this, when he was allowed to speak freely, and often did. Nobody else was present in the room. He might have been wanting leave to settle his land dispute at his native place. He might have wanted a transfer for his children's education. He might have a genuine complaint about his sub-inspector.

This aspect of Inspection went right up to the Inspector General of Police. After all, the very title indicates that Inspection was a very important part of the work of all superior police officers. The IG cannot inspect all districts, nor can the DIG, perhaps. But he could do them in turn. When I was the IG, and had gone to Ratnagiri for an inspection, I found that this district had not been inspected by any IG for the previous 17 years. Now, instead of an IG, there is a DG (Director General) with several 'stepneys' to assist him, in the Capital city and in the State, but it would be worth our while finding out how many districts in the State have been inspected during the year. If these inspections had been carried out regularly, the outbreaks of disaffection and mutiny that took place would never have occurred.

A probationer ASP had to investigate six important cases spread throughout the year, from the stage of FIR (First Information Report) to that of sending up the charge sheet. I thought that this was also a very useful practice. We heard of one ASP (from Sholapur) who had forgotten to do this chore, till his reader reminded him of it on the 15th of December. He sent telegrams to all his police stations not to investigate any serious crimes like murder, dacoity, etc. till he arrived on the scene and took them over for personal investigation. His DSP, Abernethy, told me that when he learnt about this order the next day, he not only cancelled it, but made a strong report against the ASP.

An ASP had to visit scenes of serious crime in his charge at once and stay at the scene to supervise the investigation. Telegrams and Express Reports (where there were no telegraph offices) were sent to the ASP about serious crime, which included murder, dacoity, highway robbery and serious rioting. To these were added the sabotage offences that began to occur with increasing frequency. Dacoities with murder, looting of trains, treasuries, post offices, cutting of telephone and telegraph wires came within the purview of serious crime, but wire-cutting offences could occur anywhere - on some hill or in some deep gully, By the time the police reached the spot, the saboteurs would have gone some thirty miles away. They would certainly never choose a place near their hometown or village, and yet, I was expected to camp somewhere near and comb the area searching for them. This was my first experience of the 'wooden' attitude of the British in ruling the country.

I sometimes used to have eight or ten express reports in my hand, and my heart would sink, when, after 15 or 20 days of chasing after murderers, dacoits and saboteurs, I would be rolling down a high hill within sight of Satara (and home), I would espy a constable standing under the shade of a tree, waving a paper in his hand - another express report. I had to take the report, turn about, and go back much of the way I had traversed.

When Yates was the DSP, the ASP of the other division (the western division) was a British officer named Michael Mountain. That summer, for two months, Yates sent him on a special ARP (Air Raid Precautions) course in the hill station of Mahabaleswar, which was in Mountain's division. As far as I know, Mountain had no occasion to make use of it till the British left India. Yates gave me the additional charge of the western division for those two months. I had to do all the paper work for that division in addition to my own. Moreover, I had to visit the scenes of all serious crimes that occurred in it. I ceased to count the express reports in my hand; their number was legion. In the Police Manual it was laid down that if the ASP had two or more ERs in hand, the DSP should relieve him of some of them. Yates did not offer to do so, nor did any DSP during my entire tenure as ASP.

My Circle Inspector was an elderly man named Borkar, who had a couple of years left to retire. He was a very sound and experienced officer and I can never forget the guidance and support he gave me. I do not know why he had been superseded; DSPs never let me see the

ACRs (annual confidential reports) of Inspectors and sub-Inspectors. I felt Borkar should have easily been given the charge of the other division for two months. It would have made the old man happy and the cost to the Government would have been very little. But, perhaps, even that amount had to be saved for 'the War Effort'.

Then there were plenty of departmental enquiries against officers. Hobson had a mania for them, and he would load me with them, even those from the other division. I had to ensure that every clause and sub-clause of the Rules was observed. 'If you don't, I shall jump on you!' he said. His favorite phrase with all officers was, "I shall jump on you". This much I shall say for Hobson - he taught me the ABC of enquiries, if the hard way. Had it not been for this background, I could never have completed the enquiry into the fire in the State Bank of India High-Rise Building, and certainly, never in five weeks.

A series of dacoities had been committed in the area of Vita and Kadegaon police stations. According to the definition in the Indian Penal Code, a robbery becomes a dacoity if it is committed by a gang of five or more persons. The District Magistrate, a man called Chambers, was worried.. He had Hobson and me in for a conference. "The depredations of this gang are causing great concern," he said. " I had a telephone from Drew (the Home Secretary). A rich `sowkar` was killed in one village. In another, a retired engineer was robbed of thirty four thousand rupees in jewellery and cash; he came crying to me." This has got to stop."

"How many dacoities have there been in the last fortnight?' Hobson asked me "All from Vita or Kadegaon. They seem to be the work of the same gang".

"Nine dacoities, Sir," I said. "Yes, they seem to be the work of a gang of Ramoshis led by Dnyanu Ramoshi. I'm trying to get the jump on them.We did get some information about their presence in a place near Vita, and followed them, but they disappeared after six miles of chase."

The Ramoshis were one of the 'criminal tribes' of the Presidency of Bombay. We had learnt in the PTS from Kennedy's then famous book that each one had a peculiar modus operandi in committing its crimes. The Ramoshis carried swords, axes, *tamanchas*(country made pistols which used twelve bore cartridges), and as in the case of Dnyanu's gang, one or two shot guns and rifles. Before committing a dacoity, they would 'case the joint' (to use an American expression). They had some informer in the village, perhaps one of the village watchmen, also Ramoshis, who would give them correct information about the rich people in the village, location of their houses, the amount of wealth they (foolishly) kept with them, and the condition of the defences - whether the police patil (the village headman) was a strong man, what kind of following and watchmen he had, and the like. After getting the all-clear signal from their informer, they would strike, announcing their arrival by throwing *apat bars* (potash bombs) which made a lot of noise, but did little damage. Before entering the house of the intended victim, they would latch the doors of the houses nearby from the outside, If the victim or any other inmates of the house showed any resistance, they would beat them senseless, wound them with their swords or daggers, or even kill them without any mercy. Ramoshis were spread all over the district. In Belgaum, they were called `Berads`.

And yet Ramoshis, as village watchmen, made fine trackers. When a dacoity was committed, it was the duty of the Ramoshis of the village to follow the tracks of the culprits to the borders of the next village, and convince the Ramoshis of the next village that the tracks were genuine. It was the duty of the watchmen of that village to follow the track to the next village. All this was done under the vigilant eye of the police. I have, myself, followed these trackers and wondered what they saw; I could see nothing. Often, these tracks ended up on the rocky side of a hill, or near the bank of a river. It was impossible to follow them any further.

The number of criminal tribes in Bombay Presidency was very large. Besides Ramoshis, there were Mangs, Lamanis, Ghantichors and Pardhis. During the days of the British, many of these people were put into wired settlements in Sholapur, Hubli and other places. They had to take written permission to leave the settlements. After Independence, one of the first acts of the Congress Government was to open these settlements and set the inmates free. I well remember the fanfare with which the Minister in charge cut the wires of these places. They maintained - and they were right - that you could not brand anybody in an independent country with the mark of Cain. But, unfortunately, the Government provided neither employment nor guidance for them. The result was that many of them have continued their criminal activities even to this day. At this time of writing, I have been reading in the papers of the dacoities committed on the outskirts of Pune by unknown persons armed with swords, axes, and sticks. The same weapons! The same modus operandi ! And the police haven't a clue. I have told anybody who has cared to listen that the gangsters seemed to be Pardhis who live in shanties by the side of the railway track, fifty or a hundred miles away. There are over 70 trains (of all kinds) coming into Pune every day. How convenient for these criminals to appear and disappear at will!

I first met head constable Pisal outside the house of a retired prostitute in a village in Vita. Dnyanu Ramoshi's gang had attacked her house the previous night. They had robbed her of all her jewellery and cash, amounting to a lakh of rupees, and, in addition, had unnecessarily beaten her. I was not favourably impressed with Pisal. He was doing plain-clothes duty - investigation. His clothes were plain, but they were not clean. He had a *pan*- stained mouth, a day's stubble on his chin and a glazed look in his eyes. I was about to reprimand him when Inspector Borkar whispered to me that he was the best investigator in my division, and had the best sources.

Pisal explained to me that Dnyanu Shahu Ramoshi's home town was Atpadi in Sangli, more than 25 miles east of Vita. "He can always take shelter there when things get too hot for him here, Sir," Pisal said. "There is nothing we can do about it."

"What about the Sangli police? Won't they help?" I asked Borkar. None of these States' police will help, Sir", he said. "Neither the police from Sangli, nor Aundh, nor Miraj, junior or senior; why should they? At a lower level at any rate they're paid by these dacoits. At a higher level, they create all sorts of difficulties, Aundh in particular. And their villages are all mixed up with ours. What's the word, I beg your pardon?"

"Enclaves, " I said. "Yes, I've seen it on the map.

"They kick up a big shindy, if we make any searches and arrests in their territory, as you will soon find out", Borkar said. "They want us to first inform them, take their PSI, and then enter their villages, by which time the culprits escape."

A few days later, while I was in a village at the foot of a hill, looking at a telegraph wire that had been cut. Pisal came in hot haste, panting and sweating. He said," Sir, Dnyamu's gang has been sighted on top of the hill. Let's follow."

"Good luck for me," I said. "Yes, I think we sighted him all right - that's what I have learnt from other sources, also. But he was far away. Can't you get a really good source through whom we can catch him unawares?"

"My informants are keeping a close watch on Dnyanu's movements", he said. "I have told several of these Ramoshi watchmen."

"We know their limits, Pisal," I said. "I don't mean people like them. Can't you contact an actual member of his gang? I'd like to meet him and get his willingness to help. I would then instruct him on what he should do,"

Pisal's eyes gleamed. For a moment they lost their habitual glaze. "I'll try hardly, Sir", he said.

"Don't tell anyone about it, not even your sub-inspector. Not anybody", I Said Pisal shook his head vigorously, gave his usual sloppy salute and shuffled out of the room.

I did not hear anything from Pisal for a fortnight. Then one morning at six, when I was sipping a cup of tea on the veranda of my cottage, ready in my uniform to go on parade, my orderly came and told me that head constable Pisal of Vita police station was waiting outside and wanted to see me. Pisal came in looking dirtier than ever. He said that he had got a lift in a truck at night after walking five miles. "I am succeeding, Sir", he said. With great difficulty, I was able to make him sit on a chair opposite and sip a cup of tea, which he gratefully did, slurping tea from the saucer.

"Tell me about it," I said.

"I have contacted a member of the gang," he replied. "His name is Lakshya Ramoshi. He is willing to work for us and take instructions from you. He knows about the reward of a thousand rupees offered by the Government for Dnyanu's capture."

"Where and when do I meet him ?" I asked.

"The place will be somewhere near Tadsar, Sir" he said. "I shall let you know the date and time by wire. But Lakshya insists that you come alone. If there is any police party with you, he will simply not appear."

I nodded and asked Pisal to see me again in the afternoon.

Later, at 10 o'clock I went to see Hobson in the office with Pisal's service sheet. I gave him a succinct account of my talks to date with Pisal.

Hobson smiled at me in disbelief. "Do you expect me to swallow all this balderdash? ", he said. "In my entire career I have never come across a member of a gang willing to work for the police. You have been reading too many detective novels instead of working," he said.

I could feel the hot flush rising in my neck. I stood up, saluted and began to walk away, when the DSP called me back. "Don't get so het up, young fellow," he said. " I won't dampen your enthusiasm. Sit down. You want to learn things the hard way, so be it."

"I have been learning things the hard way ever since I came to Satara, Sir," I said. The sarcasm was lost on him.

Hobson's large, pale blue eyes stared at me through his horn-rimmed glasses. He said,"Tell you what. You can meet this man, but you must take an armed party of one-three with you". (One head constable and three constables). I didn't argue. "Sir," I said. "If we succeed in getting Dnyanu and his gang, could I promise Pisal a promotion on your behalf? I mean, in view of his record?" I gave him Pisal's sheet. I again stood up to go.

He glanced at it. "Well, you can hardly call him a good man," he said, handing it back to me.

"Unfortunately, Sir, good men don't seem to have good sources", I said. "I can give him a reward of up to Rs.30.00 and a GST" (Good Service Ticket), Hobson said.

"What's the use of GST to him, Sir. It will be too late for him to do any good. As for the money, if as you think, he's mixed up with criminals, he could get thirty times that amount from Dnyanu." I got up to go.

"Wait", said Hobson. "It's only the IG who can give the promotion in a case of this kind. He had phoned me only last week from Poona about Dnyanu and his depredations. I think I can persuade him to give it".

"May I make a promise to Pisal on your behalf, Sir?" I asked.

"Yes", said Hobson. "You can".

Ten days later I got a telegram from Pisal as follows: RENDEZVIS ARRANGED STOP MEET ME TADSAR TOMORROW 2 AM SHARP.

I drove that night to Tadsar in my car with my driver, Bashir, beside me. Kadegaon is 42 miles from Satara and Tadsar is 4 miles from there. I had decided to ignore the DSP's injunction to take a police party with me either from the HQ or from Kadegaon police station. I slowed down and stopped near the Inamdar's *wada*. The whole village was asleep. I got down and asked Bashir to wait in the car. The time was 5 minutes after 2 AM. If I did not return by 5 AM, he was to inform the PSI at Kadegaon.

Pisal, who had been sitting on the ota of a big banyan tree in front of the *wada*, came up to me. I went alone on foot with Pisal on the track to Devarashtra, a small village perched on top of a hill, 7 miles from Tadsar. (Devarashtra happened to be the native village of Mr. Y.B.Chavan). We did not switch on our torches so as not to attract attention. We could see faintly with the aid of the crescent moon. I followed Pisal, who was sure of foot and walked fast in spite of his dissolute ways. After a couple of miles Pisal turned into a field and we walked up a further furlong. Sometimes when my foot slipped on the way, Pisal held me firmly by the shoulder. At last we came to a well in the field beside which stood a *neem* tree. I could make out the shadow of someone sitting under it. The man got up when we approached and touched my feet.

"This is Lakshya," Pisal said.

A month later, I got another telegram from Pisal: PROGRAMME ARRANGED STOP MEET ME VITA. I showed it to Hobson. "Go ahead, " he said,"And best of luck!"

The next day two covered bullock carts set out from the Inspection Bungalow at Vita. After travelling on the main road for six miles, they took the track on the left to a village named Shelakbav. To any people on the road, the carts might have appeared to contain a marriage party. There were eight persons inside the carts, including two 'women'. There were, besides me, the PSI of Vita, Shinde, Pisal and an armed party. My inspector, Borkar, was in the second cart.

When we went on the track leading to the village, a light drizzle had started. Pisal took the opportunity to draw the curtain across the front of the cart. An old man was returning from the bazaar to Shelakbav with his family. "Where are you from, strangers?" he asked "and whither bound?"

Pisal acted as our spokesman. "We are from Khatav," he said. "Marriage party. Seeing a prospective bride."

"From which family?" asked the curious villager.

"From Patil family," Pisal said. It was a safe name, one of the most common. "Know them?"

"Who doesn't?" the man said. "They are very rich and have a big house. It must be their daughter, Sita. The girl is nubile and quite comely."

"So is our boy," said Pisal, pointing to me. Pisal turned his head to make it clear that he was in no mood for further conversation. The man took the hint and moved away.

We were now passing through the bed of a nullah. The drizzle had become a downpour. The old man and his family took shelter under a tree. He decided to give us some parting advice. "You're lucky you came through before the rain has really started, friends," he shouted. Within an hour this nullah will become a raging torrent. It practically surrounds our village, and you would have been cut off. Do come and visit us. Though we have a small house, you'll be welcome. We're at the other end of the lane from the big house you are visiting."

Pisal gave an appropriate reply and the carts moved forward. When we came to the outskirts of the village, we were met by a lookout from the gang. Normally, he would have alerted them about the presence of strangers. But on this occasion he was working for Lakshya, which meant for me. He whispered to Pisal, "The gang's in Lakshya's hut." The carts were directed right up to Lakshya's hut in the Ramoshiwada. I jumped down, revolver drawn and cocked, and entered the hut, PSI Shinde beside me also with drawn revolver. An armed HC was behind me with his rifle at the ready. Seven of the dacoits, including Lakshya, were sitting on the earthen floor, chewing *paan* or smoking *bidis.* Obviously, they had just finished their meals. The man siting in front picked up his *tamancha.* He was leaning on a wooden post behind him; I fired one foot above his head and the bullet embedded itself in the wood. Dnyanu (for it was he) dropped the pistol as if it was red hot. By this time the other members of the posse had entered the hut. The dacoits offered no resistance when they were handcuffed and roped.

We went to the '*chavadi*' with the prisoners. Borkar spoke to the police patil (village headman) who had arrived there by this time. "Sir," he said to me " the PP says that the nullah will not be fordable for several hours. We might be able to wade through it after a couple of hours from the west side. I am sending for the police bus from Vita to meet us at Wangi, which is four miles away." He again spoke to the PP. "The PP says that in the meantime we can rest; he is bringing some refreshments." We soon had cups of hot tea and thick chappatis, which I dunked in the tea. It felt like food for the gods.

After two hours, the whole party left for Wangi. We had to wade through the nullah, which was waist deep in water. We surrounded our prisoners and went through, holding our guns and ammunition above our heads. By the time I got out, I was soaking wet, my teeth chattering in the cold wind that blew with the rain. Someone threw a blanket round my shoulders. The bus was waiting at Wangi and we drove to Vita. I sent off a telegram to Hobson and went to the Inspection Bungalow, utterly exhausted, but triumphant. I toweled myself, drew on my pajamas, and sank into the cot. Within minutes I was fast asleep.

Lakshya had been "arrested" along with the rest of the gang in order to avert suspicion. He was released after ten days and got his reward in due course. I had asked Pisal to enjoin upon him not to splurge his money, and to be circumspect in his talk. Dnyanu's brother was still at large. He was not present at Shelakav as he had gone to Atpadi on some work. I learnt that in a drunken bout Lakshya boasted about what he had done. A month later, Dnyanu's brother and two of his friends caught Lakshya alone and cut off his leg. I was eventually able to get a compensation of Rs.1000/= sanctioned for Lakshya. With this amount, together with the Rs.1000/= sanctioned to him as a reward earlier, Lakshya was able to buy an artificial leg in Poona and a small farm in Shelakbav. He was reasonably happy.

I was not. I had made a report to the DSP about the entire episode and requested him to promote Pisal to the grade of *Jemadar*. A month later, I got a shock when I opened the district police gazette and found that Pisal had been given a reward of thirty rupees and a GST. There was no mention of a promotion. I rushed to Hobson, the gazette in my hand.

"Sir," I said, " there must be some mistake. Pisal..." Hobson looked up from his work. "Ah, Modak", he said. "I was about to call you. The IG (N P A Smith) Is pleased with your work" (Not even a D.O. to me. That much for man-management.)

"Thank you, Sir", I said. "But what about Pisal? Where is his promotion?"

" I am sorry about that, but I'm afraid that it can't be helped," Hobson said. I have spoken to the IG about it, but he says he can't give the HC a promotion in view of his bad record. It might encourage delinquency."

I said," Sir, I promised him on your assurance that he'd get the promotion. How can I look him in the face?"

" You have to learn a lot about the police, young fellow," Hobson said. " I don't think what Pisal has done is all that outstanding. Such types are two a penny."

"Are they, indeed", I said. Then in desperation, "Sir, can I not meet the IG and explain things to him?"

"Meet the IG? You? When I'm the DSP? Above my head.Are you out of your mind? That's enough! The matter is closed..."

I saluted and left. I was to learn through much bitter experience that because of the semi-military nature of the police department, I had no alternative but to suffer fools gladly.(In the police department, there were many such, and the IAS took full advantage of this fact.)

(In my first novel, and in a short story, based on this true incident, I gave Dnyanu the name, 'Mhatarba' because I liked the sound of it. There was, in fact, an ex-dacoit named Mhatarba, who used to hang around Kadegaon police station. The PSI of Kadegaon had told me that Mhatarba was his *khabri* (informer). Pisal once said that the information that Mhatarba gave was very little, and that he used to take money from both the sides to eke out a tolerable existence.)

CHAPTER II

THE PATRI SARKAR OR THE GOVERNMENT OF THE BASTINADO

One morning I got a telegram from the PSI of Tasgaon that a major dacoity had taken place at Kupwad, a large village with a police outpost. The gangsters had stolen jewellery and cash worth one and a half lakhs of Rupees. Besides this, the sowkar (rich merchant of the village) had been severely beaten. I showed it to the DSP, and left *ek dum* for Kupwad. Kupwad was 85 miles from Satara . It was five miles off the Sangli-Miraj road. The whole of the outpost area was an enclave between the States of Sangli and Miraj. As I had found by this time, very little help would be forthcoming from the police of the States. The gangsters could easily have taken shelter in the towns of Sangli or Miraj.

I left my car in the precincts of Willingdon College, and went on foot to Kupwad. The facts of the case that I got from the police officers were be repeated again and again: the pattern was the same - only the specific details were different.

The gangsters were fifteen in number. They carried between them a rifle, two shot guns, spears, swords and jemmies. The village watchman recognized Pandu Ramoshi, a notorious dacoit operating in the southern part of Satara, but he was not the leader. Their leader was a young man in his early twenties. He wore khaki shorts and a sola topee. He had a whistle and all the other gangsters jumped to his commands. They first went to the house of the sowkar, Durgadas, and dragged him, half asleep to the chavadi. Some of them remained behind and broke open his safe. Besides jewellery and a large amount of cash Durgadas had kept in his safe the title deeds to several plots of land that the farmers had mortgaged to him. I was to find such broken safes in many large and medium-sized villages where the saboteurs struck.

All the male villagers were assembled in front of the chavadi. The leader made a short speech in which he said that they had come to destroy the enemies of the poor. The poor had no reason to fear them; they were working for the independence of the country from the foreign yoke. He collected all the title deeds and IOUs which the gangsters had brought from the safe, and made a bonfire of them.

The leader then said that he would administer such a punishment to the sowkar that it would dissuade, not only him, but also other like-minded persons from harrassing the poor villagers. They tied Durgadas's feet together, and put a stick between his legs. They up-ended him, and two of them held on to the stick, one at each end. The third man then took a lathi and began to systematically beat the sowkar on the soles of his feet. Durgadas at first coughed and spluttered, and then began to scream. The beating and the screaming went on and on. At last his screams ended; he had fainted. His feet were a mass of flesh and blood. They threw him down on the floor.

The leader drew two short, sharp blasts on his whistle. All the gangsters collected round him. Some of them were loaded with the loot, which they had put in *thailies* - cloth bags, which they had brought with them. The leader again blew on his whistle. They all shouted:'Mahatma Gandhi ki Jai! Vande Mataram'! and melted unto the darkness

A head-constable and a constable were in charge of the outpost. I asked them where they were at the time. They said they had both gone on beat duty to other villages.

We questioned the police patil and the watchman. Apart from the fact that one of them had recognized Pandu Ramoshi, no one had a clue. He also said that the two others besides him were Ramoshis, but the rest were not. He said they seemed to be 'political' people. I took all the routine steps that were necessary. Borkar went to enlist the 'help' of the police from Sangli and Miraj. He reported that they had made routine promises.

While I was questioning all the witnesses, speaking to Durgadas on his sick bed, I had noticed two young plain-clothes PCs hanging on the outskirts, grinning at me whenever I glanced in their direction. I had learnt from the PSI of Tasgaon that they were from the LIB (Local Crime Branch), and always came for crimes with political overtones.

They were to become familiar figures to me in the months and years to come. That night, in the chavadi after dinner, I was sitting at a little table, catching up with my office work, when my cook said that the two LIB PCs wanted to see me. They came up, saluted, and grinned wider than ever; I learnt that it had become a sort of trademark. They told me that their names were Mohite and Ganeshkar, and that they had been asked to work on information about one of the saboteurs from Babalal Tamboli's list."Which one?" I asked. "A young man called Vasant Patil". (He was the same person who later became Vasantdada Patil, Chief Minister of Maharashtra, Governor of Rajasthan.)

"Was he the leader in this case?" I asked.

"I am almost sure that he was,"Mohite said. "He comes from a village named Padmala in Tasgaon police station"

"Please go there, and see what you can discover," I said."By the way, did you know Babalal Tamboli?"

"We did, Sir," Ganeshkar said. "I had taken him to my PSI (LIB), who in turn, took him to Yates Saheb."

"What has happened to him? Can't he help?" I said.

"The saboteurs sent him a message that they'd kill him, if they got him," Ganeshkar said,"So he's run off to Bombay. I understand he's got a job there in some factory".

The DSP had sent me a memo that the IG had called a conference of all police officers at Satara the next day, and that I should report at the office at 11 a.m.

There was one other reason - a personal one - why I wanted to return to Satara. I had asked for, and got seven days' casual leave. I wanted to go to Bombay. I had earlier met a young lady there who had done me the honour of agreeing to accept my offer to marry her. She was coming with her father all the way from Calcutta, for a formal engagement in my parent's house.

The IG of Bombay Province, NPA Smith, was a tall ruddy Englishman with a bulbous nose and deep, penetrating eyes looking through a pair of gold-rimmed glasses. He was said to have tremendous powers of concentration and a quick grasp of problems. Within a year and a half he was promoted to the highest police job in India, that of the Director of the Intelligence Bureau.

In fifteen minutes he made it clear to all of us present that he would brook no nonsense. He began with Karad police station, the heaviest in crime, and started going through the crime register, case by case. The sub-inspector in charge was a man called Walawalker. He soon showed that had produced 'results', (though, as Borkar often told me, his methods were questionable). In case after case, especially property offences like dacoity, house- breaking and theft, he showed that he had detected them, and caught some culprits. Smith (the IG) had no time to see that when in an offence, the stolen property was worth Rs.20000, Rs.6000 was recovered, the rest of it divided between Walawalker and the other criminals most of whom were still at large.

The IG said he was particularly concerned with the new kind of sabotage crimes that were being committed in Satara. All officers of the rank of sub-inspector and above attended the IG's conference. Several officers from the Crime Branch of the State CID were also present. They were working independently of the district police; so far as I knew, they had not caught anybody.

The IG gave us the tongue-lashing of a lifetime. 'These saboteurs are not professional dacoits'" he stormed. "They are *chokras* out of school and college. Callow youths! Instead of your chasing them, you allow them to lead you a merry dance. You have to be on their tails all the time, yes, all the time. How far can they go?"

He cross-examined me closely on the Kupwad dacoity, which was the most recent sabotage case. "This man, Durgadas, might be a bounder, but what right has anybody to take the Law into his own hands? What a horrible beating he's been given! I'm told that he'll be hospitalised for six months. Whose writ runs in this district, anyway? That of the British Sarkar, or that of the *Patri Sarkar*, or whatever they call themselves?"

He brushed aside the difficulties that some of us put forward, including the attitude of the Princely States,"Let them kick up a row," he said. "You must press on."

I felt the effect of this lecture the next morning on the parade ground. I was going to take my seven days' leave after breakfast. I had packed up a few things, and was to go by car to Bombay.

Hobson called me from the other end of the parade ground." Ah, Modak," he said, "about your casual leave. I'm afraid it's off. The IG has ordered that you must go back to Kupwad and stay there for six months, if necessary, till you catch this man, Vasant Patil."

My heart sank. "B-but Sir," I babbled. "The girl who had agreed to marry me is coming for the engagement to Bombay with her father from Calcutta, all the way! The date for the engagement has been fixed. Many relatives and friends have been invited for the party. There's no guarantee that this saboteur or any of the others will be caught, even in six months. And why am I alone to be blamed? What about the old hands here? What about the State CID?"

"Orders are orders." Hobson said

"Very well, Sir" I said. "It's not the case that I am not going on a prolonged holiday to Mahabaleshwar at the expense of the Government like mountain. I shall put in an application to the Government for four month's leave. Let the IG refuse that, also."

I saluted, turned about, and began to march off, when Hobson called me back. "Not so hasty, young fellow!" he said. "I tell you what. On my own, in spite of the IG's order, I'll give you three days leave. How's that?"

"Thank you, Sir," I said. "I'll take it. One day to drive to Bombay; another to drive back; and the third for the engagement."(For my wedding, which took place later in the year, I asked for two months leave; I got fifteen days)

In Bombay, after the engagement, I as strolling, hand in hand with my fiancée, Kiron, daughter of Mr. N N Sen Gupta. I described the situation in Satara to her as briefly as I could. "I'm afraid you won't see much of me when you come there," I said. "My life seems to be one long chase - after either dacoits or saboteurs."

"I'm prepared for it," she said, pressing my hand. "You know, of course, that my father was a former terrorist in Bengal. Isn't it strange that I should be marrying a man whose job is to catch terrorists? Would it make any difference to you career?"

"Would what make any difference?" I asked.

"This. I mean my father having been a terrorist. You know, he threw a bomb at the deputy police commissioner of Calcutta, Chatterjee. It missed him, but killed a police constable."

"That's all ancient history." I said. "Much water has flown in the Hooghly since then. And what's the worst that they can do to me? Transfer me? I shall be delighted if they do."

"My father says Satara is the land of Shivaji." Kiron said. "In the *anushilan* movement, they were all great admirers of Shivaji. Shivaji built many forts, we read in our history books."

"I should know," I said feelingly. "I had to climb up to quite a few of them. But enough of this serious talk. No one can deny the fact that you are a very beautiful woman."

"My father says that beauty is but skin-deep," she said. (I'm going to hear a lot of her father's sayings, I thought.) Aloud I said, "I'll settle for that!"

N.P.A. (afterwards Sir Norman) Smith was considered by many police officers (both British and Indian) to be one of the ablest police officers that the Indian Police ever produced. His main qualities were said to be his tremendous powers of concentration and his grasp of detail. It was said that he could size up a problem within minutes, and give a clear and prompt decision.

Smith's superior, Shillidy, who left India long before I joined the police, did not think so. He had not only superseded Smith, but also made him DSP of Alibag, a district given to junior officers on their first promotion. Strangely enough, it was the Congress Government which had first 'discovered' his outstanding qualities. K.M.Munshi was the Home Minister in Bombay in 1937. He was so impressed by some of the reports that N.P.A. Smith made, and by his personality, that he made him Joint Secretary in the Home Department, something unheard of in those days.

The Congress Government thought that Smith had repaid their gesture with base ingratitude. They thought that it was at his suggestion (when he became the I G) that the leaders were arrested at the Gowalia Tank maidan on 9th August 1942 ; he was present on the spot when the arrests were made. Maybe he was doing his duty but, as the sequel will show, the action seems to have made as much of an adverse impression on his mind, as on theirs.

I have been one of the few who never had a high opinion of N P A Smith. It was not due to his treatment of me. On the contrary I found that he had appreciated my work. I just felt that he never understood the ground realities of the situation in Satara. He never asked me, even once, for my views on the subject - nor did any of the other senior officers for that matter. What the British needed at that time in Bombay as I G was a man like Sir William Sleeman ('Thugee' Sleeman)[1]. Unfortunately for the British, no such man was forthcoming.

Lord Wavell, who was Viceroy when Smith was the Director of the Intelligence Bureau (DIB), had this to say about him: " Smith, D I B, gave a most gloomy forecast of the law and order situation, said he considered the country ripe for serious trouble, thought that the Constituent Assembly would be made the instrument for a coup de'tat by Congress, which would declare the Constituent Assembly to be a sovereign body.and set it up as a parallel Government. I wonder how far his judgment is sound!"

Wavell was a pretty shrewd judge of character as ' The Viceroy's Journal' shows. He should have acted on it and sacked Smith immediately.

Shillidy was right after all!

In anticipation of arrests after the 'Quit India' resolution, the members of the radical wing of the Congress, the Congress Socialist Party had already gone underground. They began a campaign of sabotage of communications with the object of hampering the war effort. The two districts most affected in India were Satara in Bombay, and Arrah, in Bihar. The leaders directing the movements were Achyut Patwardhan in Satara and Jai Praksh Narain in Bihar. I doubt if Patwardhan ever visited Satara, but he directed it brilliantly from Poona and Bombay. In Satara they organized six or seven gangs, all coming under the cognomen of *Patri Sarkar* - the Government of the Bastinado.

1. Major General Sir W H Sleeman was called 'Thugee' Sleeman in admiration, because it was under his dynamic leadership that Thuggery was wiped out in India.

The term 'Bastinado' is of Italian origin. Mussolini's Fascists used it against their opponents with doses of castor oil added. The *patri sarkar* omitted the castor oil (perhaps it was in short supply) but they followed the rest of the procedure with scrupulous attention to detail..

This procedure, the result of which I saw in Kupwad, was repeated ad nauseum all over the district. The villagers were happy. They got their lands back and no longer worried about their loans; the moneylenders had no records left to prove anything. And why should they give any information to the police? Especially when police informers began to be killed (not just beaten) with sickening regularity?

Hobson once made the two SDO's (sub-divisional officers), ASP's or Deputy SP's organize two large beats in the affected areas. S G Pradhan had come in Mountain's place. At he end of the operation, we reported to Hobson, who was sitting in the Karad Inspection Bungalow, that we had found nothing. He visited a couple of the large villages, and asked us to round up all the villagers in front of the *chavadi.* He held up a ten-rupee note and said, "Tell them that I'll give them 500 of these if they help the police catch Vasant Patil or Nana Patil." We told them. I observed the faces of some of the men; they were openly smiling. Could he not understand, I wondered? Which of these villagers would be willing to risk almost certain death for the prospect of winning 5,000 rupees? Or, 10,000 or any higher sum?

It then dawned on me that Hobson regarded the entire operation (or all operations to catch the dacoits or criminals)as a chase or *shikar.* The criminals could easily be flushed out, and pointing them out was a routine for the lower ranks. (Even dumb animals, like dogs could be trained to become pointers on hunting trips in the jungles). I could understand this attitude on the part of Hobson; he was a former British Tommy in the ranks. But I had discovered that the best of them - India's top policeman, N P A Smith - had the same mind-set.

I was, therefore, not a little surprised when Hobson called me some weeks later and said,"Modak, do you think you'll be able to work the same trick again? "

"What trick, Sir? I said. " As far as I know, I have not played any trick on anybody."

"Don't get me wrong," he said. I don't mean to disparage. I had a phone call from Sir Charles Bristow (Adviser, Home). The Government is beginning to get rattled about the saboteurs. Couldn't you get an informer like that man Lakshya?"

"Informers can only be got through the lower ranks, " I said. "And they won't work for 30 rupees and a G S T, I'm afraid. They all want promotions, not petty sums of money."

"I am sorry about Pisal," Hobson said. "But he had a bad record and even the IG couldn't go against the rules. I tell you what. If you can get an informer through a HC or a PC, provided he has a clean sheet, I can promise you that I'll get him a promotion."

"I don't know if they will have any faith in me after what happened to Pisal," I said, "But I'll try hardly as Pisal used to say".

I called the grinning duo, PC's Mohite and Ganeshker to my house one night. I explained to them the situation. I asked them to leave everything else and work on Vasant Patil's gang. They were to try and get an informer in the gang. The DSP had promised to give them both promotions. (In the meantime, I had taken their service sheets to Hobson. Their records were good, but one had put in only 8 years service, and the other, 6. Normally, a promotion was given after 15 years. I had taken the police manual with me, and I showed Hobson the rule that said that the IG could give promotion out of turn in an outstanding case, on the recommendation of the SP and the Range DIG).

"I'll speak to the IG and the DIG," Hobson promised.

I reminded Hobson about it a couple of days later. He said,"I was about to call you. Yes, you can go ahead with your project. The IG has agreed to promote them if they help you catch Vasant Patil. You'll be glad to hear that the IG is specially sending Bill Moore Gilbert to deal with the saboteurs. He'll take all the weight on his broad shoulders." He looked out of his window. "Do you see that hill?"

"The Ajinkya -Tara Fort? I said."Of course!"

Bill could climb that hill from the side within ten minutes, you know."

"Why would he want to do that, Sir?" I asked. "There's a regular road going up to the Fort."

"You don't understand," he said. "When he starts chasing the saboteurs, they won't stand a chance."

(Catching a criminal or spy to the British was always a chase. James Bond and his fast cars. In the meantime, the KGB had moles operating right inside their organizations.)

After some days Mohite and Ganeshker came to see me. They said that they were unable to get any member of the gang to work for the police. In fact, they were not able even to meet any member of the gang. "They are a closely knit and fanatical outfit," Mohite said. "Besides, the result of exposure is too awful to contemplate. No amount of reward would be worth it."

I was disappointed. "I'll tell the SP," I said. "You've done your best."

Mohite grinned. "I have been able to get a man who has some contact with Vasant Patil," he said.

I sat up with a jerk. "Who is he, and how does he happen to be in touch with Vasant Patil?" I asked.

"He is a school teacher from a village named Vadgaon under Tasgaon police station. His name is Mahind - Vishnu Bhau Mahind. It seems he and Vasant Patil were classmates in school in Padmala," Mohite said.

I said," The main questions are: would he be willing to do the job, and will he have the guts to see it through?"

"We think he might, Sir," Ganeshker said. "You must meet him and then decide for yourself.

"What's his age?, I asked.

"27 or 28", Mohite said. "No doubt he's only a school master, but so are many of the saboteurs in this district"

"If that's the case, why hasn't he joined the gang"?

He said that Vasant Patil has urged him many times to join his gang, but he has refused to do so."

"Why?, I asked".

"He says it's a question of principles. He's a Gandhian, and does not believe in violence, however noble the ends might be. But that has not prevented him from giving shelter to Vasant Patil. After all, Patil and his gang claim they are fighting for the country. It seems that Mahind took part in the previous Satyagraha movement of Mahatma Gandhi when he was in his teens, and was in the Belgaum jail for one year."

"When can I meet him and where?"

"Anywhere, but Vadgaon," Mohite said.

"How about Sangli City?", I said, "in a tea shop ?"

It was arranged that I would meet them on the day fixed, three miles outside Sangli, where I would leave my car. They would bring a spare bicycle for me. What about my attire? Mohite was of my size and build, and he brought me a spare set of mufti, freshly washed and pressed.

We were all drinking tea in a small restaurant in Sangli, a fortnight later. There was some *puri bhaji* also on the table. The customers who were at the other tables looked at us curiously. Ganeshkar wore a turban and a dhoti.

Mahind Master was a small, thin man with bright grey eyes. After a great deal of palaver, he, at last agreed to work for me.I said to him," I want you to win the complete confidence of the gang before we act. How will you do it?"

Mahind Master was quick on the uptake. "There is only one way." He said. "For three or four months I shall have to go with them and take part in their offences. I agree that winning their confidence is absolutely necessary. Vasant does not even sleep in the same place for one night. He changes it once, sometimes twice. Then they keep a watch on each other. In fact, when I join the gang, it will be very difficult for me even to contact these two."

"I see," I said. "Who is the brain behind all this *patri sarkar*?"

"From what I have heard, it is Achyutrao Patwardhan."

"Has he ever come to Satara to direct them?" I asked.

"I have no idea, frankly", he said. "Sir, I have one condition before I start work".

"What's that", I asked.

"I must have a revolver."

"How can I give you a licenced revolver?, I said. "The SP sahib will never agree to it."

"Then get me an unlicenced weapon," he said.

"Where can I get it?" I said helplessly. "Why do you want it?"

"To protect myself against these very gangsters if they come to know what I'm doing. My life is at stake, Sir, not yours. No pistol, no work."

On that note we parted.

I saw clearly that unless I supplied Mahind with either a revolver or a pistol, he would never agree to join the gang. I explained the position to Hobson. I asked him (a little nervously) whether we could give him a revolver from the stock in police headquarters.

"Give your so-called informer, a ha'penny, tuppenny man, a police revolver?" Hobson exclaimed. "Have you taken leave of your senses? He may well join the saboteurs and use the weapon against us. I shall become the laughing stock of the whole police force. No way."

He refuses to work without a weapon," I said. "Suppose I get him an unlicensed handgun, will you agree to my giving it to him?"

"What you suggest is all against the rules," Hobson said.

"Please to remember, Sir, this is like a boxing bout in which the Queensberry Rules do not apply."

"Are there unlicensed weapons doing the rounds in Satara?" Hobson asked."You ought to have seized them all. You ought."

"None that I know of," I said. "I propose to get it from outside."

Hobson thought for a long moment. He tapped at the papers on his desk with his glasses. "A letter from Bristow and another from the IG, yes, you can go ahead," he said slowly. "Don't mention it to the DM, or anyone else."

"I won't" I promised. I shall not detain my reader with a review of all the steps I took to get the revolver. All I can say is that the entire transaction eventually cost me six hundred Rupees, not a small sum, considering my starting pay of Rupees 350 with an annual increment of Rupees 25. This much of glory for the Indian (Imperial) Police! The SP of every district has a sum of money under the Secret Service Fund to be used at his discretion. I requested Hobson in vain to reimburse my expenses from this fund. He absolutely refused to do it.

To continue with the narrative, Mahind Master joined the gang, and for the ensuing month, took part in all their operations. He would somehow keep in touch with Mohite or Ganeshker, and they would report to me faithfully whatever he told them. They would go on bicycle a distance of 50 miles, sometimes, to meet him. Travelling by bus would have aroused suspicion.

The Miraj railway rest house was in British territory (as was Miraj Junction station). All around it was the area of Miraj (Senior). I used to often camp there whenever I had work nearby. I sometimes went to the Miraj railway refreshment room for a change of fare. The lunch or dinner was the same: it consisted of mutton cutlets with green peas, potato chips, and caramel custard - my favourite dessert. One day, when I was having lunch there, the railway sub-inspector, Talekar, informed me that the DIG CID, O'Gormon, was camping in the bungalow.

I went to the bungalow and paid my respects. "I have been reading your diaries and I am most interested in the activities of the *patri sarkar*,

" he said. (ASP's were required to maintain diaries of all the work they had done. The first copy went to the SP, two others went to the Range DIG and the DIG CID).

F W O'Gormon (Freddie O'Gormon) was an outstanding officer in the Indian Police. He had been awarded the King's Police Medal and two bars for gallantry. I was flattered that he was interested in the work of a humble ASP.

"Is there no clue about this Vasant Patil? He asked. "I believe he is from these parts and moves around here."

I explained to him the difficulties encountered by the police, and asked his permission to describe what I was doing with the aid of Mahind Master.He seemed to be most interested, and we talked for about an hour. That was the most that any senior officer had given me, and I was delighted. O'Gormon wished me luck before I left. (Unfortunately, in spite of his three medals for gallantry, he was no Sleeman.)

On the Saturday following, Mohite and Ganeshkar both came to my house at night. "Mahind Master has told us that Vasant Patil will definitely be in Sangli next week," Mohite said. "We want you to camp in the Miraj bungalow from Sunday."

On Sunday I went to the railway bungalow, prepared to camp there for a week, if necessary. I had taken an armed party of 1 and 3. The head-constable was a short, wiry young man named Gaikwad. I had asked Borkar to be there, and he had come. Another officer whom I had asked to be on call was sub-inspector Talekar of the railway police. The railway police had their own superintendent, and were not under the SP Satara. So much the better, I thought. The less the district police know about what I was doing the better.

I had spent four days in the rest house at Miraj. I had decided that none of us would, as much as, show his face outside the compound of the bungalow. I began to appreciate what a prison would be like. However, I had taken a few books with me. The Shakespeare volume, of course, and 'The Grand Rebel' by Dennis Kincaid- a biography of Shivaji.

On the fifth night, Mohite came to the Rest House. He told me that Vasant Patil was coming to Sangli the next morning, and that he would stay there for the night. As usual, he would change the house in which he was sleeping, twice, or even thrice. It would not be possible to give information the previous day of where, exactly, he would be. I called Borkar, and we decided that we would wait in a field on the outskirts of the city. We would all wear disguises. Mohite would be with us in the beginning so that he would know where to report when Mahind gave him VP's exact location.

At about nine that night, we gathered in the field after going to the city in two's and three's. We were eleven in all. Since rifles would have been conspicuous, we carried pistols, bayonets and knives. We all sat down in the field and waited. Borkar had thoughtfully brought a cloth satchel full of groundnuts, *shev and murmura*, which we ate with relish, At about one in the morning, Mohite reported that he had, somehow, lost touch with Mahind, and that the raid was off for the night. It was a tired and dispirited party that returned to the Miraj Rest House. I began to feel that, maybe, I had relied too much on the capacity of my informer to work out the plan. I could imagine Hobson's mocking smile. Yes. It had now become obvious that Mahind Master didn't have the guts to carry out such a daring plan. Now my problem was how to get back the revolver. After stringing along the two PCs and they were, after all, only PCs, he might become a full-fledged member of the gang and use the revolver against us. Hobson would never forgive me. The entire responsibility for the operation was mine; Borkar knew nothing about it; the railway sub-inspector, Talekar, had come because I had called him. He knew nothing, either.

My head had barely touched the pillow, when Bashir woke me up and said that Mohite was waiting outside. I jumped out of bed and ran out. Mohite was panting and gasping for breath; he had cycled hard for eight miles. He said that Mahind had, at last, contacted Ganeshkar. Vasant Patil was sleeping in a house behind the police HQ. Ganeshkar had seen the house. He was waiting for us outside the city.

I asked Bashir, my driver, to get the car. It was a 1934 V8 Ford, which I had bought from an Anglo-Indian engine driver in Igatpuri; it had never let me down even once during all the rushing about that I had done in Satara up hill and down dale. We all piled into the car. In those days cars had running boards. Three men stood on each side, on the running board. Some were on the roof. There were eleven of us, including the driver.

The car went slowly down the Miraj-Sangli road. Just outside the city, we met Ganeshkar. He got on to the bonnet. While we were passing a street light, I saw the time on my watch; it was 4 o'clock, still quite dark, not a soul stirring. Under Ganeshkar's direction we came to the entrance to a small lane which was right behind the looming police headquarters. We stopped in the dark. The lights of the car had been switched off when we entered the city.

Ganeshker came to me and whispered,"Vasant Patil is sleeping in a one-room apartment. The front wall is not flush with the ceiling, there's a gap of six inches. The door is locked from outside, but he has the key. He has a whole arsenal of weapons: one rifle, two 12-bore guns, four hand grenades and six revolvers, along with the ammunition. Five members of the gang are sleeping outside (Mahind Master was one of them). They're all unarmed. The others are not in Sangli. Mahind says you should also arrest him along with the others."

"Has the room got a back door," I asked.

"No Sir," Ganeshker said. " I had specially asked Mahind."

The whole party tiptoed right up to the veranda. All the gangstera sleeping there were quickly seized, including Mahind.

I asked the leading man, "What's your name?"

"Hindurao", he said.

"Who's inside?"

"Nobody, as you can see, the door's locked."

"You lie," I said giving him a slap. "We know who's inside." Vasant Patil must have heard the commotion, because I heard the sounds of movement. I knocked on the door.

"We're the police," I said, "Who's inside?"

" Vasant Patil "came the reply.

"Your friends say that the key of the door is with you, " I said. "Throw it over, there is no escape for you."

"I won't give you the key," Patil said. "If you break open the door, I'll come out shooting, and, as you know, I have got hand grenades. Before I die I shall account for a few of you, at least".

I conferred with Borkar and Talekar. "Let's break open the door and rush in," I said.

My wise old Inspector differed. "My advice, Sir, is that now we should go slow," he said. "After all, please remember that we are in 'foreign territory'. No one can take exception to our conduct so far. We can say that we came up here in hot pursuit of the gangsters. But now we must call the SP of Sangli. It is only with his assistance that we can proceed further."

There was a great deal of sense in what he said. I knew perfectly well that if anything went wrong, neither Hobson nor Chambers would support me. We sent for the SP, Kulkarni, who arrived within minutes in his pajamas. He gave me a sticky smile. The three of them had a further powwow.

They spoke to Vasant Patil. Then they praised him high and low, called him heroic, valiant and worthy of admiration, a prince among men. They said they had an overwhelming force with them. He would kill a few, but he would surely be killed and the grenades might destroy the lives of innocent neighbours. At the most, he would have to undergo a term of imprisonment, but that was what the great leaders were doing. Eventually, after the war, they were all going to be released, when his role in the freedom movement would be rewarded. (It was).

Vasant Patil at last asked where was he going to be kept, in Sangli Jail or in British India?

"In Sangli Jail, of course", Kulkarni said, looking at me sideways." I will not allow the British police to take you to Satara". (That was one promise that he kept).

At last, Vasant Patil agreed to surrender. After ten minutes he came out, with his hands raised. We handed him over to the Sangli police along with the others the arms and ammunition from the room.

By this time the dawn had come. News of the arrest had spread like wildfire throughout the city and curious crowds were pushing into the lane.

Our job in Sangli was over. Under my prior instructions, my officers did not hand over Mahind to the Sangli police. They allowed him to disappear in the crowds.

I went to Miraj and sent a telegram to Hobson. With great daring, casting aside the rules and the chain of command, I sent a copy to F W O'Gormon, the DIG CID. Then I went to the rest house at Miraj and had a breakfast of three fried eggs, marmalade, hot toast and butter, washed down with scalding cups of tea. I paid my bill, hastily collected my things together and dumped them in the car, took the wheel from Bashir, and drove like mad for Satara.

On reaching home, I narrated the episode to my wife. After lauding my success in the appropriate manner that a bride should, she said," But his is exactly what my father did when he was in the *anushilan* movement."

"Tell me about it," I said later.

"My father used to say," she began, "that the terrorist movement (as the British called it) in Bengal, was entirely the outcome of the partition of Bengal by the then Viceroy, Lord Curzon. My father said that brilliant men sometimes behave stupidly"

"I can name one of the British IGs who could easily fit into this category," I said.

"Bengalis actually felt that their mother was cut in two. You know how emotional Bengalis are !"

"I know one Bengali who is," I said. "I like it".

"I am my father's daughter," she said, drawing herself up.

"My father's people came from Noakhali, near Dhaka. Their family name was Sen Gupta. My grandfather died when my father was eight years old. He had a small estate, which was put under the Court of Wards. His wife, my grandmother was practically a *pardanshin* woman. The estate was put under the control of Miss Cornelia Sorabjee, the first woman barrister in India. She exercised only remote control over my father and his brothers. They could have run wild; but he joined the *anushilan* movement from the age of eleven.

The good thing about the anushilon was that the young men and boys who joined it were moved by high ideals; they led Spartan lives, sang patriotic songs, and practised *lathi khela*. They would not allow a single foul word to be used in their hearing. The idea of driving out the British by revolution dominated their thoughts completely."

"But didn't his studies suffer?" I said. "Surely, Miss Sorabjee would have noticed that!"

"Well, that's the amazing thing. He did not neglect his studies. In his Matriculation, he stood among the first ten in the Calcutta University." She paused for a minute. "Miss Sorabjee got him admitted to the Presidency College in Calcutta and made him stay in the Oxford Mission Hostel."

"Didn't you once tell me that he was a contemporary of Subhas Chandra Bose?"

"Yes, they were classmates - both among the first ten. My father used to tell us that he knew Subhas Bose very well. He said that Bose was absolutely brilliant in his studies, but very solemn in his deportment. He had joined an idealistic group led by Dr. Suresh Banerji, which believed in plain living and high thinking. He used to come sometimes to college, barefoot, sometimes wearing only a *chaddar*."

Didn't he join this anushilan movement?"

"No, though he knew what they were doing. My father said that perhaps at that time he was thinking of taking the ICS."

"You father told you that what they were doing was exactly like what these saboteurs are doing,"I said. "Tell me about his bomb case."

"It was known as the *Musalman Para* bomb case. It became, a what do you call it?"

"A cause *celebre*?"

"A cause, whatever you call it. Six of them got together and decided to throw bombs on the house of Basanta Chatterjee, the Deputy Commissioner of Police, CID. Though my father was only eighteen at the time, and not the nominal leader, he had planned the entire operation and procured the bombs. He also became the lone scapegoat."

"What happened?" I asked.

"They had observed the place for several days. Mr. Chatterjee used to meet his subordinates every evening in an outhouse adjacent to the street. The gang was ten minutes late - they couldn't help it. The officers had all gone out, and Chatterjee was standing in front of the room. My father and another man threw two bombs at the outhouse. One went inside killing a HC instantly and injuring two others. The second hit the wall, the shrapnel ricocheting and hitting my father. He said that blood began to gush out of his thigh like water out of a fountain. He somehow managed to drag himself to the next lane, Mistry Street, before collapsing. But before he became unconscious, he did manage to pull out the revolver from inside his coat pocket, and threw it a couple of feet away. The others ran away."

"Where did the police say they found the revolver? On his person, or where it lay?"

"Where it lay."

"Amazing! What about fingerprints?"

"In those days they took no fingerprints. At least, none were produced in the trial."

"On what date did the incident occur? Do you remember?"

"24 November 1914"

"To think that the art of fingerprinting was discovered in 1902 in Calcutta by Sir Edward Henry. Your father was lucky!"

"And what about the trial?" I asked.

"It was conducted in the High Court before a Full Bench. The Chief Justice, Sir Lawrence Jenkins presided. Sir Ashutosh Mukherjee was one of the members. I can't remember the name of the third."

"Never mind! You're doing very well. It's a wonder that you remember all these details."

"Not really. The case has been discussed so often in our house that all three of us sisters know the details by heart. To continue, Sir S P Sinha (you know, Lord Sinha) was the Government prosecutor. Miss Sorabjee, (herself a Barrister, remember?) selected Mr. Langford James as the defence counsel. He was brilliant lawyer then; this case made him famous; my father was acquitted. If he had been found guilty, he would have been hanged. It hinged on the fact that the revolver was not found on his person

'What made him change his whole attitude?"

"As you know, he was sent to England for his studies by Miss Sorabjee. He had a brilliant career in Durham, in chemistry, He stayed in England for eight years with the help of the estate funds, and scholarships. The Oxford Mission people sent him to Durham because, one of their kind, Canon Trotter, a humble priest, kept him in his house as a member of the family. Gradually his outlook changed and he began to hate violence. You must ask him for the details."

"Tell me something, love," I said. "What does he think of my chasing these saboteurs?"

She smiled. "I asked him that, too,"she said. "My father said to tell you this: 'Whatever thy hand findeth to do, do it with all thy might.'

"Ecclesiastes," I said. "I don't have much time for preachers, but that one, I like."

My father was also very happy that I was going to Satara. 'Satara is the land of Shivaji,' he said. 'We in the anushilan, were always great admirers of Shivaji.' So was Tagore, for that matter. I must read to you soon Tagore's poem on Shivaji, called 'Pratinidhi.'"

In those days my prestige with the constabulary was very high. PCs, HCs, and some PSIs used to wend their way to my house at night with offers of information about the hideouts of this dacoit or that saboteur. Most of it was vague and infructuous, but what I valued was the vast fund of faith and good-will that the lower ranks reposed in me - all of which I was soon to lose due to the stupidity of Hobson and the British system.

A week later I was told that one of the underground workers, Gaurihar Sinhasane, wanted to surrender to me. He did this at Kadegaon police station. Over a cup of tea, we had a friendly chat. I found that he was educated and a man of culture. He said he was really a Gandhian who had, somehow, got caught in the vortex of the sabotage movement. I asked my officers to treat him with consideration and respect. Sinhasane was a close associate of Y B Chavan. By a strange coincidence, Chavan was caught (he apparently did not surrender) in Phaltan by Inspector Deshmukh of the State CID. I was glad to learn that Deshmukh was awarded the Indian Police Medal for this meritorious service. The reward for both Sinhasane and Chavan was Rs.500 each; for Vasant Patil and some others it was Rs.5000. I must explain here that the reward was meant for private informers, not for the policemen who slogged for it.

There are some further developments in the matter of the arrest of Vasant Patil, which I must narrate here. On my report, the home department of Bombay wrote to the Sangli Administration to give us the custody of Patil for a fortnight for interrogation. They point blank refused to do it, and the political resident, Colonel Edwardes, supported them. We asked that the Sangli police should at least allow our Inspector to be present during his interrogation. This was also refused. It seemed to me that the Bombay Government was afraid of crossing swords with the Resident, who occupied a privileged position in the relations between British India and the Princely States.

Eventually, as a special favour, the Sangli police sent us a copy of Patil's statement, which they had recorded. I remember one particular passage. When he was asked what he had done with the jewellery from the Kupwad dacoity, he said that he had crushed it into powder with a big stone, and thrown it in the river.

A month later, Patil and his associates escaped from the rickety old Sangli Jail, after overpowering the guard, and taking their weapons. They ran along the river and were pursued by the mounted police of Sangli State. Vasant Patil was shot in the shoulder, and was recaptured; the others escaped. At last the Government woke up. Things must have moved pretty fast in high quarters. Within two days I got a direct order from the home department that I should go to Sangli at once and escort Vasant Patil to the Yeravada Jail in Poona, which I did.

There are two postscripts to this episode. Several years later I was astonished to read in a magazine, a highly fanciful and imaginary account of how Vasant Dada Patil (later the Chief Minister of Maharashtra) was caught by the Satara police and taken to a special interrogation cell, where he was brutally tortured. I called on the then editor of the magazine, Arun Gandhi, grandson of Mahatma Gandhi,and told him what truly happened. I said that there was no special interrogation cell in Satara, nor with the CID (so far as I was aware), and that we were not even allowed to be present at Patil's interrogation by the Sangli police. I requested the editor to allow me to publish my rebuttal, but he refused to do so for reasons best known to himself.

The second postscript that I want to add is that when I was the IG of Police of Maharashtra, 'Vasant Dada' became the chief Minister, I invited him to address my officers at the police club in Bombay. The first thing he said was that the gentleman on his right (myself) was the man who had arrested him. I don't think he ever forgot or forgave. In complete contrast, my father-in-law, Nagendra Nath Sen Gupta, became a very good friend of Basanta Chatterjee, the DCP CID, Calcutta. They used to visit each other in their homes in Calcutta. As material standards go, 'Vasant Patil' did quite well for himself. In comparison, Sen Gupta, who escaped hanging by the skin of his teeth, got nothing. When his widow applied for a measly pension of Rs.150 per month, the Government would not sanction it on some technical grounds.

As part of her 'dowry', my father-in-law had given my wife a seventeen volume, leather bound set of the complete works of Rabindra Nath Tagore in the original Bengali. Whenever I took her on tour, she would carry one of these volumes with her, and read it aloud and explain it to me at night when the day's work was done.

This time I told her that I was going to inspect Dahiwadi police station, and would show her the memorial of Shivaji at Shingnapur. She took the volume, which contained the poem titled:'Pratinidhi', and read it out to me at Gondavle, where we had camped. Tagore wrote that he had based this poem on the 'Ballads of the Marathas' translated by Acworth. In this poem Tagore has described in his own inimitable style how Shivaji had made over the title deeds of his kingdom to his Guru, Ramdas, and how Ramdas had returned them to him, asked him to rule as the "Pratinidhi"- the representative of God, which, I think he did, to the best of his ability.

The next morning we went to Shingnapur. I had warned my wife that the ascent up the stone steps was pretty steep, but she thought it would be no problem as she used to go regularly to Darjeeling and Kalimpong. We were a small party consisting of, besides the two of us, the local PSI, some policemen and the Trustees of the Mahadev temple and some others. I had already visited it before. We went past an old T-shaped tank, and began the climb; some of the steps were a foot high, but we reached the top, at last.

After taking *prasad* at the temple, we went about a hundred yards along the edge of the temple to a block of three buildings with memorials inside. The central memorial was that of Shahji, father of Shivaji while to the east of that was that of Sambhaji. We paid our respects to Chatrapati and to his father and son. I stood at Shivaji's memorial for a long time thinking of what Kincaid had written about him.

While returning, we stopped for a while on a small promontory beside the Temple. As I stood gazing at the scene below, I reflected that from these very hills and valleys must have first arisen the battle cry of the Marathas, 'Har Har Mahadev!', which for a short time at least reverberated through the length and breadth of Hindustan.

That night I gave my wife the gist of what Dennis Kincaid had said about Shivaji in his book ' The Grand Rebel'.

I have had occasion to read Kincaid's book again recently, and, in the light of all my reading and study of military history and warfare, my opinion of Shivaji as an army leader, and of Kincaid, as a writer was greatly enhanced.

Ever since the First World War, Liddell Hart had been advocating the doctrine of ' The Indirect Approach', both in tactics and in strategy. He had said that from the time that mobility had been restored to the armies with the invention of the Tank, the 'Indirect Approach' had become the most effective and the least expensive method of warfare. We know that his doctrines were ignored by the British, and studied with great interest by the Germans - in particular, by Guderian - and utilized by them in World War II.

Liddell Hart advocated his theory, not only for war, but also as a philosophy of life. In his books, he gave examples of the great captains of history - beginning with Alexander who had practiced the Indirect

Approach to win his empire. However, what has surprised me is the fact that Liddell Hart has not as much as even mentioned the name of Shivaji as one who used it most successfully in all his campaigns.

Dennis Kincaid was an ICS officer and the District Judge of Karwar when he was drowned while swimming. Surely, his book, published in 1937, must have been available to Liddell Hart. Kincaid, obviously, knew nothing of Liddell Hart or about warfare, and yet his book proves (and anyone can verify this statement) that Shivaji was an exemplar of this doctrine. When he found that Aurungzeb was moving to the Deccan, and was going to campaign against him with all the resources of the Moghul Empire, he decided to move on through Karnataka, and fortify himself on the eastern coast, in case he was forced to withdraw.

Shivaji's own campaign in the Karnataka with 70,000 Horse would have beaten Sherman's march through Georgia (during the American Civil War), by any standards of generalship. However, far from following Sherman's scorched earth policy, he not only prevented any vandalism by his troops, but also paid for all the supplies on the way. (I was reminded of Sherman, because at the time we were camping at Dahiwadi, the Army were conducting their firing practices with the new Sherman tanks, which had just arrived at Ahmednagar. The cordoned-off area was about 20 miles from Dahiwadi. The Army had invited the district civilian officers and their wives from Satara to see the tank maneuvers, and they gave some of us short rides in the new tanks.)

There is one other fact that I would like to mention about Kincaid, namely, his felicity of expression, and power to hold his readers' attention. According to Somerset Maugham, the three essential qualities of a good writer are lucidity, simplicity and euphony. Kincaid had all these in good measure. Further, he loved India, just as his father (also an ICS officer and a writer on India) did before him.

I explained all this to my wife while we were in Gondavle and asked her if she followed what I said.

"Sort of", she replied.

The next day, the sub-inspector of Dahiwadi asked me if my wife and I were interested in hearing *pavadas*, the ballads of Shivaji and other heroes, sung by his policemen. We were interested, and once my officers came to know that we both enjoyed them, these ballads became a regular feature during my inspections, whenever my wife accompanied me. Though, at first, I had to translate them, she began to follow them with ease as she picked up Marathi.

And when, on the eve of my departure, the police gave us a farewell, they even composed a *pavada* in our honour!

When I returned to Satara and went to my office, my Reader, Yaravdekar came inside with a peculiar look on his face. Silently he placed the district police gazette on my table. One of the notices said that PC's Mohite and Ganeshker had been given rewards of Rupees One Hundred each and GST's for their work in connection with the arrest of Vasant Patil.

I realized that Hobson had given me a new version of the original Hobson's Choice. Thomas Hobson was an English liveryman of the 18th Century who gave his customers a choice between the hack nearest the door of the stables, or nothing; James Hobson of this A.D. had given me two choices, each of nothing.

I shall draw a curtain over the scene that took place when I rushed to his room. The police is a para-military department, and you can 'rave and rant' to your superiors only in circumscribed limits. I don't know what an officer of the ICS would have done. However, I told Hobson that thereafter no policeman would give me his trust.

Hobson said that I have always overrated the role of the lower ranks in catching these wanted men.

"Bill Moore-Gilbert arrived last night, for your information," he said. The IG has put him in special charge of these operations. Within a couple of months he will catch the whole lot of these louts. All I expect you and the others to do is to follow him, and carry out his orders. I won't need any help from your PCs".

I told my wife that evening what had happened. She sympathized with me, but what else could she, or anybody else, do?

I said to her, "I have come to one definite conclusion: the British are not fit to rule India or any other place."

"My father always used to say that the British have no moral right to rule" she said sententiously.

"I know what your father used to say," I said. "I am not talking of their moral right. I am talking of their *fitness* as rulers. There are no Clives or Warren Hastings or Lawrences left among them. You see what has happened at Singapore. While all their big guns were pointing to the sea, and two battleships were brought to reinforce them, they exposed their ruddy backsides to the enemy. I am sure that Yamashita must have read Liddell Hart- in translation, of course."

As for the grinning duo, Mohite resigned from the police. I gave him full credit for it. Many times during my further stay at Satara, I felt like doing it - but there was my precious family to consider - my hostages to fortune. Where would I go? And what could I do?

Many years later, when I was IG of Maharashtra, I had gone on a visit to Satara in connection with some strike. The SP, S K Seth, took me to a meeting in the office of the Municipal President. A white-shirted man in a khadi kurta was grinning at me all the time. I asked Seth who he was; his face seemed familiar. Seth said he was the Municipal President. This man came up to me and said in Marathi," Sahib, haven't you recognized me? I told him his face was familiar, but I could not place him. He said," Sahib, I am your constable Mohite, who helped you catch Vasant Dada Patil. I have now become the Municipal President on behalf of the Congress Party." (This much for Vasant Dada's attitude towards the old servants of the British Raj!)

" I am very glad you have ", I said. "How I wish I too could have also resigned.!"

S M (Bill) Moore-Gilbert breezed into my office next morning, and after a friendly handshake, sat down for a pow-wow. He had been given the post of Additional ASP (not even SP) in charge of anti-sabotage operations. He said he was on his way to Belgaum to deal with a much more serious law-and-order problem. (I never learnt what it was) when the IG had called him and asked him to go to Satara. "I don't expect to be here for more than a month. I have been told that you have already caught a few of these gangsters; I'll mop up the rest within a month," he said. (S M Moore-Gilbert stayed on in Satara for a year and a half, and caught nobody, not even one single dacoit or saboteur).

Bill Moore-Gilbert was a handsome blonde giant of a man (he told me once that his mother was a German), with a frank smile and an engaging manner. Some of the senior Indian officers had told me lurid tales of his behaviour in the I P Mess. They said that he was an overbearing bully during guest nights. To me, at any rate, all during his entire stay in Satara, he was polite and pleasant. As for the ladies, they were all charmed with his ''shy' smile and his boyish behaviour'

I had trained a small armed party at the HQ consisting of head constable Gaikwad and three young PC's who had been *pahelwans* (wrestlers), and I used to take them with me on raids. Gaikwad was a stocky, tough man with great strength and agility - he was a marvellous performer on the *malkhamb* (the single gymnastic pole). Bill Moore-Gilbert appropriated them, and armed them with the new sten guns he had brought with him. He would take this party with him wherever he went in his Ford stationwagon.

Soon after his arrival, Bill paid lightning visits to all the affected police stations. I was told that he would address the policemen and offer rewards and promotions to anyone who gave him information about the absconders. I was not surprised that during his entire stay of a year and a half, nobody gave him any information. And the only man who got a promotion within three months of his arrival was Gaikwad, who became a Jemadar with a ''cross-belt'. When I protested to Hobson that he had superseded 26 men (when Pisal and the two others were refused promotion) he replied," I don't know anything about it; it's the IG's order. It's between Bill and the IG."

Police officers at the level of sub-inspector or inspector should never have been prevented from working out their own information about the gangsters, unless the operation was beyond their resources. But when Bill found that he was not getting any clue at all from them, and not getting any results, he made it known (very indirectly, of course) that every bit of information - be it big or small - had to be given to him. He explained to me that the IG had ordered it 'for better coordination'. There was no arguing with the IG's orders. But it did seem to me a little strange that the IG began to issue a great many orders directly through Bill. And none of them was in writing.

Sub-inspector Shinde was transferred from Vita police station, and a young man named Thakur was posted in his place. During the investigation of a robbery, his subordinates had rolled steel pipes on the legs of a suspect, injuring him badly. The Magistrate of Vita had reported the matter to Hobson. The SP sent me a telegram asking me to take up the investigation of the case personally. In the meantime, the suspect had died, and I had to register a case of murder against the PSI and his subordinates. Eventually, the PSI, who had been present during the interrogation, was convicted to 5 years' rigorous imprisonment.

A somewhat similar case took place in the other division, which was in charge of SG Pradhan, a direct deputy superintendent. In this case the famous Walawalker (now an Inspector) was involved. He had caught a big dacoit, Mahadu Ramoshi, in some place under Karad police station. Pradhan reported to the SP that the Inspector had to struggle with the dacoit. In the struggle Walawalker had very bravely snatched the sword carried by Mahadu, and hit him on the leg with it, injuring him seriously. Pradhan had recommended the Inspector for the award of the Indian Police Medal for gallantry. It was learnt that Mahadu Ramoshi had offered no resistance when he was captured, and that Walawalker had inflicted to wound on him subsequently.

Bill Moore Gilbert somehow got wind of the true facts, and informed Hobson. The SP ordered me to make an enquiry into the matter, even though it was outside my jurisdiction. By now it was known that I would make a thorough enquiry no matter against whom. I made the enquiry. Inspector Walawalker was suspended (and later dismissed). Pradhan was transferred outside the district by telegram. In the result, I became less and less popular with the police force of Satara.

And sabotage offences began to increase, in spite of the Pimpernel-like presence of Bill Moore Gilbert, running all over the district with his sten gun squad.

F W O'Gorman had now become the IG, and he came to Satara for a conference to discuss what was to be done.

Perhaps he remembered me. When my turn came to speak, he said,"Can't you get any information at all about these saboteurs, Modak?"

I said,"No Sir, I cannot get any information any more, nor can anybody else."

"If we can't catch these men, at least these offences have to stop." He said. "The writ of the British Government no longer runs in Satara."

"We can stop these offences, Sir" I said.

"How?" the IG asked.

"Two steps are essential," I said. First, the Satara police must be allowed to operate freely inside the enclaves of the Deccan States - especially, Aundh. Aundh, in particular, openly gives them shelter."

"We have tried," the IG said wearily, "I'm afraid it's no go. And the second?"

"Every one in a village does not give them shelter and support. A few - their trusted adherents do - the rest are afraid of their vengeance. If we arrest these people, the saboteurs won't be able to function. I know that for a fact."

"How many would they be?" O'Gorman asked.

"About a hundred in my division; the same number in the other. I have already got a list in mine; I am sure the other SDO has it in his, or he can get it easily from his police stations."

"What will you do? Have you enough evidence to prosecute them?" he again asked.

"We have no evidence to do that, Sir," I said. "For that matter we have no evidence against the saboteurs either. Vasant Patil was detained under Rule 129 of the Defence of India Rules. This rule can be used against these men also."

It was decided at the Conference that the police would put up proposals for detention against the 200 men. However, the District Magistrate, Chambers, turned down every one of them, saying that even detention orders needed some concrete evidence. And this concrete evidence was not forthcoming.

Chambers was a very nice man, friendly and considerate. His wife was a charming woman. She had been, particularly helpful to my wife, and neither of us can ever forget her manifold kindnesses. But Chambers was quite unfit to be the District Magistrate of Satara. He didn't seem to understand what was happening to the British Raj. Eventually, when he was transferred, and A L Dias became the District Magistrate, I put up a similar proposal to the SP, Abernethy, and to Dias. No more evidence was forthcoming than before, in any of the cases. But by this time a lot of water had passed through the Krishna, and we had to detain 800 persons, and not 200.. The offences completely stopped, but we were unable to arrest any of the saboteurs.

Willy nilly, I came into close contact with Bill Moore-Gilbert.during the next year and a half. Through him and through his observations, I came to understand the key to the hold of the British Administration in India, and of their 'steel frame'- the handful of British officers, and a small standing army of British troops. They ruled the country with basically a simple system of Laws, clearly understood, and a simple system of rules- in particular for the police. All that was needed was rigid enforcement, and this they secured through the Services - more specifically, the ICS and the IP.

The competitive examinations for the IP were held simultaneously in England and in India, but while the minimum qualification in India was a graduate degree, in England it was only the 'O' level; perhaps, the British equated the two. But whatever be their level of education, I was impressed with their method of work. I saw again and again that British officers were thorough in whatever they did. What they taught us in the police training school was scratched on steel, not written on sand.

I used to watch Bill Noore-Gilbert's movements sometimes. His whole attention was concentrated on every single action, whether he was reading a report or writing a note. Whenever I travelled with him in his stationwagon, he would slowly and deliberately do a double de-clutch when going into low gear. Once I asked him why he did it; he said that was the way he was taught driving in London; he didn't know why it was done. (I later found out that it was necessary in the days before the synchromesh gearbox.) He had carefully kept files of all his school certificates, prizes he had won and letters of appreciation. I learnt later that all the British police officers did this. He had once mentioned the name of his public school - one of the five famous ones. Perhaps they taught something else besides Latin and Greek!

This system was good enough for normal times, but the times were no longer normal. Ever since the Morley-Minto Reforms, there had been a great awakening among the masses. The intellectuals who have always led national movements wanted self-rule, not British rule, whatever the benefits of Pax Britannica. And the Second World War rudely interrupted this peace - the once invincible British seemed to be withdrawing on all fronts, and they began to lose their prestige. After all they had ruled the vast sub-continent with a small standing army and a tiny band of civilian officers mainly because of their prestige built over the years through a judicious mixture of bluff and bluster.

The British officers who constituted the 'steel frame' did not understand till almost the very end that the time had come for them to fold their tents and go. Once I met Crosthwaite, the new Assistant Collector in Islampur, and we were chatting over a cup of tea. The morning newspaper had announced the landslide victory of the British Labour Party in the General Elections. I said to Crosthwaite that from what was known about the Labour Party leader, Clement Attlee's views, Dominion Status for India was round the corner. Crosthwaite had been Assistant Private Secretary to the previous Viceroy, Lord Linlithgow, before coming to Satara. He said to me,"My dear fellow, you've got it all wrong. Take it from me that the British will not leave India for another forty years." We know now that this had been Linlithgow's view all along.

Since the District Magistrate had refused to allow the arrest of even a single one of the friends of the saboteurs under the Defence of India Rules, Moore-Gilbert tried to dissuade them in another way. He could hardly use the Bastinado, but he could do something faintly akin to it. He would go to an important village, collect their friends, take them to the chavadi, where the police patil and his watchmen had gathered all the male villagers present in the village. Then he would begin to thrash the suspects, one by one, Gaikwad assisting him all the way.

I had accompanied Moore-Gilbert twice, but had not taken part in the proceedings. I told him that all the muscular effort on his part would do no one any good. The saboteurs continued their activities without let or hindrance, and the hatred that the general public had begun to feel for the British, only increased.

Bill Moore-Gilbert, apparently, lost no time in reporting my views to Hobson, because from that day I began to notice a distinct change in Hobson's attitude towards me. Not that he had ever gone overboard in showing any warmth or kindness.

During our return from the second village, we had to cross a nullah to get to our bus. It had rained hard somewhere upstream, because when we came to the nullah, which had been dry before, now it was full of knee-deep water. I took off my stockings and boots and began to wade into the nullah. Bill Moore-Gilbert had done neither. A giant of a man, he was riding piggyback on Jemadar Gaikwad to save himself the trouble of removing his stockings and boots. Many years later, I was reminded of this incident when I read in Neville Maxwell's book about Lt. General Kaul riding up the mountain path towards the Sela Pass on the back of some hapless porter.

CHAPTER III

THE SATARA POLICE AND THE PRINCELY STATES OF THE DECCAN

I have already written about the obstructive practices adopted by the Deccan States towards the (British) Satara police during the sabotage movement. In the case of Aundh, there was positive connivance. Most of Aundh was within the boundaries of Satara district. The old Raja of Aundh had given constitutional powers to an 'elected' Assembly. The 'prime minister' was his younger son, Appasaheb Pant, who later became the Indian High Commissioner to the UK, and Ambassador to Cairo.

Appasaheb openly professed that he was a Congressman. He used to wear a khadi shirt, shorts, and a Gandhi cap. There could be no objection to this, but under his orders, saboteurs of all kinds were given shelter. We had definite information when they were hiding there, but we were not allowed to take our armed police inside Aundh, or make any searches. In fact, ever since my arrest of Vasant Patil under the very noses of the Sangli police, all the Deccan States had become very vigilant about any 'encroachments' by the Satara, i.e.'the British' police, on their so called territorial independence.

It is patent that all this would not have been possible without the consent and knowledge of the political resident in Kolhapur, Colonel Edwardes. We had represented the matter in the strongest possible terms to the home department of the Government of Bombay. The Adviser (Home), Sir Charles Bristow had the powers of the Home Minister under provincial autonomy. Bristow had not visited Satara even once during my entire stay in Satara. Surely it was the duty of the Adviser (Home) to have acquainted himself, personally, with the problems of the most difficult district in India (at the time)! Further, for some reason, which I did not understand, he did not want to tangle with the political resident who became increasingly intransigent.

The reason became clearer to me as the days passed and I began to get acquainted with the cognoscenti in Kolhapur and Miraj during the course of my visits there. While the British boasted (not without justification) about the incorruptibility of their administration, since the take-over by the Crown, there was one branch, namely the political department, dealing with the 'native' Princes which retained its old ways. It was in the charge of the political secretary who was directly under the Viceroy. Sir Conrad Corfield was the then political secretary. He worked with the single-minded aim of preserving and strengthening the *apparat* that enabled him to loosen or tighten the reins of control over the Princes as and when required. We know now that Corfield had kept minute dossiers of every princeling containing details of his misdeeds-from small peccadilloes to murder. (When at last he came to know that the princes were on the way out, he burnt all these records, to prevent the successors of the British from exploiting them).

The system of giving *Nazranas*, *haftas* or installments, did not originate in the police or the PWD, or any other department. From the beginning, it was the special privilege of the Viceroy, and was, I think, respected as such. The princes gladly gave, their dues to the paramount power, the Viceroy, because it had always been part of the feudal system of old. But now, in view of the impending transfer of power, the position of the princes had to be strengthened for the bargaining that was to ensue. If this happened during the British regime, so much the better. The democratic Indian parties could not say that it was done deliberately by the British before handing over power.

One of the steps taken was to make every petty 'Chief' of the Deccan States, a 'Raja'. And he was given a gun salute to boot. The more of the 'elected' Assemblies these princes had (all under the control of their relatives or stooges), the better. If all of them collectively wanted to be independent of the Congess ruled provinces, it was in the interest of the political department to encourage them.

Colonel Edwarde's arrogance extended to his family. Whenever I was in or near Miraj, I used to go to the refreshment room in the railway station and order a light lunch or dinner. I used to park my car in the yard, and go into the refreshment room, not from the platform, but through a swing door at the back. One evening I had gone there, accompanied by the railway sub-inspector and a couple of the PCs, all of whom were in uniform. After I sat down and ordered my usual meal, they saluted and left.

I saw a young British army officer with the insignia of a major sitting in a corner. The train from the south had just left, so I thought, idly, that he must be waiting for somebody. He had seen the police officers with me and must have felt that I was someone in authority in the police. He smiled at me, and came over and asked me if he could join me. We introduced ourselves, and I offered him a beer. He told me that he had traveled from Mountbatten's Headquarters in Kandy, and was going on a posting to Delhi. He had stopped over at Miraj Station to see his fiancée, who was in Kolhapur.

"That wouldn't be Miss Edwardes, would it?" I asked.

He was surprised. "Why, yes," he said,"do you know her?'

"Not at all," I said. "Nor her father, for that matter."

He seemed mystified, and his eyes asked a question.

"I just guessed it." I said, laughing. "There are only a couple of European families in Kolhapur, and I had heard that Colonel Edwardes had a grown-up daughter."

"You seem to be in the police," he said, and asked me what I was doing. I told him about the saboteurs, he was most interested. We passed half an hour happily, thus, when I heard the sound of a car horn. A few minutes later, an elegant, slim young woman came into the refreshment room followed by a gaudily dressed peon.

After they had embraced and kissed, she sat down and the major turned to me, and said to her, "This is Mr....."

I was about to give my name, when she said disdainfully,"It doesn't really matter, does it...?"

"No, indeed not, to the likes of such as you, madam," I said, getting up. "I beg your pardon, I thought this was *my* table." The other tables were all filled up, except for one chair. I went and sat on the chair, and was paying my bill, when the sub-inspector came in. The major looked embarrassed. I waved the bill to him, indicating that I had paid for the drink, and went out through the rear swing doors.

Many of the isolated Inspection bungalows had been burnt by the saboteurs at the early stages of their activities. While I could stay in *chavadis* and the like for quick visits to the scenes of crimes, I needed something more substantial for my inspections of police stations which could last for six or seven days. We had some tents in the headquarters and I tried making tent camps a few times. But the question of transport became difficult. Police officers were not allowed to use police buses or trucks to transport their kits. Hiring private vehicle was out of the question for an ASP, and I could have hardly taken the tents in my car. Moreover, the police did not have a steady, settled programme of tour, like the Assistant Collectors. I could be called away at midnight to go anywhere in my charge. The times were unsettled, and unless armed guards were posted at every tent camp, the saboteurs would have made short work of it.

I had, therefore, to exercise my ingenuity in finding some unused bungalow, or part of a bungalow in which I could stay for a few days. The bungalow at Islampur where Crosthwaite had stayed was 'discovered' by me. It belonged to the American Mission, was fully furnished and had sanitary fittings with a septic tank. None of the Inspection bungalows and hardly any of the district officers' bungalows had such furniture or fittings. Another one was in an isolated place a few miles outside Tasgaon. The Tasgaon Inspection Bungalow was the first to be burnt by the saboteurs - by Vasant Patil and his gang-no less. His native village, Padmala, was not far from there.

The bungalow I found in Tasgaon belonged to Mr.Parshurambhau Mali, the owner of Mali's world famous circus. His native place was Tasgaon, and he had built this large house for his retirement.. He hardly came to stay in it. During the time I was in Satara, he was out with the circus, touring all over the country, and even taking the circus abroad - to Africa and the Middle East. He had locked up half the bungalow, but the other half was available, though sparsely furnished. It had a kitchen of which my cook made full use, a living room and a clean bathroom.

The manager of the estate was an old man who had once been a roustabout in the circus. He told me that he had gradually risen to the post of assistant animal trainer. In the compound at one end, there was a cage in which a Bengal tiger was kept. The manager told me that the tiger, which was very old, had been a pet of Mr.Mali. Both the manager and the tiger had been superannuated and sent to this place to live in comfortable retirement.

The tiger used to roar and snarl in the beginning, whenever he saw me. The manager said that he only did that to strangers. Gradually, he came to recognize me and gave a friendly toss of his head, whenever I passed by and saluted him.

On my first night at the house, I was fast asleep when I heard what sounded like a blood-curdling roar, not far from my pillow. I practically jumped out of my skin, and yelled as loud as the tiger. The manager came and apologized. He said,"I'll tell Dasarath to keep the tiger away from your window."

"Who be Dasarath?" I asked.

"Dasarath is his keeper, and walks with him at night in the compound to exercise him." He assured me that the tiger now had only friendly feelings towards me. Even so, from that day onwards, before going to sleep, I made certain that all the doors and windows of the house were securely bolted from inside.

Everybody (including the saboteurs, I am sure) knew about the night rounds of the tiger. I did not have to keep an armed guard of 2:6 or even 1:3 in the compound, nor would the guards have relished the prospect.

I was in this house one afternoon when I heard a terrific commotion outside. The noise of the tiger's roars was mixed with the sounds of motor cars' horns and shouts. I left my piled up *tapal* on the table and rushed out. It was Bill Moore-Gilbert in his stationwagon. Behind him was a police bus with some policemen, villagers and what looked like a female figure in a sari.

I met Bill and we both walked inside. "Not a friendly fellow that, tiger of yours, is he?" Bill said.

"He's not exactly my tiger", I said. "But he grows on you".

"I am sure of it," Bill said. "The sub-inspector of Tasgaon says the tiger practically eats out of your hand."

"I haven't tried that as yet", I said, But what brings you here, Bill?" I asked.

He then expounded his tale. "It concerns sub-inspector Malhar of Patan police station."

"I know him, of course", I said. " Isn't he the chap who recently arrested the gang of dacoits - Balbhim was the leader. A good officer, I thought, what's happened?"

Moore-Gilbert pulled out hid pocket diary. " You know, of course, about this gang of Bhaskar Jadhav - he is as bad as your Vasant Patil."

Not quite, I thought, but there was no point in making an issue out of it, so, I nodded.

"They used to take shelter frequently in the house of this man (he looked at his books again) Govind Nikam. Malhar raided the house. The gang, which was there escaped, Nikam along with them."

PSI Malhar arrested his sister and took her to the police station where he tortured her to give him information about her brother and the gang. "You should see her. She's a very beautiful woman - I mean for a villager."

"My dear Bill," I said. " Why shouldn't there be very beautiful women in the villages? I have seen a few during my countless visits. Do they exist only in cities in India, or in any other country? And haven't you noticed the unconscious grace with which many of them walk? They don't practice with books on their heads, as do some society ladies, or so one is told."

"Well, it's about this torture. Malhar has made several burns with his cigarettes, on her thighs and near her private parts. She showed them to me."

"She-actually-showed-them-to-you," I said. "And since when has a police officer taken on himself the role of a paramedic? Why in Heaven's name didn't you send her to the Medical Officer at Patan?"

"I did, but he had gone on leave."

"Then why did you not have her examined by one or more female panchas (witnesses) as required by the rules?"

"My *Jemadar*, Gaikwad, tried to get them," Bill said, " but nobody was prepared to come. They are all afraid of Malhar. That's the whole point. I've brought her here so that you can send her to the Medical Officer in Tasgaon."

"Tasgaon is fifty miles from her village," I said. "But what have I to do with it? It's not in my jurisdiction. Why didn't you take her to the other SDO?"

"I don't trust him any more than I trusted Pradhan", Moore-Gilbert said. I want you to take up this case for personal investigation, same as you did in Walawalker's matter."

"Why don't you take up the case for personal investigation yourself?" I asked. "You have jurisdiction over the whole district".

"I can't," Moore-Gilbert said. "The IGP has asked me to concentrate on catching saboteurs and dacoits."

"No inspections, no enquiries, no investigation," I said.

Then it hit me in a flash. I remembered my Inspector, Borkar, telling me that he had heard from the grapevine that Moore-Gilbert was furious with Malhar because he did not inform him about the raid on Bhimsen's gang. This was his way of making sure that he would be taken by an officer for every single raid that was made, so that Bill Moore-Gilbert got the credit for it. According to British police officers (and many Indians too), the raid was the important part of the action, not the really difficult and delicate task of getting the information, and laying the plans which would make the raid successful.

"In that matter, I was ordered by Mr. Hobson in writing to take up the case, and I had no choice, Bill", I said.

"If that's all that's worrying you, I could get the order within fifteen minutes on the phone from Jimmy Hobson," Moore Gilbert said. "And if you're so punctilious, you could send the girl for examination to the M O at Tasgaon *after* you get the order."

"You could get an order from Mr. Hobson, Bill," I said. "But please remember this. The fact that you have -ah - seen this girl's injuries will come out in the enquiry."

"It doesn't have to," Moore Gilbert said. "You don't need to mention my name. You could say that Hobson sent her to you. The girl won't say anything; I promise you that."

"You are going to suspend the sub-inspector, and have him arrested. In the Court his lawyer will reduce the girl to tears within fifteen minutes, and make her come out with what happened. I hope you were not alone with her when you - examined her?"

"No, her uncle was with her."

"You've brought her in the bus which is outside? All the persons in the bus will be examined in Court. Perhaps people from this house, even, my friend, the tiger might have to give evidence."

Bill Moore Gilbert got up to go. As we passed the cage, he snarled,"A lot of help you've been, I must say."

"That's how the matter stands." I snarled back. "Don't forget that Nasik fracas!"

The tiger seemed to have got a whiff of the atmosphere. He gave the loudest snarl of all as Bill passed by. He did not seem to like Bill Moore-Gilbert.

(I must say a few words here about the 'Nasik fracas.' This incident took place in Nasik at the beginning of the Quit India agitation. Moore Gilbert was the ASP Nasik. Several ladies had taken part in the Satyagraha, and were courting arrest. One of them, a portly person, was finding it difficult to climb up the steps of the bus. According to Bill, he gave her a friendly assist on her posterior with the palm of his hand. He showed me exactly how he held the palm at right angles, when he pushed her up. Perhaps in the U K or the U S the lady would have simpered and thanked him prettily. But this incident led to an immediate uproar, turmoil, furore, storm, outburst, explosion (to use only half the list from Roget's Thesaurus) The incident was widely reported in the Press. Somehow I felt that Moore Gilbert would not have liked the far stronger reaction that was bound to occur when his examination of the girl's injuries became known.)

I was right. I heard nothing about the case from Hobson, but from that day onwards he became openly hostile towards me. Not only did he load me with work, but also he tried to find fault with everything I did.

An ASP was required to maintain a weekly diary giving details of everything that he did, such as attending parades, performing night rounds, holding kit committees, visiting crimes, inspections, ad infinitum. During my inspection of Vaduj police station, I had gone to Budh outpost, 5 miles away in a *tonga*, as my car was sent for some repairs. I wrote that it took me 30 minutes to reach Budh and two hours to return. Hobson wanted my explanation for the difference in times. I wrote back that when I went, there was plenty of light, but when I returned, the *tonga* driver had to walk the horse back because it was dark, and he had no lights. I enclosed his statement and the receipt for the hire of the *tonga*.

As for my expenses during camps, I was always prepared for an enquiry that he or anybody else cared to make. Yates had taken me with him to see his inspection, when I had newly come to Satara. He told me that officers were sometimes in the habit of obtaining nominal receipts from their sub-inspectors of rupees two and eight annas, during the whole stay of several days, when everything was paid for by the officer. Since then my wife used to give me a wooden box in which she put all the rations necessary for a week or ten days: rice, dal, flour, tea, sugar and condiments. In those days there was no powdered milk, so I had to buy locally milk, kerosene, and sometimes meat.

The only exception was the brief halts I had to make at scenes of crimes when I reached a village at three in the afternoon or eleven at night. On such occasions, the police patil supplied me within ten minutes of my arrival, three or four thick chappaties with two hard-boiled eggs which I washed down with scalding cups of tea. It would not only have been churlish to insist on paying him for this light repast, but it would have been bad PR.

In brief, Hobson began the parlour game of twenty questions with me on each and every report I made to him. I was prepared for it, because the 'Discourses' of Socrates had been one of my favorite books since my boyhood. And it made me undertake any enquiry given to me with clarity and speed, such as I would never have got otherwise. With this background of the numerous enquiries given to me by Hobson, I was able to complete the enquiry and draft the report on the fire in the State Bank of India high- rise building in 1997 within a month, as required by the Government.

All this I was ready to put up with, but when Hobson refused to give me any armed parties for raids, and when he did give them, refused to give me transport, I protested, both in person and in writing.

However, deliverance was at hand sooner than I expected. Moore Gilbert was suddenly transferred. One fine morning he just disappeared without saying good-bye. And the order of Hobson's transfer followed within a week. Before Hobson left, the IG, O'Gorman, paid a visit to Satara and met all the officers in a conference. The day before he was to come, Hobson called me to his office. He was all smiles.

"I want to know what armed parties you want, and how many buses for them," he said. "You also wanted some officers shifted? Give me their names." He noted it all down, and issued the orders within half an hour.

During the conference the next day, O'Gorman specifically asked me why the offences were increasing in my sub-division. "I thought you said, Modak, the last time I was here that you would definitely stop these saboteurs, even if you couldn't catch them?"

I explained that I was given neither the armed parties I wanted, nor the transport. I had protested both orally, and in writing. I took out a sheaf of reports and weekly diaries.

O'Gormon looked enquiringly at Hobson. The latter took out the order he had issued the previous day.

"I have already given Modak the men and the buses he wanted," he began to say.

I got up and interrupted him."Sir," I said. "The SP has issued these orders only yesterday." I waved the papers in my hand. "I have been asking for these men for the last three months. Mr. Hobson has refused to supply any, and he told me that I could walk on my own flat feet."

Hobson had nothing to say, for once.

I had often wondered why with the combined efforts of both Hobson and Moore Gilbert, they were unable to get me out of Satara. They had got Pradhan out by telegram. Not that I would not have been happy to go, but not 'with a bad chit' (as they would have put it in those days). On thinking it over, I realized that it was entirely due to that little talk that I had had with Freddie O'Gorman long ago in the Miraj railway bungalow, followed by my telegram a few days later, on the arrest of Vasant Patil.

Indubitably, F W O'Gorman was the best police officer the British had in Bombay Province, but, even so, Freddie O'Gorman was no William Sleeman.

Have I given the impression that, according to me, all British police officers in Bombay were like Hobson and Moore Gilbert? There were plenty of good capable officers like Abernathy, who succeeded Hobson. I was unlucky enough to have to deal with two of the worst. And we had to confront a situation that needed special skill and resilience. In general, the policy of the British in India was to run the administration as efficiently as possible at as little cost as possible. After the onset of WWII, the idea of saving money for the War Effort reached absurd lengths. Eventually, the British Government had deposited upwards of eighteen thousand pounds sterling, in the Bank of England, which they dutifully (and honestly) handed over to the successor Governments on the subcontinent.

Since Independence, I have often heard and read a great deal about the alleged 'brutality' and high-handedness of the British administration in India. These allegations have sometimes been made by senior Indian police officers who have had no experience of the administration, themselves.

From the point of view of the British, Satara was the worst district in India. Both NPA Smith and F W O'Gorman admitted in conference that the writ of the King Emperor did not run in Satara. I am persuaded that with all his outward toughness, deep down there was a strong negative trait in NPA Smith's character that led him to make the gloomy forecast to Wavell that the Congress party would sabotage the Constituent Assembly, and set up a parallel Government in India. That Wavell did not set much store by this view is another matter.

I have no love lost for the British because they were unfair to me, and unfair to my father, but what did these 'atrocities' amount to in Satara, the 'worst district in India'? I was in Satara from the beginning to the end of the sabotage movement.I can vouch for the fact that, not more than 25 people were killed in the police firing that took place there during this entire period of three years and a half. These 25 people included the 5 who were shot in Vaduj when they were demonstrating peacefully in front of the police station. This was done under Yates' personal orders. It happened before I went to Satara. As a corollary I might mention that after this incident, no British police officer of the rank of superintendent of police, in Bombay State took or wanted to take the onus of opening fire on political agitators.

As for torture or high-handedness by the police, I have shown how, in the districts of Satara, in the grip of the *patri sarkar*, under the SP's order I was responsible for sending one officer to jail and sacking another, when these allegations were proved. The enquiries were not instituted on anybody's formal complaint; they were instituted *suo moto* by the SP (however bad he was to me), on information received.

During the sabotage movement, the police had to face a lot of virulent criticism from the vernacular Press; we felt that a good deal of it was unfair. The police represented the matter to Government, and suggested that some control (not censorship) should be imposed on the Press. We got the reply (when the British had their backs to the wall), that the Government could not interfere with the freedom of the Press!

Very soon after their transfer, the announcement came that both Hobson and Moore Gilbert were awarded the Indian Police Medals for their meritorious services.

I got nothing.

This happened in December 1946. In November of that year, I got my first promotion (in turn) as Superintendent of Police of Bijapur. At that time, the IG was H B Kidd, the last of the British IGs. All the political detenus had been released, and provincial autonomy announced. B G Kher was the Chief Minister of the Congress Government installed in Bombay. Sardar Vallbhbhai Patel was the Home Minister at the Centre, in the Viceroy's new Council.

Kidd had come to Bijapur on an inspection (really a farewell visit). My wife and I had invited him for dinner with some district officers and a few friends. After dinner and after they had all gone, Kidd indicated that he would like to have a private chat with me, and we both repaired to the veranda.

Over coffee and a cigar, Kidd seemed to be in an expansive mood. "Well, lad," he said, "you are soon going to get your reward for all the hard work you did in Satara."

I said nothing. Normally, a British officer would never have been so frank with a subordinate-with an Indian, never. Perhaps it was because he was to leave for the U K and retirement shortly - all the British were to leave.

"You should have got it earlier," he said. "In fact since the arrest of - what's his name?"

"Vasant Patil," I said.

"That's right, Vasant Patil. You know, the department recommended your name year after year, but Bristow, Adviser Home, came in the way every time. He used to say, you were too young, or something."

"He didn't consider Moore Gilbert too young, Sir," I said.

He puffed a couple of times."I see what you mean. I don't know why he was against you. Did you know him?"

"No Sir, I've never met him," I said. "He never came to Satara."

"Not even once - during all this trouble? Strange!"

"Not ever, to my certain knowledge," I said. I did not think it proper to say anything about his relations with my father.

On the 30th of December 1946 I got a D O letter from the Governor of Bombay, Sir John Colville, congratulating me on the award of the Indian Police Medal for meritorious service, in the ensuing New Year's Honours List.

The Medal was at last given to me, not by the British Government, but by the Congress, more specifically, by the Home Minister of the Interim Government, Sardar Vallabhbhai Patel. He was, obviously more generous and practical than the British.

In the mail, I also got a telegram from the PSI Sindgi police station, about a murder in Sindgi town. Bijapur was not a fully sub-divided district; one of the sub-divisions was with the SP. I had, therefore, to visit the scene of the murder, like any ASP.

On my arrival at Sindgi, I went through all the routine required: visited the scene, questioned all the witnesses, scrutinized all the case papers, and so forth. The PSI then took me up to the office of the *panchayat* where he had arranged for my stay. It was a small, dusty, stuffy room, but I had to make the best of it. After my dinner, consisting of sandwiches and coffee provided by my wife, I tried to sleep on my camp cot, but sleep would not come.

At last, well past midnight, I went downstairs and began to walk up and down the single street, in my pajamas and sandals. The street was deserted; everybody had gone to sleep. It was lit by a solitary oil lamp, just below the office. I stopped under the lamp, pulled out Colville's letter from my pocket, and read it for the umpteenth time

After all the hindrances and obstacles, I had got the Medal - within five years of my service. Not bad going! If you left out the one and a half-year's training (at the PTS), I had got it within three and a half years.

A feeling of exultation, a surge of triumph, swept over me. It was a feeling I had never had before, and would never have again.

I walked up and down, till I was too tired to walk. Then I went up the narrow staircase, to the poky little room, and fell on my camp cot into a dreamless sleep.

CHAPTER IV
Section-I

TRAINING IN UNARMED COMBAT

The constabulary of every district police force is divided into the Armed and Unarmed branches. The unarmed police are distributed in the police stations, urban and rural. The armed are centred at the district police Headquarters. Several of them are deployed in police stations for guard and other duties.

I was posted to Kolhapur as District Superintendent of Police in March 1950 and stayed there for two years. Kolhapur was the capital of the former princely state of that name. Princes were then allowed to retain their titles and privy purses, and the Maharaja was still addressed as the 'Chatrapati' - the descendent of the great Shivaji.

The unarmed police of Kolhapur were, by and large, third-rate and inefficient, but the armed police were something else. They were, probably, the best-armed policemen that I have had the honour to command. They were originally *jawans* from the Rajaram Rifles - the Kolhapur State Army - and were housed in the buildings which had belonged to the army. I had never seen such a loyal, disciplined and enthusiastic lot. They were prepared to do anything that I asked them to do; they even staged two plays of which one was about Shivaji. And the man who was in charge, Jemadar Bhosale, was a leader non-pareil.

As part of the HQ force I had with me the *Red Risala* - the mounted bodyguard of the Chatrapati. It consisted of 150 mounted horsemen whom I trained for dacoit operations. (Unfortunately the Government on grounds of cost disbanded the Red Risala. I had pleaded with Morarji Desai that they could be used effectively all over the State, and that the cost was only one lakh of rupees per month, but Morarji Desai was unconvinced.)

My bungalow was next to the HQ and the parade ground. Whenever I was in Kolhapur, I used to visit the HQ three times a week, morning and evening. When I did not, I would go out riding. One day I called Jemadar Bhosale and a few senior instructors. I said that I had come to the conclusion that the lathi was too unwieldy a weapon for the cities, and that the baton was too short, both for offence and defence. If a lathi hit a man on his head, it could prove fatal. Our object was not to kill rioters; it was to incapacitate them. I showed them a book written by a former I.P. officer from Bombay whose name was H G Lang. He had devised a system of stick drill which he had based on the experiences of a Frenchman called Vigui, who had defended himself successfully from an attack by a gang of the apaches of Paris, with the aid of a plain walking stick. He had also based his training on the stick play of tribes on the West Indian islands, called 'Bois'.

In using the lathi, both the hands had to employed, and even then, it was cumbersome. As for the drill on the parade ground, it was comical, and often evoked laughter from the waifs and strays hanging on the boundary of the parade ground. Lang argued that man is an easily vulnerable animal, and has many soft parts - the knee, the shin, the elbow. These could be attacked to incapacitate him, using a stick with only one hand. And, he said, better than a stick, would be a cane - not a schoolmaster's cane, but a stout Malacca cane, about three feet long. The advantage of the cane over the stick was that of *the glancing blow*, the whipping effect that could crack a bone.

Jemadar Bhosale and his men were quick to learn. Within a few months they became experts and taught the 'new' cane drill to as many men as possible.

In those days the Chinese and Japanese Martial Arts were not practiced or taught anywhere, though people spoke about them with respect, and said they had seen them performed on film. As far as I could learn, unarmed combat *was* taught in the Army, but not Judo, or Karate or Kung Fu. I decided to get some books and study how it was done. I was, perhaps, too naïve to understand that some things cannot be learnt from books.

It appeared to me that the main object in these Martial Arts was to catch your enemy off balance, and to try to remain in balance all the while. But what if you were caught off balance and fell? The first step was then to learn how to fall, without hurting yourself. When falling, you had to study two things. First, the Break Fall, and second, the Roll. When you were about to fall on your right side, you learnt to put your right hand out straight, and slap it hard on the ground. It acted exactly like a shock absorber. For the left side, it was the left hand. And if you fell on your back, you slapped both hands on the ground. I tried it out on a mat first and then on the hard floor. It worked! Seeing me do it, my men tried to do it too, and it worked with them.

If you fell on the front, you had to roll. You tucked your head in, and took the force of the somersault on the lower part of the neck. While this was easy to perform on the mat, it needed a lot of practice on the hard floor. As I saw it, the main idea behind these movements was to protect the head. We then learnt some basic throws and defence exercises.

While doing all these judo movements, I forgot one important fact, or more correctly, there was no instructor to guide me. They were learnt by the martial artists from the age of ten, not thirty. Long after I had forgotten them, this truth was brought home to me when I had to undergo a hernia operation in 1954 in Bombay. I had to undergo two more similar operations in later life, My colleagues in Bombay laughed at me when they saw me in the police hospital; hernia was supposed to be an ailment for the elderly. I did not enlighten them about the cause; I doubt if they would have believed me.

Was all this time and effort a waste? Well, I am not so sure. Consider these three incidents, separated from each other by several years. When I was the IG of Maharashtra, I was once invited to give a lecture at the Y M C A at Byculla in Bombay. After finishing my talk on the first floor, I had started to go down the marble steps. Halfway down, there was a landing with a wall in front leading to steps on the opposite side, going to the ground floor. While saying goodbye to the Secretary, I missed my step and went rolling down. I landed in front of the wall on my feet in a crouching position. I was unharmed, and even my glasses were intact. The Secretary said he saw a marvellous thing, he found me turning a somersault and landing on my feet with my head inches from the wall. If my head had hit the wall, I would certainly have suffered a concussion, if nothing worse.

Some years later, after my retirement, I had gone to the United States on a visit to my son and my brother. I had bought a Greyhound bus ticket to Chicago and came by the bus to the Greyhound stop underground, below the Chicago railroad station. My brother was to meet me outside the station at the top and I went on the long and steep escalator with my heavy bag. When I was almost at the top, the suitcase got caught in the railing and I fell down backwards the entire length of the escalator. Some kindly people came to help me, but to their amazement, I was in a squatting position, none the worse for wear except for a few bruises.

I went to settle in Pune in 1984. Some years later, I was standing on the East Street (in the Camp) which was one way, looking to the right at the traffic, waiting to cross the street. Suddenly a man came fast on a bicycle from the wrong side and hit me, knocking me down. I did not see him coming, and did not have time to put out my hand. I was knocked down and fell on my right side. My leg was bleeding, but my head was unhurt. And yes, my glasses were intact!

I can only say this by way of explanation of my 'miraculous' escapes. Those exercises in Judo (without even an instructor to guide me properly) had created a reflex action in my subconscious, which came to my help in my moments of physical danger.

But coming back to Kolhapur, we also used to have a drill in attack and defence with dummy knives. After watching it for some time, I said to Jemadar Bhosale," Don't you think these fellows are slow? I mean when *goondas* attack with knives during a communal riot in Bombay, they must surely be faster than this!"

Bhosale said," You are right, Sir. They certainly are much faster."

"How do you know?" I asked him.

" I have seen them practising."

"You have seen *goondas* practising? Where? I asked.

"Here in the *akhadas*."

The *akhadas* were the gymnasiums in Kolhapur run by private organisations where wrestling had been practised for generations. I knew that the wrestlers from Kolhapur were famous in India, but I did not know that they also practised knife drill.

"Who are these people who do this kind of drill?" I asked, my curiosity aroused. "Do you mean to say that you know somebody who practises it and has also committed stabbings in Bombay?"

"They are mostly mill- hands who work in Bombay and come home during holidays. I do know one such young man who is actually an instructor in a well-known gymnasium here."

"Would he be willing to show me his skill?" I asked.

There was a long pause. "If he is given an assurance that no police action will be taken against him, he might be willing to meet you," Bhosale said slowly.

"Is there any police case against him here, or in Bombay, or anywhere else that you know of, or that he knows of?" I asked.

"None," Bhosale said emphatically. "That much I can say definitely. You see, Sir, he is my nephew."

I said," I wouldn't have caught the dacoits I did without the aid of dacoits, and I wouldn't have caught Vasant Dada Patil without the aid of a saboteur. Bring him in."

The man whom Bhosale brought to the drill shed was a wiry trim young man of medium height. He touched my feet as wrestlers do and after a brief warming up, began his demonstration. None of my instructors could come anywhere near him in knife work. All I could say was that if this was the way *goondas* stabbed during the riots in Bombay, the police had a long way to go in getting the better of them. He agreed to teach my men for the next three months. I always found it a pleasure to watch the economy of his movements, his speed, and, yes. his grace, if there could be grace in stabbing.

Once I asked him where he had learnt his skill. He said that he had learnt it from his guru who used to consult a book. Could he show me the book? Yes, he could, because his guru had bequeathed it to him. He brought it to me: a tattered volume in Marathi giving detailed diagrams and instructions on knife play, and other kinds of attack and defence. You might even call it a 'Manual for *goondas*' It had no covers, and the names of the author and publisher were missing. I asked my L I B (Local Intelligence Branch) to trace it, but they could not find another copy in Kolhapur. Nor did any press in Kolhapur acknowledge that it had printed the book.

Eventually, with the help of my staff, I prepared a Manual of Drill and Unarmed Combat (i.e., combat without firearms) written in Marathi, and got a thousand copies printed privately. No Government funds were available for the purpose, nor any to pay the special instructor in knife drill. My enthusiastic staff arranged for a cricket match for the Ranji Trophy for the first time in Kolhapur. The profits were credited to the Police Welfare Fund. Out of the Fund I paid for the printing and I gave an adequate solatium to the expert in knife drill for the pains he had taken.

CHAPTER IV
Section-II

THE COMMUNAL RIOTS OF PUNE OF 1965

I was the Member - Secretary of the Maharashtra State Police which gave its report to the Government early in 1964. One of its main recommendations (made at my instance) was that posts of Police Commissioners should be established in Pune and Nagpur cities. The Government accepted this recommendation. On 6th March 1965 I was posted as D I G, Pune Range. Within a short time of my taking charge, I received a letter from the Government that it had decided to establish a commissionerate in Pune as soon as possible. I was asked to formulate my proposal and submit my report to the Government through the I G within a fortnight. I was also told separately that I would be the first Police Commissioner of Pune. At that time, J F Ribeiro was the SP of Pune. I submitted my proposal through the I G, after collecting all the necessary information from SP Ribeiro's office. On 7th July 1964 I took charge as the Police Commissioner.

Rebeiro claims in his book that the IG asked him to submit his proposals for the commissionerate to him. Could any IG have ever been so foolish as to ask my subordinate to send him a parallel proposal?

Three Superintendents were appointed as my Deputy Commissioners (DCPs). Rebeiro, the former SP of Pune was made the DCP HQ (Headquarters), Parthasarathy was made the DCP CID, and Misar was the DCP in charge of the police stations. I had worked in Bombay city for some years, and knew their functions. I called them together and individually, and explained what was expected of them. I told Ribeiro, in particular, that he was my second-in-command, and had to use his initiative in all times of crisis, as I had done and other

DCP HQs had done in Bombay. All this becomes important in view of the communal riots that took place in Pune shortly thereafter, and of the remarks that Ribeiro has made against me in his book.

The riots took place in Pune at the time of the *Ganesh Utsav* in 1965. One of the biggest *Ganapatis* during the festival is always installed in the *Mandai* not far from the police *chowkey*. A middle-aged man named Shaikh (possibly a hawker) had been drinking and moving about in the vicinity the previous night. Early in the morning, in an inebriated condition, he climbed up on the stage where the Ganapati had been installed and relieved himself. He felt hungry and wanted to scrape the kernel of the coconut in his hand. Not seeing a knife nearby, he helped himself to the *trishul* (the *trident*) in the hands of the *Ganapati*. A crowd soon gathered and there was an uproar.

B J Misar was the DCP in charge of police stations. On getting a phone call from the control room, I went to the *Mandai* immediately. The crowds had dispersed, but Misar, who was already there, had not taken the elementary precaution of removing the culprit as far as possible from the *Mandai*. I found him sitting in the *chowkey*, in the room below. I had Shaikh sent away in a van and called for an armed posse from HQ. I gave Misar the following oral orders: 1) I asked him to divide the armed policemen into sections and send them out for patrolling under his officers, in the area; 2) Neither Ribeiro nor Parthasarathy had arrived at the *chowkey*. I asked Misar to tell Ribeiro to move around in the area and contact any political leaders that he could, and ask for their help in restraining the hotheads. As he had been the SP, he knew them better than any of us. I asked Misar to instruct Parthasarathy to round up all the known *goondas*; and 3) I asked Misar not to leave the *Mandai* till further orders.

Neither Ribeiro nor Parthasarathy carried out my orders. Even if Misar had failed to convey my orders to them, it was their duty to take action on their own initiative; otherwise what were they there for? Further, as my second-in-command, Ribeiro should have interrogated Shaikh. From the wrong description that he has given of Shaikh in his book, it is clear that Ribeiro did not even see him. As for Misar, he was no Casabianca. I learnt later that he left the Mandai soon after I did. Had he remained there, he could have scotched the riot when it began. I went to my office thereafter.

Since I did not hear anything from Misar or the other two, I naturally took it for granted that the situation was normal. (I learnt later that Misar had left the *Mandai* soon after I did contrary to my order. This is also proved by the fact that he would not have waited to phone me till 1.30 when large-scale rioting was taking place all over the city). I went home at 1.30 PM., and was about to sit down for lunch, when I got an excited and frantic call from Misar. He said that rioting was taking place on a large scale in the *Mandai*, and that it was spreading to other areas besides the *Mandai*.

It was obvious that none of the DCPs had carried out my orders. Even assuming that Misar did not convey my instructions to Rebeiro and Parthasarathy, it was their duty to act *suo moto*, and do what I had asked them to do. It was their duty to have moved around the locus of the incident till complete peace prevailed. If they expected to be spoon-fed at every step, then why have these DCPs? I would much rather have preferred efficient ACPs, or even Inspectors, of whom there was no dearth in the State.

However, in spite of these shortcomings, the riot was well under control by the evening, and we had not fired a single shot. None of the DCP's had asked that they should be allowed to do so.

At that time D S alias Balasaheb Desai was the Home Minister. He had the habit of turning up in Pune every weekend on his way to Satara. He would come in the evening on Saturday, camp for the night, go early in the morning to Satara, return at night and go the next morning to Bombay. He had ordered that all officers of the rank of SP and above should line up in uniform on each of the occasions that he came and went. There were eighteen of us.

When I learnt that he had come, I went to meet him with my DCPs. We discussed the riot situation with him. He was happy we had controlled it without resorting to firing. At night, he went round the city with me, and saw the police patrols and pickets. He went on to Satara next morning. The police had kept up their vigil during the whole of the night and next morning. Not a single incident had occurred to disturb the peace, However, the rioting began again at about 11 AM. I could see that many of those taking part were young men, students and others. They seemed to me to be cadres from all political parties. This had happened soon after the war with Pakistan, and the atmosphere was still surcharged.

In the forenoon, I was standing with Ribeiro and the other DCPs in Kasture Chowk. We were discussing the question of opening fire, and I had decided to give the orders. Let it be noted that at no stage had I given orders to any of the DCPs, or to any of the subordinates not to open fire, nor had Ribeiro, or anybody else, suggested that I should. At Law, if a magistrate is not available on the spot, even an officer in charge of a police station can open fire.

In the meantime, unknown to me, the Home Minister had turned up at the Circuit House from Satara. He must have got my location from the Control Room. His security Officer came to Kasture Chowk in the Minister's car. He said to me in terms loud enough to be heard by all the officers, "Sir, The Minister has ordered that you should not open fire under any circumstances. He is sure that the riots will soon peter out."

Now, while theoretically, it may be true that the Minister cannot issue such an order, in practice you have to follow the orders of the Government (Minister) provided they are not contrary to Law. Further, while Ribeiro is now making such a brouhaha over my not ignoring the order, as my second-in-command, my chief adviser, he didn't urge me to ignore the Home Minister and order firing. When I was DCP HQ in Bombay city during the Samyukta Maharashtra riots, I did not ask for the CP's permission to open fire. No one said a word. Ribeiro did not suggest to me to meet the Minister and argue with him that the time had come for me to order the firing. As the sequel will show, such a situation did arise for me in the State of Jammu and Kashmir within a year, and I had to leave the State because of my disagreement with those in authority over the use of force (among some other reasons).

I left the Chowk and went about doing my best to control the riot without opening fire. When I felt it was hopeless, I went to the Circuit House to meet the Home Minister and try to persuade him to rescind the order, but when I reached it, I learnt that he had left for Bombay.

At about 7.30 in the evening I was taking a short breather in my house, The orderly informed me that a 'Colonel Saab' wanted to see me urgently for a few minutes. A gentleman dressed in mufti was ushered in. I had never seen him before. He said his name was Lt. Colonel Godbole. He further told me that he was in charge of the battalion from the B E G[1] that would have been sent to aid the police, if such aid was requisitioned. I said that I had not asked for aid from the Army, and had no intention of doing so.

1. The Bombay Engineering Group

He replied,"I understand that now, Sir. But in case the police did require aid from the Army, I wanted to take a recce of the situation, and I got Ribeiro's permission to accompany him in the city - in mufti as you can see."

I was somewhat mystified, and asked him what I could do for him. "Nothing," he said. "But there is something I want to do *for you*." Seeing my look of astonishment, he continued, "You did not notice me, but I was standing right behind Ribeiro at Kasture Chowk. I heard loud and clear what the Home Minister's security officer said to you." He repeated it for my benefit. "I have a feeling," he said, "that some enquiry may be held against you for not ordering the firing. I have come to tell you that I am prepared to give evidence in any Court of Law about the Minister's instructions to you. I observed the face of the security officer closely, and I am prepared to spot him in any, - what do you call it?"

"Identification Parade," I said. "Colonel, you're not an army officer sent to aid the police. You're an angel of mercy sent to aid this man. Thank you! I shall never forget you as long as I live."

Soon after Col.Godbole left, I got a phone from the Chief Minister, V P Naik. Without any pre-amble he said, "Why haven't you ordered firing?"

I replied, "Because Sir, the Home Minister ordered me not to fire under any circumstance."

He said,"Treat the order as cancelled. How soon will you be able to control the rioting?"

I replied,"Within two hours, Sir. If any daylight had been left, I would have said, 'within one hour'. We shall have to be careful not to fire on innocent people in the dark."

He said,"Do you want any help from the Army?"

I replied,"None Sir. If I wanted it, I would have called them. Further, may I request you to kindly note that in spite of my not firing, there has not been a single incident of stabbing?"

He said, 'Noted." And rang off.

The rioting was controlled well within two hours. The next morning, there were a few stray incidents but the rioting was definitely over. In the police firing, 2 persons were killed and five or six injured. Not a major riot compared to what I had faced and what I would have to face. Ribeiro says that the Army was called in for flag marches. This is not true. The Army was *not* called in at any stage for any purpose whatsoever.

My troubles, however, were not over. A couple of days later the Home Secretary, Paymaster, asked me to meet him in Bombay. He told me that the Home Minister (Balasaheb Desai) wanted to order an enquiry against me for *not* giving the order to open fire earlier. I said that I thought that that was a peculiar subject for an enquiry. I then told him about the Home Minister's order not to open fire. Paymaster said,"The Home Minister denies it. He called his security officer in my presence, who denied that he ever visited Kasture Chowk or spoke to you." I told him that my DCPs were present and would support me. (I did not know at the time that they had 'honestly' turned against me.) The Home Secretary said, "the Home Minister says they are your subordinates and are bound to support you."

I then told him about Col.Godbole. After that I heard no more on the subject of my not opening fire. But the Home Minister began on a different tack. At his behest, the I G, Majeedullah, began an enquiry into my alleged failure to take adequate preventive action. He asked me why I had not kept a list of goondas in my office, and why I had not arrested them before and during the riots. I did not put the blame on ny subordinates, particularly on Ribeiro, where it belonged. It was Rebeiro's duty when he was SP to have kept such a list, and it was his duty and Pathasarathy's to have ordered the arrest of the *goondas*, without waiting for any orders from me. I took it all on my shoulders, and gave suitable replies (into the details of which it is not necessary to go here.)

It has now been revealed (in Ribeiro's book) that while I did not bring my DCPs into the picture, these not-so-loyal officers gave their 'honest'opinions against me in the magisterial enquiry by R C Joshi. As far as I recall it, Joshi did not record my statement. Had he done so, he would have been forced to call Colonel Godbole, to testify.

And adverting to Colonel Godbole, I had often wondered what impelled him to come to me. Why did the possibility of an enquiry for not opening fire come into his mind? The only reason that now emerges is that he must have heard the not-so-loyal talk of my 'loyal' subordinates.

Let it also be noted that I did not make any adverse remark against any of these three officers - Ribeiro, Parthasarathy, or Misar - in their confidential reports, then, *or at any later stage.*

As for Majeedullah's enquiry, the questions and answers went on for some time, till the enquiry died a natural death. I do not know where Ribeiro got the information that there was a rivalry between Majeedullah and me. There was another officer between us, and I had to wait for eleven years before I became the I G.

I had spent part of my childhood and boyhood in the beloved city of Pune, and I was delighted when I was appointed its first police commissioner. Normally I would have been loath to leave it, but this episode had disillusioned me about many things. So, when, a couple of months later I was asked whether I would like to go on promotion as the I G of Jammu and Kashmir, I accepted the offer. As to what happened to me there, I shall relate it in the next chapter.

CHAPTER V

INTERLUDE IN KASHMIR

A recent writer on Kashmir has stated that despite all the efforts made by the secular forces in India to win over the hearts and minds of the Muslims of the Valley, these efforts have failed because whenever the Muslims have a majority in an area, they want an Islamic state. Further, their's was not only a matter of ideology, it was also a question of 'realpolitik'. *This*, according to him, was the great tragedy of Kashmir.

The ensuing discussion will show that at that critical period of time when such efforts would have borne fruit, they were not only not made, but the very opposite was done, by those holding the reins of power, entirely for selfish and personal reasons, in spite of the repeated warnings of this writer. *That* is the real tragedy of Kashmir.

In the middle of June 1966, when I was the Commissioner of Police of Poona, I got a phone call one morning from D S Joshi, Cabinet Secretary in New Delhi. He said that the Government of Jammu and Kashmir immediately wanted the services of a police officer from Maharashtra to be the I G of Police, and that the Union Government had suggested my name. The appointment was for a period of three years in the first instance. Was I interested?

I knew Joshi well. I had worked directly under him for several years as the Director of the Anti-Corruption Bureau, when he was the home secretary of Maharashtra.

I was fed up with the situation in Pune, following the riots (which I have described in detail earlier). I thought that Kashmir would be a welcome reprieve. I said to Joshi that I would consult my wife and would ring him up in a couple of days. He said,"No! the matter is extremely urgent. They want you there immediately. I must have your answer within an hour."

I went home and talked to my wife. Neither of us had ever visited Kashmir. Besides, she loved the mountains.

"We must visit Pangong Lake,"she said.

"Where on earth, is it," I asked.

"In Leh," she said. That settled it. I went back to the office and phoned Joshi.

"Barkis is willing," I said.

"Who?" he asked.

"I am willing to go to Kashmir as soon as possible, Sir," I said.

We packed up and left within a week. En route, I had to stop at Delhi where I met Joshi and the Home Minister, Y B Chavan.

I said to Chavan," Sir, I am told that there is a lot of politics in Kashmir. You have known me for several years. I am no politician or courtier, but a plain, blunt policeman".

"I know that very well, Modak," Chavan said." The Chief Minister, Sadiq Saheb, *wants* such a man; that's why I have specially suggested your name".

I also met the Union home secretary, L P Singh, who told me that the Chief Minister wanted a complete overhaul of the police department, which was probably the most corrupt and inefficient in India. " You will have my full support," he said. What more could I ask?

After a night's halt at Jammu, I went in my Fiat car to Srinagar, over the tortuous 200-mile route, on which I would be travelling frequently over the next year and a half.

When I reached Srinagar the only police officer who met me and welcomed me was Surendra Nath, the D I G, C I D. He was an officer from the Punjab cadre, on deputation to the State. I asked him whether the I G's residence had been vacated, and if so, whether I could move in. He said, somewhat hesitatingly (to my surprise) that no accommodation had been allotted to the I G. The present incumbent stayed in his own bungalow. I said that I would have to put up somewhere till the Government gave me a place.

Surendra Nath said that there were two State Guest Houses on the Bund where Rustamji, DG BSF, and Ashwini Kumar, IG BSF, always stayed during their visits to the State. He had asked for a reservation for my family and me for a week, but the Chief Secretary, Mangat Rai, had refused to give it. Surendra Nath had reserved a room for me in the Tourist Quarters. It was dirty, the bathroom was filthy and it smelled strongly of urine. When my wife saw it, she burst into tears. Surendra Nath then requested me to stay in his house for a few days till something was arranged. We had no choice but to accept his kind hospitality.

Imagine my surprise, when two days later, I got a phone call from Mangat Rai. He said," Modak, I hear that you have become very friendly with Surendra Nath?"

I replied that I had never met Surendra Nath before. I explained to him the circumstances leading to my staying with him. " Oh, in that case, I have nothing to say." He did not offer to give me accommodation in the State Guest House. When I went to call on him, he disposed me off within fifteen minutes.

Very soon I learnt the facts of life' for me in Kashmir:

I was to take over charge, not as I G , but as Officer on Special Duty for a month. The I G, Lachmandas Thakar, had been given an extension of one month, ' for his own, pressing, private reasons'.(Later, I learnt from him that D P Dhar had expressly asked him to take the extension. He had no private reasons whatever.)

The headquarters of the I G had been shifted very recently to Jammu. This was done on no rational grounds, as far as I could ascertain. Kashmir was the most sensitive state in India. If the Chief Minister or the home secretary wanted to see the I G for any purpose, or if the I G wanted to see either of them, he had to travel by road the entire tortuous distance of 200 miles and back, every time.

D P Dhar used to be the Home Minister. Very recently, the Chief Minister, G M Sadiq, had removed the Home portfolio from him (he was on tour at that time).With his powerful connections in New Delhi (the High Command), D P Dhar wanted to be the *eminence grise* of Kashmir politics. He could no longer issue orders to the police himself. Mangat Rai, or Renzu, acted according to his bidding. As Home Minister, Sadiq must have at least initial inchalled these orders. Why he did so became clear to me only after a long time.

The whole object of making me an Officer on Special Duty for one month also became clear. It was to make me pack up my bags and go back. However, I did not do so, because I had faith in the pronouncements made to me by the Chief Minister. I had faith in the declared support of the Union Home Minister. I was confident of solid support from Joshi, Cabinet Secretary. And I had the belief that I could do something concrete for Kashmir, and for my country in my humble capacity as the I G of Police of the State of Jammu and Kashmir.

As I have said, I had never been to Kashmir before, and I knew nobody there; I had made this clear to Mangat Rai when I went to call on him. Surely, it was his duty to have put me wise to the situation. Had he done so, I would not have betrayed his confidence - I had been a member of an old, covenanted cadre of service, like himself. I would have quietly packed my bags and gone with no hard feelings, either. During the remaining time he was there, he did not call me even once to discuss anything. IfI had been familiar with senior officers, like Joshi, or Dias, or Paymaster, it was because they sent for me frequently; perhaps, from among police officers, they had learnt to separate the wheat from the chaff. Within the Civil Service, they had a great camaraderie; a junior officer could call a senior secretary by his name or surname. The police have been, basically, a para- military organization with its 'chain of command'. Rustamji never asked me to call him by his name, even though like V D Moray, he was only three years my senior. He must have know what was happening to me. He never discussed the matter with me.

When he was leaving his post, I said to Mangat Rai that he had never sought any kind of close relationship with me. He agreed that that was so, and said that perhaps it was a mistake, but his policy was to keep all officers at a distance. What an extraordinary policy for a Chief Secretary to follow in Jammu and Kashmir, and that too, with an I G of Police who had been especially brought to overhaul the system! I am not speaking of social familiarity either; I am speaking of a close working relationship between the Chief Secretary and the I G of police - a visible and conspicuous relationship, which was an essential prerequisite for facing the peculiar problems of Kashmir and the challenge of insurgency that was to engulf the State.

When I first met G M Sadiq, the Chief Minister, I was very favourably impressed with him. He said that the police force of Jammu & Kashmir was corrupt and rotten to the core. He wanted me to overhaul it radically. He said that I would find some junior officers quite capable, but what they needed was a firm and guiding hand. As for the Kashmir Armed Police (the KAP), they were a cowardly lot. Whenever, even a small riot occurred, they would run away. The outside forces, the Border Security Force, would have to face the music, Because of this, the crowds would always cry, 'Punjab Police Hai Hai' (most of the BSF were Sikhs). He said it was the duty of the KAP to bear the brunt of any agitation, and he wanted me to train them to be fearless, even as I was known to be fearless! I thought that his views were eminently sensible.

I told him about the recent shifting of my headquarters to Jammu. He said, of course it was absurd. He did not know how it had happened, but he would have the order changed. It seems that he either forgot about the matter or did not have the guts to rescind the order made (I learnt at D P Dhar's instance). Eventually, I had to get it changed through the intervention of L P Singh.

No bungalow had been allotted to the I G, and no help could be expected from the Chief Secretary in getting one. Eventually, the Public Works Department (P W D) found a bungalow on the Bund. It was a lovely wooden Swiss chalet with a beautiful lawn, and a wicket gate going up to the embankment.

On the sides were the flowers of the season: tulips, daffodils, pansies, lily of the valley, white narcissus and an abundance of roses - there were roses, roses everywhere. My wife fell in love with it. I soon found out that I got the bungalow because it had been boarded up for a long time. Nobody wanted to occupy it, because they thought it was unlucky. Its previous occupant long ago had been a Captain Arthur, a renegade British Army officer, who was A D C to Maharaja Hari Singh, and had wormed his way into his confidence. Arthur had blackmailed the Maharaja in the 'Case of Mr. A' - a *cause celebre* of those days. Many of my subordinates implored me not to occupy it, but there was no other house available, and anyway, neither my wife nor I believed in superstitions.

I installed an armed guard from the KAP on the premises. I was the first officer *from outside* who had ever done so. Officers like Surendra Nath and others entitled to have guards, always got them from the Punjab Police or BSF or other outside forces. In fact, he suggested to me, with his ever-present smile, that I should take a BSF guard. He gave me the sad example of Col.Hari Singh, who was in charge of a Kashmir army unit in 1947. When the Pakistani infiltrators entered the valley, Col. Hari Singh had been advised to disarm his Muslim troops. He had refused to do so, and had been murdered by them on 31st October,. Ninety percent of the KAP in Srinagar were Muslims. I took the risk till I had personally trained the KAP. After that there was no risk.

"I was confident that the KAP would follow me *anywhere in India*, not only in Kashmir." At that time, and for some months thereafter, my prestige with the bureaucracy and with the public in general was very high. They all thought that I was the blue-eyed boy of the Union Home Minister, Y B Chavan, and that I would get his full backing in whatever I did, or wanted to do. Further, I was also known to be close to the Cabinet Secretary, D S Joshi, the top bureaucrat in the land.

When I first visited the KAP headquarters, I learnt that there were originally four KAP battalions. Very recently (a fortnight before I came), an order had been passed inducting two of the battalions into the BSF. I had, thus, only two battalions left with me. I protested very strongly at this order. D P Dhar, who was responsible for the order said to me that it was much better that way. The two battalions would be entirely at my disposal; their lot would improve, and so would their discipline. I did not agree. I said that they would become part of the BSF, and would be as much or as little available as any other BSF unit; this is what happened. I said that their higher scales of pay and conditions of service would create discontent in the KAP; this is exactly what happened. I said that if the Government of J and K wanted me to radically over haul the police, and through them, establish a rapport with the public, this would have to begin with the KAP in the conditions prevailing in the State. As far as I could see that early, there was a case for creating two more battalions of the KAP, not reducing the number. This action would make the public feel that the Government, itself, had no faith in its own police. Both the armed and unarmed police had their relatives in the valley. As it happened, Shamji, SP of Baramulla, had told me that he had first got information of the Maqbool gang through the armed police.

But D P Dhar was the accredited *expert* on the Kashmir administration; and he had a stranglehold on it. I found that his views always prevailed.[1]

My first duty, given to me by the Chief Minister in charge of the home portfolio, was to toughen the KAP, and make them bold enough to confront riotous mobs, I felt that they alone could deal with outside infiltrators. All police are afraid to face stones or other missiles; maybe, the Kashmir armed police were more afraid! I had created *and led* the striking forces in Bombay during the Samyukta Maharashtra agitation in 1956. I, therefore, decided to train the KAP in facing stones by taking the lead in facing the stones, myself. There was just no other way. As Field Marshall B L Montgomery has said, 'before an officer is fit to train others, he must train himself'.

I had seen again and again that the main problem that the police had in dealing with the rioters was to face their initial barrage of stones and other missiles. Once they could do this, the initiative would pass on the police. The rioters would have generally exhausted their supply of stones collected on the spot, or brought earlier in small tempos from somewhere. The next step for the police would be to break them up by cane charges, tear gas, or whatever, catch as many as possible, pursue the rest, and prevent them from assembling. In Bombay, during the Samyukta Maharashtra agitation, the police had no shields. We would wear steel helmets, put our heads down, and somehow charge. Now I learnt that in Calcutta the police used metal shields, so I sent for half a dozen. I found them very effective, so I sent for a hundred, then five hundred. I have discussed the details of this training in another chapter.

To repeat, the only way to remove the fear from the minds of the police *jawans* was to set the example, myself. I would take up a position at the apex of the 'V' formation of a platoon. When I observed that the 'mob' in front consisting of policemen in plain clothes were reluctant to throw stones at the IG, I announced a reward of rupees ten (to be given on the spot) for every dent on my shield, or on my person. The stones then came thick and fast.

It is difficult to describe the sensation I felt when I first faced the barrage. It felt a little like being born again. I was not so young then -

1. Mangat Rai and Renzu carried out his orders as if he was still the Home Minister. Renzu's attitude I could understand. He was a local man and a Kashmiri Pandit. But Mangat Rai was a senior ICS officer from the Punjab cadre, a former Chief Secretary of Punjab!

46, going on to 47. I don't know how many IPS officers have undergone this course in shield drill that I instituted in Maharashtra in 1976 when I became the I.G. Not so many, I have the impression. They are wont to satisfy their conscience by thinking or saying, ''All this is for the lower ranks". When confronted with mutinous armed police at the HQ, a police commissioner remarked that an officer of the inspector's rank could have tackled the problem. My reply was 'An officer of the Inspector's rank, forsooth! What are you there for then, pray? To put on higher and higher insignia of rank on your shoulders, and prance up and down before chief ministers and home ministers at such times, and show how busy and overworked you are? *Fee Fi Fo Fum.*"

I gave personal demonstrations of the shield drill (by facing the barrage of stones myself) to the Chief Minister, G M Sadiq, to K F Rustomji. DG BSF, and to the Union Home Secretary, LP Singh. Mob fighting was not the only thing I taught the KAP. I improved their drill, their field training - in dealing with dacoits or infiltrators, or whatever. At the end of it the two battalions were as good as any in the SRP in Maharashtra; they would have followed me anywhere in India. And the chance to prove their mettle soon offered itself.

The SP Baramulla, Shamji, had received information about the likely entry of infiltrators in the valley. He had come to see me one day and told me about it. He said he had not informed either the DIG Range or the DIG CID. I gave him two of my specially trained KAP companies. A week later, early one morning, he telephoned me that a gang of six infiltrators had been sighted inside the border, and he was going to lead the KAP and his police against them. I said I would join him directly, and began to dress up when I got a phone from D N Kaul, DIG Kashmir Range. He said that he and DP Saheb were going to Sopore to deal with the matter, and that DP Saheb had asked him to tell me that I should stay in Srinagar, and not go to Sopore or Baramulla. I asked him why I, the IG, should not go there. He said, "DP Saheb (DPDhar) says there is likely to be some trouble in Srinagar, and you should remain there to deal with it"

I asked him,"what trouble?" He could not give me an answer, and said that he was merely relaying DP Saheb's order.

I said to Kaul, "Tell DP Saheb *that I refuse to obey his order*. Who is he to give me such a preposterous order? He is not the Home Minister, I shall obtain orders from the Chief Minister,Sadiq Saheb."

I said to Sadiq on the phone,"Sir, the gang is sighted in Sopore and DPDhar says I should not go there. Why have you appointed me the IG? And he says there is likely to be some trouble in Srinagar and I should stay here.Kaul, the Range DIG, does not know of any."

The Chief Minister said," You go right ahead. I'll deal with any trouble that might arise here."

I went to Sopore. DPDhar, Kaul and Surendra Nath were already there. Neither of these two DIGs had gone to assist Shamji. They were both hanging around the 'VIP' area. I told D P Dhar that I was leaving for the place directly. He caught my hand, and would not let go.

He said,"No! No! We are doing something very important."

He made me get into his car and we drove in the *opposite* direction. We started making short halts at the villages on the way. He would call the headman and some other persons and repeat the same thing. The infiltrators were sighted, and they should alert the villagers and make the village defence parties ready to face any challenge. I learnt later there were no active village defence parties - they existed only in DPDhar's imagination). Till late evening I wasted my precious time in this stupid exercise.

At last when we came back to Sopore, we found that Shamji had returned. His party had caught Maqbool Butt, and killed another man, named Khan. The others had escaped.

Before going to Sopore, D P Dhar had ordered another armed party from the KAP HQ in Srinagar, under a young Kashmiri *Pandit* SP named O N Kaul to go to Baramulla, and had even given them directions where to confront the infiltrators. He had absolutely no business to do this, even if he had been the Home Minister, which he was not. But he was the eminence grise of the Kashmir Government and assumed such a position because of his alleged standing with the 'High Command'(The Prime Minister).

This officer had stationed himself at a a place which was not less than five miles from the scene of action. His subordinates told me that he refused to proceed any further in spite of their urging and pleading.

A couple of days later I recommended the names of Shamji and a young Muslim inspector for police medals for gallantry. Surendra Nath came to see me and said that DPSaheb has asked me to also recommend Kaul's name for the medal. I said to him,"You know the situation. He was not prepared to come within five miles of the scene of action. How can I recommend him?"

Surendra Nath said,"D P Saheb says that you should do it for the sake of balance between the two communities."

I said to Surendra Nath," Please tell D P Saheb that gallantry medals are not given for the sake of balance." (I learnt after I had left that Surendra Nath, who took over as I G, sent his name up immediately for the medal).

That evening at Srinagar, D P Dhar gave a press conference, describing how after getting the information about the infiltrators, he had gone himself to Sopore and visited all the border villages arousing the villagers; how the villagers had surrounded the gangsters and forced them on to the police parties, who had then an encounter with them. Yes, the I G had accompanied him. After the conference, Dhar asked me if I had anything further to add. I said I had not, after such an illuminating exposition.

Apart from interrogation by any other officer, I questioned Maqbool Butt at length, alone. He said he had begun his career as a journalist. I had never met such a diehard terrorist before. He said they were all being trained in special camps, and would come in waves till they won their objective, no matter how long it took. Their first goal was to create bases in the rural population and in Srinagar. He was openly contemptuous of the Kashmir administration and the police.

I realized we would have to create a special organization and an awareness to counter the movements and activities of these persons. Surendra Nath and his subordinates (as far as I could see) had never thought of working on these lines. Their objective was to impress political leaders and high Government officers in Kashmir and in Delhi with the seizures of weapons, and vituperations about Sheikh Abdullah's party and their activities. Nor was I impressed with the Range DIG (a very conservative type) and his subordinates in Srinagar, I decided to form my own intelligence cells (as I had done elsewhere).

I would have succeeded in it had I been given the time and the support I wanted. But my attention was diverted by all that happened, much of it caused by a selfish and narrow-minded outlook on the part of, shall I say, the powers that be, both in Kashmir and in Delhi.

I have always been interested in military history and military science. Stating this as a simple matter of fact, and not of pride, I might say that I have read more books on this subject than any other civilian in India. I was, therefore, greatly impressed with Lt. Gen. J F R Jacob's book, 'Surrender at Dacca'. I had met General Jacob in Kashmir when he was the Brigade Commander at Samba. What impressed me about him were his clear mind and grasp of the problem at hand. Now though, in the war against Bangladesh, we must all pay tribute to the excellent work done by the *muktibahini*, it cannot be denied (even from a cursory perusal of Jacob's book) that ninety percent of the success of the Bangladeh War was due to the Army. How could a group of volunteers, trained for a couple of months, like the *muktibahini*, fight against a professional army? They might have worked as guerillas. DPDhar seems to have been in the background helping to organize them. Those village defence parties in Baramulla appear to have been a dress rehearsal for his supervision (or unnecessary interference, depending on the way you look at it) in the war in East Pakistan.

I spoke to the Chief Minister, G M Sadiq, on more than one occasion about this uncalled- for interference by DPDhar. His reaction was always the same. The blood would rush to his face and he could hardly speak. When he calmed down he would say that D P Dhar was only allowed to give advice on policy matters. He had no business to interfere in the internal administration of the police, that I should not allow it, et al.

It was only later- much later- that I came to realize that the removal of D P Dhar from the Home portfolio was Sadiq's one act of supreme defiance. he did not have much of a clout with the High Command. And then it gradually dawned on me that, with my so-called influence with Y B Chavan, the Union Home Minister, Sadiq expected *me* to remove DPDhar's interference in police matters. In fact, it also dawned on me that I was brought there for that very purpose.

Small incidents lead to major riots. Two such major riots took place in Jammu & Kashmir during my tenure there, which led to large-scale rioting: the second in Srinagar lasted for almost two months. Lord

Birdwood, son of a former Commander-in-Chief of India, has begun a book on Kashmir with the remark that the boiling point of Indians is very low. If this is only partly true, it is easy to see how unscrupulous persons can take advantage of it.

Trilochan Dutt, a cabinet minister from Jammu, had two grown-up sons who would easily have figured in any police list as *goondas*, and mischief-makers. One day they molested a college girl on an open street. She complained to her relatives and friends in the college. A large number of students gathered together and caught them and handed them over to the Inspector at the police station. The atmosphere in Jammu had become very tense, and students were gathering in large numbers in the squares and on the streets.

The Chief Minister called me to his office in Srinagar. D P Dhar and Trilochan Dutt were there. He asked me to go over to Jammu immediately to deal with the situation. He had arranged for an Air Force Dakota to take me there. He asked the D I G Jammu Range, MMWazir, to arrest the young men and put them in the lockup. He also ordered their prosecution. Nothing would have happened if his orders had been carried out. But, unfortunately, as usual, DPDhar interfered.

When I reached Jammu, large scale rioting was taking place. The D IG had opened fire and several students were killed and injured. At the police station Wazir told me that Dhar had asked him on the phone (Presumably from another room) not to arrest the two young men. They had been kept in the adjoining room. This soon became known to the crowd outside, and they began to throw stones, brickbats, bottles. Pandemonium had been let loose. My arrest of the culprits and the announcement thereof did no good. It was too late.

The District Magistrate, the D I G and the S P told me that the students were going to take out a funeral procession late in the evening. It would consist of at least fifteen thousand people. In the control room, I had a discussion with the District Magistrate, Sondhi, the Divisional Commissioner, Amarsingh, the S P, Khajooria, and the D I G, Wazir. The District Magistrate and the Divisional Commissioner both happened to be Sikh officers. They were among the finest IAS officers I have ever had the good fortune to deal with. They were always calm, always imperturbable, and always helpful.

In our discussion, we came to the unanimous conclusion that the only choice left to us was to allow the funeral procession. During the procession, we would keep policemen alongside. The students were most unlikely to create any trouble on the way to the cremation ground. As to the likelihood of their going back in groups and causing trouble, we had to take the risk. We decided, however, to post strong pickets at important points.

At that moment, I got a telephone from L P Singh, Union Home Secretary. I do not know who had informed him about the riots. He asked me about it, and I gave him brief details and told him about the procession and what we had all decided to do. L P Singh then urged me to get curfew orders issued immediately all over the city. I told him that the Divisional Commissioner and the District Magistrate were sitting opposite. We had decided that the imposition of curfew, if at all, could only be considered after the procession was over. He said that he had found it very effective when he was a district magistrate somewhere in Bihar. (I could not tell him that we all knew what a badly run State it had always been). I requested him to hold the line, while I spoke to the two Magistrates. They said it would be madness to impose curfew now. I then told L P Singh that they were the ones who had to decide such matters, and they were against it. He asked me what my view was. I said that I had issued more curfew orders than most police officers, but in this case, I entirely agreed with them. He then rang off.

Any callow youth in the IAS or IPS would have agreed that it was most improper for an officer from outside (be he ever so high and mighty) to give advice to the officers on the spot, But, unfortunately, the matter did not end there. Shortly thereafter, I got a signal that K F Rustamji, DG, BSF was on his way in a special plane coming to see me. He soon came to my office and took me aside. He said he had been specially sent by L P Singh to urge me to get the curfew orders issued immediately. He said he (K F Rustamji) had done it in a very big riot in Jabalpur and had found it effective. I explained that I was not a stranger to curfew orders, but there was a time and place for everything. If we issued these orders now, it would be difficult to enforce them with the police strength at my disposal. Further, the students would refuse to take out the bodies for cremation, and would not let us do it either. The time to do it was *after*the funeral, in case the students resorted to rioting. I said the judgement of whether to impose the curfew or not, was not finally that of the police, but that of the Magistrates. They were both senior, experienced officers, and were dead against the curfew. He could convince them, if he liked. He did not like.

Rustamji was of the same seniority as V D Moray (additional SP in Satara after the departure of Moore Gilbert). He was only three years senior to me, but out of respect, I called him 'Sir'. He never asked me to treat him like an elder brother, as Moray had done. Against my will, against my better judgement, I allowed myself to be intimidated by his position and that of the Great Panjandrum, L P Singh. I then went and persuaded the two Magistrates to agree. At that time, my prestige was very high.

At last Amarsingh said, "Mr. Modak, we are humble officers from this 'backward' State, but we are not overawed by Mr. Rustamji or Mr. L P Singh. In deference to your wishes, however, we shall issue the orders, knowing that the result will be disastrous". They then called their subordinates and made preparations for the proclamation.

One of the greatest regrets of my life has been the fact that I did not show Rustamji the door. I should have, moreover, asked him to first confirm his advice in writing, and asked LP Singh also to confirm his advice in writing. The Army in aid of civil power are wise in this respect. In every case of firing,, they demand an order in writing from the Magistrate before they are asked to use force. I learnt later that LP Singh blamed me for all the subsequent trouble that took place due to this foolish and ill-conceived order, on the ground that I did not execute it properly. After all, it is not so difficult to find some flaws in the execution of *any* order!

Rustamji then said to me,"Get a jeep. And let us go to the old secretariat; I know the area well." I ordered the jeep, and we got in. I said,"Why the old secretariat?" I had once passed by the old secretariat. It was more than a mile away; they told me that it was mostly filled up with old records, but housed a few offices.

"You will see." Was Rustamji's cryptic reply. When we reached the building, the streets were practically deserted; a few people were walking about. Rustamji leaned out on the side, and shouted,"Curfew is declared; go home, go home." The police driver turned round and gaped. I can still remember the look of sheer astonishment on his face. Apart from him, all the other occupants of the jeep were stunned, including myself.

The Dy. SP at the back said, "Excuse me, Sir, the DM has not yet made the papers ready. As soon as he does so, we shall arrange to announce the curfew through the loudspeakers on our vans."

Rustamji said,"Take it as done. It's only a formality."

I said, "Sir, the trouble is at the other end of the city. What's the point in announcing the curfew here?"

Rustamji said, "Modak, you don't understand! This is how we did it is Jabalpur. If we announce it at the centre where the trouble is, there may be strong reaction. By starting with the periphery, we shall gradually move to the centre."

I said, "Sir, how many people can we reach in this jeep. And how long will you shout?"

"You will see that it works," Rustamji said.

We went on and on this way, wasting a precious half-hour. Then we returned to the control room. By that time the DM had already made the announcement.

Rustamji's paradigm of riot control was some communal riot that he had dealt with in Jabalpur. As we all expected, the curfew order led to a strong reaction. The students refused to allow the bodies to be taken out for cremation, leading to a major problem confronting the police. Large-scale stone-throwing and rioting took place in parts of the city. The police were hard put to it to deal with it, let alone enforce the curfew. Almost the entire cabinet had arrived in Jammu, and they were considering what they should do. The students were now demanding that the D I G, Wazir, and the SP Khajooria should be immediately suspended, and the procession be allowed. I was caught up in the torrent of events and I do not know when exactly Rustamji left in his special transport and sneaked back to Mount Olympus. I was summoned to the C M's bungalow where the C M sat with D P Dhar on one side and General Candeth[1] on the other. There were other sundry ministers sitting all round the room on chairs against the walls.

The C M informed me that they had decided to agree to the demand of the students to suspend the police officers. I protested, saying that they were only carrying out the orders given by the ministers, when DP Dhar said that if this action were not taken the cabinet would fall. (I heard this argument more than once during the onset of any trouble.)

1. GOC XV Corps,

The C M also said that General Candeth had volunteered to help put down the riot. Later a Brigadier came to me and said that he could spare only one battalion and asked me how he should deploy it. I suggested to him that he should, first, take out a flag march and try to restore confidence. Secondly, with only a battalion, and knowing their methods of deployment, I suggested that he take a very limited area and control it - to be specific, the main street from the police station for a distance of about 400 yards. When, and if, they could spare another battalion, I suggested that they spread out slowly. This is what they did.

The Brigadier said that they expected to be there for a couple of days. I said," I don't think so. You will find that it easier to get in, but it will be difficult to get out." This also proved to be correct thought I did not press for their stay. The funeral procession was eventually allowed. It comprised of more than the expected number, but it passed off peacefully. Later, a judicial enquiry was ordered into the entire episode. Two of the main questions asked by the Commission, Justice Mukherjee, were:

1. Why was the curfew imposed when it was known that a very large number of disturbed students was going to take out the funeral procession? And,

2. Who were the officers who began to impose the curfew before the formal orders were issued, and from a distant place like the Old Secretariat?

Out of mistaken sense of loyalty to L P Singh and K F Rustamji, I went out of my way to ensure that their names were not exposed. I learnt subsequently that they both blamed me for the mishandling of the riot. I should have allowed the truth to prevail. They would have been called by the Commission for evidence, and it would have been established, once and for all, what great harm remote control by those, however highly placed, can do.

To get to know the people, I had first to get to know the police force, not only in Srinagar and Baramulla, Jammu and Poonch, but all over the state. Whenever I had the time, I used to tour in every nook and corner of the State. The previous I Gs and other senior officers from various departments hardly ever left their headquarters. This position was reflected in the fact that there were no Inspection Bungalows where one could stay. My wife accompanied me everywhere; she loved the mountains and valleys of Kashmir. As for Jammu, she still remembers Bhimbar Galli, Doda and Kishtwar.

All the brigade commanders and the officers of the Border Roads Organization gave us warm and wonderful hospitality. The Governor of Maharashtra had sent me a big consignment of used (but almost new) winter clothing and this was distributed by my wife to the policemen and their families. In fulfillment of her long-expressed desire, we went beyond Leh to Chushul and Demchok to see Pangong Lake, part of which was with the Chinese.

The GOC Leh said he was unable to give my wife permission to go beyond Leh. I asked him who he was to give or withhold permission. As IG, it was I who used to give permission to civilians (in those days) even to visit Leh. My wife was accompanying me on a visit to a police station beyond Demchok to distribute woolen clothes to the policemen. He said he could not give her any protection (from the Chinese). I said I had not asked for any from the Army. He then issued orders to his brigadiers not to entertain us. We managed without their help this time. The Intelligence Bureau had their posts there, and they were happy to put us up.

We did not merely do sightseeing during these visits. The police officers would bring many of the local citizens to meet me, and they were happy to do so. They said that nobody had taken any interest in them before. In view of the developments over the Line of Control and the throwing back of the Pakistanis, (as at the time of writing), I must mention here that we had stayed with Brigadier Ghosh at Kargil, both on our onward journey to Leh and back. He was delighted to meet a Bengali lady in that far off outpost.. He took us round the Line of Control, and showed us all the peaks and terrain. I particularly remember '13620', which he explained, was a vital point, given back to Pakistan in the Tashkent agreement. This, he said, was a grave blunder. We could see the Pakistani bunker, and some soldiers standing beside it, through his binoculars.

I remember asking him what happened in the winter when everything was covered with snow. He said,"My patrols are always on the move on the line of control, sunshine or snow; you get used to it." He explained all this in detail because he found out that I was greatly interested in things military.

The State C I D , under the 'able' leadership of Surendra Nath, and his equally 'able' assistant, Peer Gulam Husein, used to be very active in recovering huge caches of arms and ammunition. These seizures were even larger in quantity when any VIPs from Delhi were in J and K. It was only much later that I discovered that for a long time, Kashmir had been a regular conduit through which illegal arms passed. I also found that both these officers effected these seizures without ever moving from Srinagar (during the summer) or Jammu (during the winter). Another favourite pastime of the CID was constant vituperation against Shaikh Abdulla and his party. He was the bete noire of the ruling Congress. As for information against likely infiltrators, they did not give me any during the time I was there. They would also tell me how disloyal the Kashmir officers (particularly those from the police in the valley) had been to Mehra, former IG of police. Eventually they themselves turned out to be the ones most disloyal to me.

Several outside reserve police battalions from the BSF, CRP, and PAC (U P) were deployed in the State. They were under the administrative control of the IG BSF, L S Bisht, an officer of the UP cadre. Those with the Army were under the operational control of the Army, but those with the Kashmir Police were *under my operational control.* This latter fact was of supreme importance, but, unfortunately, Bisht did not understand it, probably due to the constant interference of officers from the Home Ministry.

As I have said before, when I went to Kashmir, my prestige was very high. The Government (Sadiq) and the officials, both police and civilians, were prepared to do anything that I asked (with, of course, the exception of DPDhar and his cohorts.) I behaved as if I was the IG of any other state in India (Article 370 not withstanding), and they seemed to like it. I had suggested that there should be a free transfer of police officials (I P S) out of and into J & K. Had I remained there, this important suggestion would have been implemented, and would have done a great deal for national integration. The idea of 'They' and 'We' never arose even once between us. It was given emphasis by D P Dhar, and officers cited above, from outside. I shall now relate two incidents that are not only illustrative of what I mean, but that had far-reaching consequences on the future of this relationship.

One afternoon, a football match between a Kashmiri eleven and an outside team was in progress in the football stadium. A very large crowd had assembled there. A platoon of the P A C (the U P Armed

Police Battalion) was housed in the spare rooms of the stadium below. The commandant of the unit was a young I P S officer named Luthra. He was watching the match along with several of his policemen from the unit. None of them was on duty. Even if they had been on duty, they would never have been given the job of keeping order at a football match. There were some policemen from the police station on duty at the stadium. If they had failed to keep order, Luthra should have reported the matter to the control room on the phone.

A dispute arose during the match, which ended in a riot. This was a matter for the Kashmir police. If they had failed in their duty, I would not have hesitated to take action against them. If the policemen present had failed to inform the police station and the control room, Luthra or one of his men should have done so. Instead of doing this, Luthra pulled out his revolver and fired several times in the air. (I have never understood why he had to carry a revolver into the stadium. He disappeared for several days after this incident, and I was too busy to enquire about him. It was Bisht's duty to have taken action against him.) The PAC men took this as a call to arms. Seven or eight of them rushed down to their quarters and brought up loaded rifles. Some of them remained in the stadium, while others went out to the road intersections. Then they began to fire, but *discriminately*! They would pull down the trousers or pajamas of the men, and if they were found circumcised, shoot them in cold blood.

The C M called me and we visited the hospital together, Some dead bodies from the firing were lying on the veranda; we went inside to see the injured persons. One of them spoke to us. He said he was the son of a head constable, and was returning home after shopping for vegetables. When the P A C men caught him, he fell at their feet and pleaded that he was the son of a head constable. They told him that because of that they would not kill him, but only shoot him in the leg, which they did.

The Chief Minister said," Modak, you have yourself seen how these outside police behave; and they talk of national integration. I would request you to personally supervise this case and see that the culprits are brought to book. And, whatever happens, please don't give this case to Surendra Nath!"

Not unexpectedly, Surendra Nath met me soon thereafter, and said with his usual smile, "Sir, as this case is complicated, I would suggest that it be given to the C I D I shall appoint a very efficient Inspector to investigate it."

I replied," I am told that the Inspector in charge of the police station is a competent officer, and he is reporting directly to me." After a few days, Surendra Nath came back smiling. He said,"Sir, I am told that you have seized the rifles which were used in the shooting, and are thinking of sending them to the Forensic Laboratory in Calcutta. This will take a long time. Let me send them to Phillaur (Punjab). I shall get the result within a few days."

I said,"Thank you, Surendra Nath, for all the trouble you are prepared to undertake, but I have already spoken on the phone to the Director of the Forensic Laboratory in Calcutta and he has promised to expedite the matter. The rifles have been sealed in a box, and an Inspector is taking them tonight.

The Forensic Laboratory reported that the bullets found in the bodies of the dead persons were fired from the rifles. The P A C men concerned were arrested and a case was sent up against them under Section 302 (murder) and other sections. It ended in conviction in the Sessions Court, and it was confirmed by the High Court. I learnt long after I left that it was acquitted on Appeal. My unpopularity with the U P Police and the Home Ministry must have begun from this date. (This reaction has dogged my footsteps whenever I have taken any action not in conformity with the wishes or my political masters.)

The second incident took place some time later. A Kashmiri Pandit woman clerk in the Supply Department got married to a Muslim clerk in the same department; they had fallen in love. She was a major and knew what she was doing. It was not the case that she was abducted by anybody. This was a small incident, but the reaction of the Kashmiri Pandit community was out of all proportion to its trifling nature. The Pandits wanted the girl to be returned to her family, failing which they took out *morchas* to the Lal Chowk, made fiery speeches, and began rioting.

The police could have easily dealt with this rioting if the matter had been left to them. By this time Mangat Rai had gone and P K Dave (brother-in-law of L P Singh) had taken over charge as the Chief Secretary. I naturally thought, that as a younger man, I would be able to establish some rapport with him, but this was not to be. He did not have an open mind. He never called me even once for a discussion. The Government gave an order that firing was not to be resorted to under any circumstances. Daily the Kashmiri Pandits would gather in large numbers at the several intersections leading to Lal Chowk, and throw stones and other missiles at the police. The police could deal with them only with canes, so the rioting went on and on. Complaints were then made against the police that they were very harsh in using canes, because the Kashmir Armed Police in Srinagar (as explained earlier) were Muslims. After that magistrates were kept at every intersection in Lal Chowk and the police had to obtain orders from them even in the use of canes.

I decided to work on a little scheme. Overnight, I brought the Kashmiri Armed Police Battalion from Jammu (mostly Hindus) and replaced them, removing the Srinagar battalion. These Hindu police beat up the Kashmiri Pandits even more severely than the Muslims - mind you, only *beat* them up for rioting, after obtaining the orders of the magistrates! Allegations were made that one Hindu was killed in the caning; careful enquiries revealed that nobody was killed, or even hospitalized,

On one of these afternoons, I was standing with the District Magistrate in the centre of Lal Chowk, while the rioting was going on 'as per programme'. A unit of the P A C (U P Armed Police) had been deployed at one of the intersections. My deputy S P and several of his subordinates came running with their hands and faces bleeding. I asked,"What's happened? You couldn't stand the stoning after all that I taught you?"

The Deputy S P said,"No sir! We can stand any amount of stoning from the rioters. When we were dealing with them, the U P platoon came on us and began to beat us. We could have retaliated because we outnumber them and we are better trained. But, this would have led to a far bigger riot, so we took the beating and have come to you as we saw you standing here,"

I said to them,"You have done the right thing. Don't go there. I shall take up the matter in the control room tonight". (Every night there used to be a meeting in the control room to take stock of the situation; it was attended by the Chief Secretary, DPDhar, and sometimes, the Chief Minister.)

That night I raised the issue. I told all the officers and others present that my men had exercised admirable restraint. I told them what I had done in putting Hindus in place of the Muslim men of the Srinagar Kahmiri Armed Police. I said that once I had trained the men myself, they did not work as Hindus or Muslims; they worked as secular policemen of Bharat, that is India. I told the VIPs present that the PAC of U P were an undisciplined and communal lot. I said that I had talked to Bhagwan Sahai (former Chief Secretary of U P), and now Governor of J&K, and he had agreed with me. I said that I would not use them for operational duties thereafter, that I wanted them removed, and battalions from any other State posted in their place. I made a report in writing about the incident.

After I had finished, there was complete silence for a few minutes. Then L S Bisht, I G BSF, blew his top off. He did not contradict me; he could not. But he said that I should not have raised the matter 'in public' like this. I should have spoken about this matter confidentially.

This was my reply, in effect:Is the control room a public place, or is it private? Did the U P police beat up my men in private? It was witnessed by thousands. If my men had not exercised admirable restraint, partly, at least, due to my presence and hold over them, the incident would have resulted in one of the bloodiest massacres in the history of the police in India. As for this strange order not to open fire, and not to beat the rioters severely, it was going to send a very ugly message to the Muslim majority. In fact, my own information was that it was going to produce a strong reaction among them, and lead to rioting between the two communities on a scale never before seen in Kashmir. The Kashmiri Pandit woman, Parmeshwari Handu, was making *takhrirs* (speeches) openly in mosques and in public squares denouncing the Kashmiri police for interfering with her rights.

Within a few days, D P Kohli, D G SPE (the forerunner of the CBI) turned up in Srinagar. I gathered that he had been sent by L P Singh to make an enquiry into the incident. I used to regard D P Kohli and B N Mallik as demi-gods in the police. I was absolutely sure that he would make an impartial enquiry. He heard me sympathetically and did not ask a single question to clear up any doubts in his mind (or so I thought). Alas! I found out too late that the feet of these demi-gods were mired in mud. And I should have remembered that Kohli was an officer from the Uttar Pradesh cadre.

I learnt much later that Kohli had made a confidential report to the Union Home Secretary justifying the behaviour of the P A C of U P. It seems that he had 'discovered' that at one particular intersection in Lal Chowk, the police had not obtained the order of a magistrate in making the cane charge. In fact, the magistrate was not present, so where was the question of getting his order? He also found out that the K A P men had been cruel with canes (if I may so put it). That is why those splendid men of the P A C had intervened, and their intervention was justified! In order to make the position doubly clear, Kohli had found my supervision wanting and made some remarks against me.

In the first place, why was it necessary to have a confidential enquiry in the matter? Kohli should have held an open enquiry in which (according to the elementary rule of natural justice) he should have recorded my statement, including my reply to this allegation. He should also have recorded the statements of my senior officers and the magistrates. Even if I had the slightest doubt of Kohli's impartiality, I would have demanded a judicial enquiry, in writing, from the Chief Minister.

The Government now gave another order (whether it was oral, or in writing, I cannot remember). The police were no longer allowed to use even canes in dealing with the Kashmiri Pandits. By the Government, it is to be understood it was DPDhar, acting through his mouthpiece, the Chief Secretary. We were discussing how such an absurd order was to be implemented. Bisht went out of the control room and came back with a rifle. He held it up vertically, and pushed it down, uttering the expression,"'humph!' I shall do this if any rioters come on me". He marched out, and we thought he was going to demonstrate his new method to his men on the streets. But he came back without the rifle in five minutes flat. "I thought you had gone out to demonstrate," I said. "What happened?" "I have been showing my men what they should do," he said.

I had explained to D P Kohli that I was not anti-U P police or pro anything. I had seen more of the P A C during my visits in Kashmir than Bisht had ever done. I was more interested in the welfare of armed policemen than most police officers. There was something radically wrong with their training and discipline. He should have listened to me and had the P A C in U P thoroughly overhauled. He did no such thing. Within a year, the P A C in U P mutinied and the Chief Minister (Tripathi) had to resign.

In September of 1967 Y B Chavan visited Srinagar. I told him in brief what had happened. I said that an atmosphere was building up against me, and I could no longer be of any use in J & K. They had originally told me that my term was for three years. On reaching Kashmir, I had found that D P Dhar had maneuvered to one year. That year was now over. I wanted to write to the Government of J & K to release me. Chavan heard me and said,"If you write, Sadiq Saheb will misunderstand it. Leave it to me. I shall arrange the matter."

Alas! Y B Chavan promptly forgot. I never had any illusions that I was ever his blue-eyed boy. I, who had worked under Chavan for several years, should have known that he used to rely very heavily on his secretaries (ICSor IAS) in departmental matters.

Now I come to the last episode of my stay in Kashmir.

Rioting was taking place on a large scale between Hindus and Muslims all over Srinagar city. The Chief Secretary, P K Dave, came to the control room and issued orders (at the instigation of D P Dhar) of a new method of dealing with the riots. The Kashmiri Pandits largely stayed in a small area called Rainawari, which constituted one-fifth of Srinagar. The Muslims and the others stayed in the remaining four-fifths. Dave's order was that the K A P, who were Muslims, should be in charge of Rainawari, and the B S F, who were almost all Hindus, would be in charge of the rest of the city. I protested loud and long. I said that he was thereby creating a Hindustan and Pakistan in Srinagar itself, the effects of which would be long and lasting to the detriment of the Kashmiri Pandits themselves. From what I had seen of the situation in Kashmir there had been communal amity in the State for years. It had now been disturbed over a minor incident. After all, the minority community had to also use its discretion in such matters. My views were no different when I gave them to the Madon Commission over the Bhiwandi riots.

When Dave persisted in saying that he was carrying out orders, I asked him to give me the order in writing with his signature, which he did. By the time the men were deployed, night was drawing nigh. D P Dhar, Dave and senior police officers were to go round at night and supervise the arrangements. I went to the Chief Minister, G M Sadiq, and told him what had happened. He was in his house 'indisposed' as usual at such times. His reaction was also, as usual, strong - a reddening of the neck and face with difficulty in articulation. I told him that he was the Home Minister, not D P Dhar. Indisposed or not, he had to come to the control room and take over. If he did not do so, D P Dhar and his stupid followers would lose the goodwill of the Kashmiri Muslims forever.At last he agreed to come. I asked,"Shall I tell them that you are coming, and that they should wait for you?"

"No," he said."You wait in your house, and I shall send for you from the control room."

The Chief Minister, Ghulam Muhammad Sadiq, never went to the control room, and never sent for me.

A couple of days later, I got a phone call from his P A to see the C M in his office. The stage had been set. His table was covered with files, and so was the floor around him. His P A would give him some open file and whisper something, on which he would initial it. This went on for some time. I never saw his face, only the top of his brown fur cap.

At last he said,"Your term in Kashmir is over."

I said,"Just like that?"

He said,"Yes".

I stood up, saluted the top of his cap and left.

Everybody knew that I was to go, except me. Surendra Nath certainly knew, but he told me nothing. He was to become the I G. He came out of it all, smiling through.

This was not the end of the Kashmiri interlude for me. It seems that the Government of J & K, after a public outcry, was at last forced to order a judicial enquiry into the riot, and Justice R Dayal was appointed on the Commission. He sent me a letter asking me to appear before him in New Delhi. I was at that time the Commissioner of Police of Bombay. I wrote to the Government of J & K that I needed to refresh my memory by scrutinizing the control room files and that these should be sent to New Delhi with an officer.

Accordingly, when I went to New Delhi, the Superintendent of Police in charge of the control room in Srinagar, a Sikh officer, named

Amarsingh, came to see me the day before my evidence was recorded. This Amarsingh had a history behind him. He was a police officer from Jammu, who had been suspended and prosecuted for an offence of murder (in some police action, I forget). The case had gone on for several years during which he was under suspension. Eventually (while I was there), he was honourably acquitted by the High Court. An acquittal is no bar to a departmental enquiry, if it is on different charges, and the office had recommended that a departmental enquiry should be held against him, and he should continue to be under suspension.

The file was on my table in Jammu, and I had to deal with it in turn. My orderly announced that Mrs.Amarsingh was waiting outside and wanted to see me. I called her in and asked her to sit down. I noticed that her clothes were in tatters. She said in Hindi,"Jenab, I have come to plead for my husband. We have come to the end of our tether."

I asked her,"How have you supported yourselves all these years? Your husband's pay must have stopped long ago? "

She said, "Yes. As you know, Sir, he cannot take up a job. Friends give him some work now and then. I have to work for the family."

"What work do you do?" I asked her.

"I am an illiterate person, Sir." She said. "I do any kind of domestic work that is offered."

"Such as?"

"Such as cooking, washing clothes and vessels, even cleaning latrines." She was matter of fact and completely dry-eyed, when she said it; I was not.

I said,"I think your husband's file is on my table; perhaps some kind soul told you! Let me see." I went through it. Amarsingh had been honourably acquitted of the criminal charges. He had committed some departmental defaults. I said,"Enough is enough."

I called my stenographer and dictated a letter to the Home Secretary, Renzu, recommending that Amarsingh should be immediately reinstated in his rank as S P, and he should be given all the back pay due to him. The lady tried to fall at my feet, but I dissuaded her. I sent the letter with a special messenger to the Home Secretary, who issued the order on that very day.

Surendra Nath had appointed this same Amarsingh as the S P in charge of the control room (considered an unimportant job) and he was now sitting before me with the control room file. He told me,"Sir, before you gave your evidence to the Dayal Commission, I wanted to say something to you. I think the matter is of some importance."

I said,"Go ahead."

Amarsingh said,"Sir, the most important issue before the Commission has become the question as to whether the Government had issued an order (signed by the Chief Secretary) dividing Srinagar city into Hindu and Muslim areas during the riots. While the junior officers have all maintained that such an order was issued, the senior officers have denied it. When Surendra Nath asked me to send him the control room file, I guessed that his object was to remove the Chief Secretary's order from the file. None of the other copies is forthcoming. I removed the order from the file- luckily, the papers are not numbered, and sent him the file. I am now producing it before you." He gave me the order.

After seeing it, I said,"Thank you Amarsingh. Are you the only officer then left, loyal to me in Kashmir? Let's put it back in chronological sequence, shall we?"

Next day I gave my evidence before the Commission. When I spoke about the order issued by the Chief Secretary, he said, " Everyone talks of the order, but the senior officers deny it. Where is the proof of the existence of the order?"

I said, "Sir, the proof of the existence of the order is the order itself. It should be in this control room file. May I see it?"

With his permission, I turned over the file, and 'found' the order in the place where it should have been. I gave it to him.

He said,"Ah! Now we have something!"

I said, "Sir, I have two requests concerning this order." He looked at me enquiringly.

I said," Sir, Kindly keep this order in your persoinal custody, and have it examined by the handwriting expert *in your presence*."

The Kashmiri Pandit agitation went on for two months or more. Most of the agitators were white-collar workers, and could not have sustained themselves without powerful financial and other backing. Eventually it resulted in rioting between Hindus and Muslims.

What was the object of this riot? My reader should have found the answer in all the previous discussion. It was done, with the object of showing that Sadiq could never be an effective Home Minister. It was further, brought about to show that D P Dhar could hold Kashmir to ransom; he could bring things to a standstill, if he so desired.

Some time later I happened to meet Y B Chavan in Bombay. He said to me, "You know Modak, L P Singh wanted to prevent your getting the medal (the President's Police Medal). I told him clearly that you were removed from Kashmir purely for political reasons, and that it was no reflection on your efficiency." I was thankful for small mercies!

After my evidence before the Madon Commission in the Bhiwandi riots was over, Mr. Justice Madon asked me to submit within a fortnight, my views on how such riots could be prevented. I submitted my views in writing, giving detailed suggestions on mobile columns etc. One view that I gave was that practically all communal riots were due to the playing of music before mosques during the Ganapati processions. The Supreme Court had given a ruling that people had a right to play the music. I said that there were many churches, synagogues, *aghyaris* in Bombay city, abutting right on the streets. During their prayers, the congregations did not object to the playing of music by processions. Almost always the members of the processions stopped the music when they saw the people inside in prayer. All the trouble arises because the Muslims object to the music. If they changed their attitude, I felt that the processionists would stop of their own accord.

The Commission criticized this view. He did not find fault with my supervision of the police action, after I had gone to Bhiwandi. He said that the provisions of the Law should be used for preventing the music. Perhaps I was misunderstood. It was never in my mind that in a case where there is a long history of communal trouble, we should not use the provisions of the Law. Of course, they must be used! But there are scores of small cities and towns where there is no history of trouble. How can the police use preventive sections in the case of every procession? I have been consistent in my stand. A minority community, be it Hindu, (as in Kashmir) or Muslim, (as in other places) has to live in amity with the majority.

I have found that the moment a secular officer makes the slightest remark which is not in favour of the Muslims, they consider him 'anti-Muslim'; and the moment he makes such a remark against Hindus, he is considered 'anti-Hindu'. How is a secular police officer or civil service officer to function in these circumstances?

That India is the largest democracy in the world, is an unquestionable fact; all the elections held after Independence have proved it. But it is a democracy with a difference. It is a communal democracy; it is a casteist democracy; it is a sectarian democracy.. The elections have also proved this fact. And even Christians in India, who form a minuscule percentage of the total population, have displayed, among themselves, a casteist bias, in spite of their much-proclaimed doctrine of the equality of man and man.

As for Kashmir[1], the loss was not entirely mine. To every man and woman, sometimes an Inner Voice speaks. The post of IG, J & K was not, as has been seen, a sinecure. But I venture to aver that if I had been allowed to continue there for five years or so, without any interference from the likes of D P Dhar,not as a Governor or Chief Secretary, but in my humble capacity as IG, perhaps the subsequent history of Kashmir would have been different.

1. in any abrupt and humiliating removal from the scene.

CHAPTER VI
Section-I

THE SHIV SENA RIOTS OF MUMBAI IN FEBRUARY 1969

I took charge of the post of Police Commissioner of Mumbai on 20th January 1968 from A G Rajadhyaksha, who became the Inspector General. The Deputy Commissioner in charge of the Special Branch was Dafle, the brother of the Raja of Jath. Dafle came from Jath as a direct Deputy Superintendent of Police, and was appointed Assitant Commissioner of Police in Mumbai, from which post he was soon made Deputy Commissioner.[1] Dafle was a thorough gentleman, honest and hard working, but without either the background or the brains to understand all the nuances that his job demanded. He was the wrong person for the job and Rajadhyaksha should have recognized this fact. Unfortunately, I could not replace him for reasons into which I cannot go. The relationship, which the Special Branch had with the Shiv Sena was, odd to say the least. It is not possible for me to be more explicit in the matter. The Cognoscenti would have readily agreed, that the responsibility for all that happened, or was likely to happen, was squarely that of my predecessor, A G Rajadhyaksha. However, it was I who had to bear the burden of the tragic consequences. And to add insult to injury, Rajadhayaksha started a whispering campaign against me:'Modak is riot prone'.

As part of his strategy, Balasaheb Thackeray used to make pronouncements that if the Government did not do such and such a thing by a certain date, he would take drastic action. In August 1969 he made a public statement that if the Central Government did not grant the inclusion of Belgaum in Samyukta Maharashtra by the end of January 1969, he would prevent any Central Minister from entering Mumbai. I spoke to Dafle many times that he should use his personal

1. He had had no experience of police work, and was apparently appointed police chief of Jath, immediately prior to the merger (of princely States).

influence with Thackeray to withdraw this impractical statement. Every time Dafle would answer, "Nothing will happen, I assure you, Sir. Balasaheb only says such things. He does not intend to pursue them."I did not agree. In the informal talks that the senior police officers had with the Chief Minister, (early in the morning when he was shaving in the veranda, that being the only time he could spare for us), I repeated that we were going to face serious trouble if Thackeray did not withdraw his threat.

Came the end of January 1969. Far from withdrawing his statement, Thackeray renewed it at a public meeting. I again expressed my apprehensions to the Chief Minister. Perhaps, he had more faith in the Inspector General and Dafle than in me. According to the Chief Minister, V P Naik, all that was needed to face difficult situations was tact, which was the writer was known to lack. 'Tact' and 'Firmness' were the two most important words on the Chief Minister's tongue when he spoke to police officers. That the two were often incompatible, he was never able to understand.

As the deadline approached, in desperation I asked for a *formal interview* with the Chief Minister. After narrating the whole sequence of events, I said that it was beyond my power to stop the holocaust that was bound to come. There was only one option left. I Pleaded that he, the Chief Minister call Balasaheb Thackeray and persuade him to give up his plan. And I urged that the Chief Minister act fast.

But V P Naik did nothing in the matter. Dafle told me that he (the Chief Minister) did not call Thackeray, and apparently, he had no intention of doing so. All that was needed was tactful handling by the police. Perhaps, both Dafle and the Inspector General had told him that the Commissioner was making a mountain out of molehill. Such tactful handling can go on for some time, but in the process political elements come to think that the police (and the Government) are weak, and that they can get away with anything.

Now as my luck would have it, the first central minister to send the programme of his visit to Mumbai was Morarji Desai, Finance Minister. He was to visit Mumbai on 9th Febraury, 1969, and would be coming by air from Madras. By this time, the Special Branch (Dafle & Co.) had lost all influence with the Shiv Sena. Eventually, at the eleventh hour, entirely on my own, without the knowledge of Dafle, I had managed to contact Dr Gupte of the Shiv Sena. Late at night on 8th Febraury, Dr

Gupte,Manohar Joshi and Pramod Navalkar met me in my flat on Nepean Sea Road. I said to them that it was in the interest of all to prevent the bloodbath that was going to come. We had, therefore to find a *modus vivendi* out of the impasse. At last they agreed that they would allow the minister to enter Mumbai, provided he accepted a memorandum from them addressed to the Prime Minister on the Samyukta Maharashtra issue. This was of course, subject to confirmation by Balasaheb Thackeray. Ten of them would wait at the junction at Mahim, before the causeway not far from St, Michael's Church. They wanted Morarji to get out of the car and accept it. I said that (from what I knew of his nature) he would never do that, come hell come high water. Eventually, they agreed to hand it over to him through the window of the car.

The next step was for me to get in touch with Morarji Desai and persuade him to agree to accept the memorandum. He was on tour in Tamil Nadu. The control room tried all day (the 9th) to locate him in Madras. It was learnt that he had gone somewhere in the interior, and would return to the city only in time to board the special plane to Mumbai. Somebody had, therefore, to meet him at the airport at Mumbai, and persuade him to accept the memorandum before he got into the car. I could have sent some other DCP, not in charge of a zone, but I did not think that any of my DCP's would cut much ice with him. Dafle definitely would not and anyway he was going. (Had I but known that Ribeiro was on such pally terms with 'Morarjibhai' (as he claims) I would gladly have sent him to the airport and put a more competent DCP in his place in charge of Zone III. On taking thought, I decided that I would go myself. I had worked under Morarji for several years, and felt that he might listen to me.

I did not have to go. It could be argued that it was my first duty to look after the whole city, not to persuade an obstinate, stiff-necked man to stop for a few minuter and accept a memorandum passed through the window of his car. And if did not agree to it, the consequences to the precious person of the Commissioner were too awful to contemplate. Nine out of ten police officers in my place would have preferred the (shelter of the) control room. Moreover, I repeat, I did not have to go. I owed Morarji nothing. In sum, I could not have been faulted from my angle for not going.

But Morarji was an old man, needing protection. As I have said I had worked directly under him for several years. Most important, the scheme of handing over the memorandum had been worked out by the three Shiv Sena leaders and me. The had done it in good faith, and had persuaded Balasaheb Thackeray to agree to it. This was in itself no small achievement. It was my moral duty to see it through. I, therfore, decided to go.

The special plane coming from Madras landed at Santa Cruz a little after dark. As soon as Morarji got out, I took him aside and explained the situation to him in a few succinct words. He refused to accept the memo, and would not budge from his position. I told him that if he did not agree, we would have to pass through the stronghold of the Shiv Sena,compared to which Dante's Inferno would have been a picnic. At last he said, "Let them come to Oceana. (his son's residence on Marine Drive) I will accept it there." "I said that they would never agree to that. They wanted it done in a public place. What do you lose Sir?". I said. He did not reply. He went and sat in the DV car.

I said to him. "As you see, Sir, I have come in uniform. There is only one thing left for me to do. I shall sit beside you on the right side. I shall offer you the protection on my body. That's all I can do. I doubt if we shall come out of this unharme, either of us."

I have to explain here that the Commissioner of Police was not required to receive any central minister coming into Mumbai, except the Prime Mininster. Further, the senior police officers from the city never sat in the D V[1] car. Every minister had his own security officer who sat in front next to the driver. Further, I had a security car behind him consisting of plainclothes officers. I could have sat in my own car, which would have been, as usual, the last car in the convoy. I could have taken him in a convoy with an S R P F company in front and one at the back. The rioting would have started even before the convoy came to the Mahim causeway.

But as we got into the car a thought flashed through my mind. I got out of the car and asked the D V car driver to follow me. I walked up to the pilot car and asked the pilot and driver to come near. I said to the latter, "you know when my son was a small boy, I used to take him and his friend to the docks on Sundays to see the steamers. We used to go a long way via the Port Trust Road. I have the impression that there is a road from the left of the Mahim Church which joins the Port Trust Road, Tulsi Pipe, or some such?"

1. Distinguished Visitor's car.

The pilot looked blank, but his driver said, "Of course, there is a way, Saheb. You're right. It is called the Tulsi Pipe Road."

"Can you take us through it?" I asked him.

"I can certainly take you Saheb," he said. "You have to zig zag a lot, but I know it all right."

"Good man," I said. "Now all of you listen carefully. We shall stop for exactly one minute at the Mahim Junction. The minister has refused to accept the memorandum. But, seeing the excited crowds, he might relent. If he does not, I shall tap the shoulder of the D Vcar driver like this. He'll give two sharp short blasts on his horn. When he does, you'll shoot to the left, and not take the straight road. Then you must drive like mad. If anyone comes in the way, drive regardless. Understtod?"

They said, they understood.

At the junction, the minister did not relent. We had kept the glasses of the windows closed. The drivers carried out the drill in perfect unison. There were furious shouts. *Lathis* were thumped on the cars, but we moved away-fast.

We did not stop till we reached *Oceana*. When the minister got down, I saluted him. He did not even have to grace to say, 'Thank you'. I ran to my car and drove off to my offfice and the control room.

I had a lot to do, yet. Bombay was on fire.

I hurried to the control room in the Police Commissioner's office. It was at the other end of the veranda from my office room, on the first floor. I acquainted myself with the developing situation. Shiv Sena mobs were rampaging all over. In the looting and arson that took place, *goondas* had, as always, joined. The inflammatory speeches, which Thackeray made, had contributed greatly to the rioting. We had seven companies of the S R P F with us. I sent an urgent signal to the Inspector General requesting for more help; I cannot remember the exact number of men I had asked for. I asked my DCP Headquarters to phone him. We never got any help. As for the Inspector General, he never visited my office even once, let alone offer to go round with me during the entire course of rioting. The reasons (there are more than one) should by now be obvious.

Under my orders, a Striking Force had been kept ready for me in the compound below. I had created these Striking Forces in 1956 to deal with the Samyukta Maharashtra agitation. They had fallen into disuse, but I had again built up at least three, on my taking over as the Commissioner of Police, Bombay. I shall explain their working in detail later: they have formed a very important part of my strategy in dealing with riots. I went down, got into the command vehicle, a jeep, and went round the city doing what I could to help, supervise and lead. That night I met Ramamurthi, Kulkarni, Scott and most of the DCP's almost all, except Ribeiro. Earlier, when I was sitting with Morarji Desai at the Mahim Junction, I took a brief look around. I did not see Ribeiro's tall 'commanding' figure anywhere near. The officers in my motorcade told me later that they did not see him anywhere around the junction either.

I returned to my office, and sat at my desk. I might have had my hands on my head and my elbows on the desk. If Ribeiro, or his favourite Inspector had seen me thus, he would most likely have concluded that I was saying my last prayers.

But I was deep in thought. I was about to take an important decision- a momentous decision in the life of any police officer.

My mind was made up, I phoned the Home Secretary, B B Paymaster, and told him *that I had decided to arrest Bal Thackeray.* I said that I felt that there was *no other go*. Paymaster said, "You'd better ring up the C M and get his consent."

I got the CM, V P Naik, with some difficulty on the phone, at Latur. I repeated what I said to the Home Secretary. He said, "You are the man on the spot. Take whatever action you consider necessary."

I called two gallant officers from the Special Branch, Inspector Pai and Joshi. I asked them to arrest Balasaheb Thackeray. In half an hour they reported that they had done so. The information was flashed on the wireless to all police stations and mobiles.

On page 118 of his recent book, "Bullet for Bullet" J F Ribeiro says; "Hence our only request to the finance minister was that he should not travel by train because Dadar was the stronghold of the Shiv Sena. It was the area where they were the most effective. Morarjibhai agreed to travel by air. While journeying from Santa Cruz airport to the city, his car was stopped by the Sainiks, who were waiting for him. He ordered the car to drive on. The police tried to disperse the Sainiks with lathis because they had begun to bang on the car with flagstaffs and fists. The police were successful in clearing the way for the minister's car. He drove away without meeting them, but the Sainiks were awaiting the signal to create trouble."

All this is double-dutch to me. I did not even once discuss the matter with Ribeiro. And who, exactly are *we*? What is all this about Ribeiro arranging the change the minister's programme of travelling by train, to agreeing to come by air? It is patent that his story is pure fabrication, from the beginning to the end.

Before leaving for the airport, I had sent a signal to the DCP Zone III (Ribeiro) that he should station himself at the Mahim junction with whatever strength he could muster. Now if he says that he did not get my order, did he need any order to station himself at the junction? Ribeiro says (and rightly) that Dadar was the stronghold of the Shiv Sena. Thousands of people had gathered at the Mahim junction. Thousands had lined up on the route that the finance minister was to take through Dadar (via L Jamshedji Rd., Senapati Bapat Marg). The control room was screaming out my order to Ribeiro and to others , on the radio telephone, just at it was giving the information of the CP meeting the FM at Santa Cruz, of the CP sitting beside the FM in the DV car, it should have been obvious to even a raw probationer that for the police that night, the Mahim junction was the "Hinge of Fate". If Mahim had been held firmly, the riot could have been contained, or its effect could have been minimized.

And Ribeiro does not know till this day that I had gone to receive the FM, and was with him in his car!

Where, indeed, was this *wunderkind*? I did not see him that night at all. Perhaps, (as it has now transpired from his own account) he was ensconced in some safe place, with his friends from the press, giving them his own special version of the *dance macabre*.

Ribeiro says on page 122 of his book: " My experience of these riots (the Shiv Sena), which were the worst I had faced till now, taught me that once such riots start, it is not possible or easy to control them despite one's best efforts. Big riots peter out on their own. The progress of the riot can be compared to a storm. There is something one can do about a storm. It dissipates on its own... The police have to be seen to be active, even if their efforts have marginal effect."

My reply to this inane, fatuous remark is as follows:

In the case of the Poone riot of 1965, this is exactly what the Home Minister's security officer was trying to convey to me at Kasture Chowk. Why, then, has Ribeiro made such a hue and cry over my alleged failure to ignore the HM's order?

In the firing that took place during the Shiv Sena riots (for which I take full responsiblity), 56 persons were killed and 130 injured. Any police officer, who took active part in quelling the riot- were he a DCP or a sub-inspector-could have told Ribeiro that it was the use of force that stopped the rioting, and not its imagined similarity to a storm. By making these remarks, Ribeiro has, himself, shown that in his long career as a police officer, he could not have had much of an interface with marauding mobs, all his publicity notwithstanding.

And speaking of publicity, Ribeiro tells us that some superior police officer had remarked about him that he was a glutton for publicity. I have not made that remark. In fact, in spite of all the provocation, I have made no remark against him at any time. But if we consider this remark, we shall have to recognize the fact that, whoever made it, has summed up Ribeiro's career admirably.

The question here was not only that of quelling the riot. it was that of preventing its recurrence.This involved the speedy, but thorough investigation of the riot cases, and the cases of the 56 deaths before the Coroner's court. The DCP CID and the ACP CID and their staff, deserve full credit for supervising these cases. As for the deaths during the police firing, each one of them was justified in the Coroner's court. This itself was no mean achievement.

Ribeiro has said in his book that on the occassion, during the riots, I was cowering, in his truck, squeezed between him and the driver, when a stone hit the tin roof of his truck. Now in the first place, was such a reaction from me likely in view of all that I have said? In the second place, I always went out with my striking force, sitting in my command vehicle which was a jeep with a canvass top. And why should I have left my Striking Force to get into *any* DCP's truck? I used to make, the DCP get into my jeep at the back. I was the CP. *Fee Fi Fo Fum!*

CHAPTER VI
Section-II

THE CASE OF THE PURLOINED FLAT

On page 231 of his book, "Bullet for Bullet" Ribeiro writes:

"Not everyone is so lucky, particularly if they belong to the lower echelons. In the past, my seniors had actually manipulated to get requisitioned flats de-requisitioned in their favour so that they could occupy them after retirement. Incidentally, many of them had flats and houses outside Bombay. Yet they did not hesitate to deprive serving officers of accommodation in order to benefit themselves. For example, E S Modak had a bungalow in Pune, where he went to stay after retirement. But he got the flat occupied by me derequisitioned and alloted to him. I had to leave the flat almost overnight on receiving orders very suddenly to that effect. I was quite surprised because Modak had not told me that he would do such a thing. Finally, after a few years he sold the flat and retreated to Pune where had had always wanted to stay."

In view of these slanderous and spiteful remarks, it behoves me to give, for the reader's edification, a truthful and fitting reply.

In the days of the British, in the three presidency cities of Bombay, Calcutta and Madras, bungalows had been specially built for the Police Commissioners. I believe that in Calcutta and Chennai (Madras) they are in the continued occupation of the Police Commissioners. Even the Communist Government of West Bengal has not disturbed this occupation.

In Bombay, there was such a bungalow named Corsley on Ridge Road, where the last British Police Commissioner, Caffin, used to live.

Morarji Desai, the new Revenue and Home Minister, threw him out (even though he was to retire in a few months) and began to occupy the bungalow. It was later called 'Sahyadri".

Among the requisitioned flats, there was a pool for the police department under the control of the Commissioner. The commissioners began to occupy the best of these, and after their ouster from Corsley, got them de-requisitioned and released in their names before retirement.

In the meantime, these flats became the happy hunting ground for all sorts of people with the right 'pull'. When I was the DCP Headquarters, two of the best flats on Bhulabhai Desai Road were released on demand to close relatives ofMrs. Vijayalakshmi Pandit. Other flats on Carmichael Road and Altamount Road (both highly desirable areas on Malabar Hill) were given to other VIP's.

At that time I was staying in a very good flat in a building called Deepak Mahal on Marine Drive. One fine morning, M C Chagla, who had returned from the U.S.A. as Ambassador, rang me up and said he was coming to see my flat. He came within twenty minutes and took a survey. He told my wife and me that Government had offered him the choice of either my flat or one with the Navy on Cuffe Parade. Luckily for me, Chagla preferred the one on Cuffe Parade. The naval officer was immediately ousted, and Chagla moved in.

When I became the Commissioner of Police in Mumbai in 1968, I got a good flat on Nepean Sea Road *alloted to the police in the name of the Police Commissioner*, as his permanent residence (whoever was the Commissioner), and not in my name.

One day an acquaintance happened to call on me in my office. He said, "So you'll be leaving your flat? Where will you be going?"

I was puzzled and said, "Not that I know of. What do you know about it?" He said he was sitting in the anterroom on the Chief Minister's office, waiting for his appointment, when somebody remarked that the Commissioner of Police, Modak's flat, had been alloted by the Government to an ex-minister, Rajaram Bapu Patil."

I went straight to the Chief Minister, V P Naik, and asked him if the rumour was true. He said, "Yes, yes. I had to give it to him for political reasons."

I gave Naik the whole history of police requisitioned flats as stated above, and spoke of the injustice done to the police. I said that Government had alloted the flat permanently to the police commissioner; how could it be taken away now for political reasons? I wonder how many officers- whether from the police or the IAS- would have spoken to him in that manner! I think from that moment on, I was out of favour with him.

I did not stop at that. After all this denudation of police flats, the only large one left with the police was in a dilapidated building called 'Dinath Court', on Pochkhanawala Road, near the police LA III HQ in Worli. Ribeiro occupied it. This flat was in the CP's pool and had not been alloted to Ribeiro by name, nor was it earmarked only for the DCP's. Many of them were staying in flats in Government buildings like Yashodhan. I said to the CM I had learnt that I was required to vacate my flat forthwith. I requested him to issue an immediate order, alloting this flat to me. I further said, that since everyone was doing this, I would also want to stay in the flat after my retirement. I wanted an order from the Government derequisitioning it in my favour, providing the landlord was willing to give it in my name (on rent).

The CM accepted my 'request', and issued the orders forthwith. He could not have done otherwise. Even a CM has to appear to be fair!

When I contacted the 'landlord' of 'Dinath Court', Mahmud Dinath, (who lived on the premises), I learnt that the building was in a family Trust, and that he was the chief Trustee. One of the conditions of the Trust was that none of the flats could be sold. So there was no question of my buying it or his selling it. Dinath also told me that he could not agree to my tenancy because he had already promised the flat to the IG, Rajadhyaksha, who was going to move into the flat shortly (I could hardly have objected, if had done so earlier!), and he was then going to write to the Government to de-requisition it in his favour. Ribeiro would have had to leave the flat within a month, in any case. I doubt if the IG would have graciously called him and told him what he intended to do.

I said to Dinath, that if I had known that the IG intended to take the flat, I would not have got the CM's sanction in the matter. But now, whether he agreed to the tenancy or not, I was going to move into the flat immediately to forestall Rajadhyaksha, and would stay there till my retirement. I had to vacate my flat, and Ribeiro got the same time that I got, to move. He was not left on the streets. He was alloted another flat. He says that I should have told him about it. Why? If had taken the trouble to go down from the third floor to the first floor, and ask Dinath, the latter would have explained the situation to him in words of one syllable. It was no secret. And if he is speaking of himself as belonging to the lower echelons, it was officers of the rank of Inspector who were the really aggrieved persons. I should know. When I was DCP HQ it was one of my functions to allot flats, and I had alloted Dinath Court to officers of that rank on more than one occasion.

I owned no bungalow or flat at that time *anywhere.* I told Dinath that I intended to settle down in Pune as soon as I could get a plot and build a bungalow. That would take time, and I might have to stay in Mumbai for a few years after my retirement. I gave him my promise that when my house was built, and I got possession of it, I would return his flat to him. By this time he could see that Rajadhayaksha could not get the flat. He seemed to have believed in me, and he gave me the tenancy.

The Government alloted all the best lands in Koregaon Park (where I wanted to stay) to the defence personnel and the IAS. The only plot left was an acre of land (divided into four plots) in a saddleback. At my wife's behest I want to see the Revenue Minister, Balasaheb Desai, and requested him to allot one of them to me (of course on sale). He was gracious, and issued the order on the spot.

Desai did not refer to our contretemps about the riot. "My compliments to your wife," he said. He seemed to have guessed that I had come at her urging. 'Modak, he said, Do you recall that fellow, Majeedullah?"

"Of course," I said.

" He used to cringe and crawl before me when I was Home Minister," he said. "When I left that job and was given Revenue, we met in Koyna after the earthquake. He was in uniform, but did not even salute me. He actually turned his back on me, and walked away."

"So sorry, Sir," I mumbled. "He should not have done that"

When, eventually, my bungalow was built in Pune, I had to rent it for a few years to recover the loan. After the expiry of the lease, I informed my tenant that I did not wish to renew it. He had already built his own bungalow, and gave me back mine. I packed up my household goods, and sent them to Pune. I went down to meet Mahmud Dinath. I gave him a letter that I was returning the flat to him, and gave him the keys. After that I got into my car. My wife and servants were waiting. We drove off to Pune to 122/4 Koregaon Park where we still reside.

CHAPTER VI

Section-III

THE COMMUNAL RIOTS OF BHIWANDI IN MAY 1970

On the 7th of May 1970, my wife and I were having dinner with a friend when the phone rang. It was for me from my senior colleague, A G Rajadhyaksha, Inspector General of Police, Maharashtra. He said that large scale rioting had broken out in Bhiwandi in Thane district, and that the Home Secretary, L G Rajwade, had ordered that I should go there immediately and deal with the situation. The Home Secretary had also ordered that *I should stay there for a month and a half.* This time, by my watch was 8.30 p.m. I went home, packed a few things, and left for Bhiwandi in my staff car.

On my way to Bhiwandi, I stopped for about 20 minutes at the police control room in the office of the SP (superintendent of police) in Thane to acquaint myself with the over-all situation. I learnt from the officer in charge that the SP had sent for the fire brigade from Bombay, but it had not arrived. I then went on to Bhiwandi. In the distance, on the horizon, I saw a red-glow Bhiwandi was ablaze. As I came within three kilometres of Bhiwandi, I saw a long line of fire tenders from Bombay city parked on the side of the road. The officer in charge told me that they were waiting for an escort. There had, obviously, been no contact between them and the control roon in Thane. The responsibility for the poor co-ordination in the control room was that of the SP, Thane. Much valuable time had been lost. A good deal of arson could have been prevented if the fire tenders had reached earlier. I was alone with my driver in my car. I asked them if my escort would do. They gladly came behind me.

The police station was in the centre of the town, opposite a fish market. I had never visited Bhiwandi before; I had no occassion to. The police station consisted of one small room for the Inspector, and an adjoining room for the sub-inspector and the rest of the staff. Only half the room-really a tin shed-was available. The other half was piled up with kerosene tins and liquor bottles seized in prohibition raids.

In front of the police station, I met the Distric Magistrate, D N Capoor, the Deputy SP, Divate, and a police *jemadar*. Nearby there was a Special Reserve Police Platoon inside a truck. Fires were raging furiously in the town, but the rioting, as such, was over. Incidents continued on the outskirts, however, and I was told that the Superintendent, S V Bhave, and the DIG Bombay Range, V A Gokhale, had gone to deal with them.

The fire brigade was immediately deployed to put out the fires. From the two officers I learnt a few relevant facts. The Inspector in charge of the police station, Pradhan, had reported that he was seriously injured, and had gone home. Except for Divate and the *jemadar*, the entire staff of the police station had melted away. They had no quarters in Bhiwandi-not a single quarter-and they stayed in places near the railway stations, as far away as Kalyan and Ghatkopar. They used to commute to the police station every day.

The District Magistrate, Capoor, told me a strange story. A platoon of the Reserve Police was kept in a truck near the police station (the same one that I saw). He asked them to follow him, and charged into the mob that was attacking the police station. None of the Reserve Policemen followed him, and he found himself entirely surrounded by the mob. Dy. Superintendent, Divate, was able to extricate him with great difficulty. Perhaps some of the leaders of the mob recognized him and took the mob in another direction. When Capoor asked the policemen why they did not follow him, they said that they were not prepared to do so without their firearms. All their rifles had been taken away, and *lathis* given in their place.

The Superintendent of Police, Bhave, had at least five companies of Reserve Police with him besides a hundred armed men from what was called, 'the IG's Reserve'. I subsequently learnt that the asinine order to remove their arms was given by Bhave, with the approval of the DIG, Gokhale. The fact that their arms were removed is confirmed in the report of the Madon Commission. It is stated therein that there were in Bhiwandi 741 unarmed men and 24 men armed with muskets (not rifles). The police had only a fraction of the men armed with rifles. The rest were, therefore, armed men whose firearms had been removed (under the SP's orders). It was not the case that Thane had any 'striking forces' as trained by me, (where their composition and training were different). Apparently, this order had been issued to show how these two 'brilliant' officers could handle the situation 'tactfully, but firmly'.

The first order that I gave was that all the armed men should be given back their rifles forthwith. I then went around the town with Capoor and Divate. I did not encounter any rioting mobs.

Capoor took me to the small hospital to see the persons injured in the rioting-rioters, innocent bystanders, and policemen. Among them I saw a sub-inspector lying on the bed on his stomach. He was flailing his arms about, and would raise his buttocks from time to time. I said to the medical officer, "Doctor, this can't be a case of hysteria, can it? I thought that hysteria only afflicted women?" The Doctor agreed. One of the SRP Police Constables said helpfully, "Sir it must be the *bhanamati*" (The Bhanamati is a poltergeist, a spirit that is said to afflict people in the villages.)

I said, "I agree with you. It is the *bhanamati*, poor fellow! I believe that the approved method is to beat it out of the one possessed, is it not? I tell you what. Two of you stand on either side of him, with the *lathis* at the ready.They did. I said, "When I say the word "Go", start hitting him on the buttocks which are moving up and down. Mind you, all present here. We are not really beating him, We are beating the *bhanamati* which is tormanting this poor man." Before I could say 'Go", the sub-inspector turned over, scrambled to his feet, saluted and fled.

In the meantime, Inspector Pradhan had arrived. I had asked an SRP officer to bring him, dead or alive. Pradhan was fat and he was sweating. Maybe the sweat was due to the heat of the fire. He held a handkerchief on his mouth. I said, "Shall I have you examined by the doctor, or is your injury only on the mouth?" He nodded holding the handkerchief tighter. I said, "Take it off!" He took the handkerchief off. There was only a bruise on his lip. All his teeth seemed to be intact. I said to him. "Put on your uniform and get ready within fifteen minutes. If you are not, consider yourself under suspension."

The DIG and the SP returned from their expeditions. They brought in a large number of rioters whom they had arrested. After some time they both went out on another foray. It is worthy of note that most of the arrests were made by these two officers. As I said, their subordinates were just not visible. Apropos the remarks of the Madon Commission, was it not their responsibility to ensure that they did not concentrate only on one community? And why should I have doubted their bonafides? They held high rank.

The only really capable *police officers* that I found in Bhiwandi were the District Magistrate, Capoor, and the Dy. Superintendent, Divate.

Round-the-clock pickets were posted in Bhiwandi and its environs to prevent a recrudescence of the rioting. Incidents were reported in the surrounding villages; police parties were sent out to deal with them. The IG had sent the DIG Crime, Goverdhan, and two SP's from the CID to investigate the cases of rioting in Bhiwandi. Madon has reported that these officers made out false and biased cases. The report unfortunately came out after four years-in November 1974. This might be, the reason Rajadhyaksha, still the Inspector General long after that, did not take the strong action against the senior officers that he ought to have. But the I G does not necessarily have to wait for such experts!

Bhiwandi was originally a small town with people living cheek by jowl on either side of the labyrinthine streets and narrow gullies. The power-loom industry, (which, in places like Bhiwandi and Malegaon) was going to ruin the textile mills of Bombay, had led to a vast influx of labour into Bhiwandi from places as distant as UP, MP and Andhra. *Zopadpatties* had sprung up in every square yard of available space, and the town was full of dirty gutters, ponds and filth thrown everywhere. There were power looms also in every small tin shed and *gotha*. Many of these were owned by the merchant class in Bombay, and they made hay while the sun shone on them. Though Bhiwandi was a small town, it had one of the riches municipalities of Maharashtra.

Bhiwandi was a keg of gunpowder even before the communal virus took possession of it from 1964. The trouble began when the Jan Sangh and the newly formed branch of the Shiv Sena insisted on taking out the procession, during the Shiv Jayanti Utsav, past the main Nizampura Jumma Mosque, and also on throwing large quantities of gulal, on the route. Each incident that occured took on a communal colour. Communal and extreme parties established their branches in Bhiwandi, communal propaganda became a feature of electioneering, and communal politics became the order of the day. In 1968 a communal riot took place in Bhiwandi, the forerunner of the trouble to come.

The Congress Party had no hold of any kind in Bhiwandi. The MLC, Zumberlal Kalantri (MLC not MLA) began to play the part of the honest (?) broker. Through him, the Minister of State for Home (Kalyanrao Patil) interfered in the administration, and the DIG and the SP were not strong enough to resist him.

In March of 1970, serious trouble was expected during the Shiv Jayanti procession. In a report of 26 March 1970, Dy. SP Divate stated that the Shiv Jayanti procession would not pass off peacefully, unless preventive action was taken against the leaders of both the communities. He recommended the detention under the Prevention Detention Act of eight of the rabid leaders of both the parties. If the SP had approved of this and sent his report to the DM, Capoor, I have no boubt (from what I saw of Capoor) that he would have issued the orders,The SP and the DIG did not forward it due to pressure from Kalantri via Kalyanrao. Divate was a seasoned and able officer. He had worked under me for several years, and I knew him well. He would, most certainly, have made a better superintendent of police than the incumbent.

The important point here is that the IG, Rajadhyaksha, could not have failed to know all this. If the DIG and SP had not personally apprised him of the facts,they had made their written reports to him from time to time, so had the CID. The IG had never visited Thane (so close by) even once, to discuss the whole issue with the officers and the leaders of both the communities, which it was his duty to have done. And if Kalyanrao had interfered with the police, it was his duty to make it clear to him (in writing, if necessary), the grave consequences of such interference. If I could take on DP Dhar in Kashmir, Rajadhyaksha could have easily have taken on Kalyanrao.

Had action been taken as suggested by Divate, the riots of May 1970 (for which I was required to stay in Bhiwandi for a month and a half) would not have occurred.

I felt that the oral order, given to me by the Home Secretary through Rajadhyaksha, was preposterous. Perhaps he thought that I was a subordinate of the Inspector General, meant to do all the dirty work for him. It was obvious that he had not read the G R on my appointment. Our duties were clearly defined. Of course, the Inspector General was the head of the department in charge of Law and Order: I would not have disputed the fact. But in this particular case he was cognizant of all the facts and background of the case. (I was not, I had never visited Bhiwandi before). It was Rajadhyaksha's duty to have gone to Bhiwandi and dealt with the riot. He could never have issued the order to me. He had, obvoiusly, made the Home Secretary issue the order.

However, if the Home Secretary considered my stay over there of such importance, I wondered why he did not visit Bhiwandi even once to discuss the matter with me and the local officials. I have no doubt that Paymaster or Dias would have done so. and if Rajwade had no time to spare for a visit, why did he not send for me, even once, to discuss the case?

The only time that the Inspector General and the Home Secretary came to Bhiwandi was in the motorcade of the Prime Minister. While she was discussing the situation with the leaders in the rest house, they deigned to visit the police station. They spent about fifteen minutes there. The only remark that Rajwade made to 'Raja' was, "Raja don't you think that the men of the Border Security Force look very smart as compared to the SRP?" Raja' sniggered.

I tried to explain the situation to him. The SRP had been on duty for over 20 days. They were on continous duty without any relief; they hardly got time to eat or answer the call of nature. They would, sometimes, sleep at their posts due to sheer exhaustion.

A battalion of the BSFhad been sent to me a couple of days back. Their commandant told me that, according to recent orders, they operated on the lines of the army; a platoon could not be split up into sections, as was done in the case of the SRP or the CRP. Further, if two platoons were on duty, one had to be given complete rest. It was small wonder that their turnout was smart and would impress a man who had not bothered to acquaint himself with the nitty-gritty of riot control.

While getting into his car, the Home Secretary said to the IG "Raja, I think the BSF are definitely smarter."

Raja took out his cheroot and gave another snigger.

A perinent question might be asked by my reader; 'When you found the action and behaviour of officers like Ribeiro or Bhave so poor, why did you not report against them?

The answer is that I did not want to spoil the careers of all these young officers. Maybe I was soft. Maybe I thought that a ticking off, face to face, would have the desired effect. That is how I was brought up in my early career. Apart from the British, I wonder how many of them could have stood the kind of treatment given to me by the first of the IG's, N M Kamte! I was the recipient of this special consideration at his hands merely because he had got the wrong impression (which he later acknowledged to be wrong) that I had 'wangled' a posting to Belgaum as SP.

But I did not take into account the fact that each one of these officers considered himself a prima donna. They took even a mild reproof as a personal insult. Perhaps their early training was responsible. Ribeiro has said in his book, that his first commandant at Mount Abu, Mehta, used to come to the parade ground on horseback (and, presumably, stayed on horseback throughout the parade).He hardly ever spoke to the probationers. The next one behaved like a kindly uncle. No wonder the products of such training lacked an elementary sense of either discipline or loyalty. No wonder their work and grasp of police problems was superficial and perfunetory!

CHAPTER VI
Section-IV

THE POLICE MUTINY OF 1982

Since Ribeiro had stayed in the same third floor flat in Dinath Court on Pochkhanawala Road, Worli, which I took over, he would remember the front enclosed veranda. When the windows were opened, you could see the road extending to the intersection several hundred yards away, with the *maidan* on the left.On the right, you could see the road upto several hundred yards towards the police LA III armed headquarters.

On the morning of the day the police mutiny occurred, I had kept the windows wide open, and got a grandstand view of all that took place right in front of me.

Ribeiro (the then Police Commissioner) is chary about calling what took place, a 'mutiny'. He has called it 'trouble'. Whether the policemen themselves initiated the action, or whether it was the result of the arrests of the Union leaders, what took place was clearly a mutiny, by any definition of the word.

In the morning, I saw about one hundred policemen, a few in plain clothes, the rest in uniform (but without their insignia) come walking along from the LA III headquarters. There were two police buses on the road. They took out the air from the tyres, and went further to the intersection and stopped a BEST bus. They made the passengers get out, and one of the mutineers drove the bus to the centre of the crossroad. They then systematically removed all removable parts from the bus- the battery, dynamo and distributer.

A van carrying tinned goods was coming along. They stopped it and looted the contents. By this time, their womenfolk and children had come up. The mutineers handed over the tinned goods to them, and I saw the latter carry these goods towards their headquarters. I phoned the police control room immediately. Other tenants in the building also did so. Nobody came for two hours. Eventually, I saw a truck bringing Central Reserve Policemen to the place, but by this time, the mutineers and their families had disappeared.

Now, I have had a special relationship with the armed men (the loyal ones) and the traffic policemen of the Bombay city, since I was the D C P Headquarters in 1954. This might have been due in part, at least, to the fact that both my wife and I had taken a great deal of interest in police welfare.

Whatever be the reason, some policemen were keeping me well informed about what was happening- this was after my retirement, when I still remained in Bombay for a few years.

During the first police mutiny, I was getting hourly reports from different parts of Bombay. I did not ask anybody to give me such reports; they just came. The then Commissioner, M S Kasbedkar, used to treat me with respect. For some reason he still does. I told him on the phone that the armed policemen at Naigaum had not returned their rifles or the ammunition and were milling around on the parade ground. Later, when I phoned him, he said he had sent his DCP Special Branch, Ubale, to Naigaum, but he had reported that the information was not correct. I continued to get the same information that I had got before. It was Ubale's duty to have gone to the Naigaum HQ himself, but this he obviously failed to do. By this time it had become dark. Luckily, the armed men did not do any mischief. I was told that eventually the Additional Commissioner, Ramachandran, went their on his own with two ACP's,one of whom was Temkar. These two ACP's managed to persuade the men to return the arms and go home. It might be worthy of note that when Temkar was a young sub-inspector, in 1956, I had selected him to head one of the striking forces. He was an officer that I would liked beside me in any riot.

Now, during this second mutiny, I learnt that policemen from LA II and LA III had looted a big cloth shop on the main Worli Road. I got the confirmation of sorts after about a fortnight. In the evening, I used to go walking with my wife to the Worli promenade. Many times policemen in plain clothes, perhaps off-duty, would pass by. After a fortnight, I began to see several of the young PCs sporting new terylene safari suits.Once, three of them in brand-new safari suits were walking in front of me. One of them slapped the other on his back playfully, and said in Marathi, "This fellow is a *pukka bevda (drunkard)"*.

Any seasoned police officer who has *actually* dealt with riots (and not with imaginary scenarios got up for the benefit of the press) would agree with me that Ribeiro's sequential order in dealing with the police mutineers was all wrong. He says that Maharashtra State was the only one that had agreed to the crackdown. Hence, enough Central Reserve Police forces could have been obtained. Six to eight battalions should have been flown in at night. Private buses or trucks should have been kept ready at the airport. On their arrival, detachments from the Central Reserve police should have been deployed at the four armed headquarters, the Commissioner's office, and important police stations.

According to Ribeiro, it was very important to ensure that the plan to arrest union leaders was kept a secret. Why was it necessary to make such a fetish out of this secrecy? He says that only one man from among the fifty odd union leaders, Shevale, could not be found. He had gone underground and could not be traced at night. And yet, he suddenly appeared in the morning. Is he supposed to have led the policemen single-handed from all the three armed headquarters- at Worli and Naigaum on the streets? How could any professional police officer, reading all this rubbish be prepared to swallow it? I think J F Ribeiro was unduly afraid of the union leaders and his officer in charge of the armed police was more afraid.

Some time earlier I was invited to a function at the LA III headquarters in Worli. I met Ribeiro there and a young police officer named Shinde whom Ribeiro had placed in charge of the armed police. Ribeiro told me that he was 'a good boy. On making enquiries, I learnt that his officer had put in less than 5 years in the police; a wrong choice on the part of Ribeiro, for which the whole department had to suffer.

I learnt on that morning, when the rioting took palce in front of me, that this officer was cooped up in the office of the LA III headquarters with one armed company of the SRP, too frightened to act. The DCP could have easily dispersed the rioting policemen when they assembled on the parade ground. As it happened, eventually an officer from the Central Reserve Police arrived at the headquarters *with only one company*, beat up those men, and dispersed them without firing a single shot.

But suppose that the secrecy of the operation was lost, and *all* the union men had gone underground and then turned up in the morning to incite the police to revolt on a grand scale. There would have been enough armed reserves from the Central Reserve Police to deal with them in one swift, ruthless action. I took such action once at the Flora Fountain in 1956 against the Samyukta Maharashtra rioters, and I know whereof I speak.

And now I come to the saddest part of this sorry episode. On the morning of the second or third day of the riots, I was standing at my usual place in the veranda, when I witnessed an amazing scene. I saw a convoy of three Army vehicles go past towards the LA III headquarters. The first was the army pilot; the second was a brigadier's car with flag and the lone star. In it, at the back, sat the brigadier and beside him the 'super-cop', J F Ribeiro. Behind them was the army escort. I learnt from my sources that this was the first time that the Commissioner of Police was visiting LA III after the mutiny.

The reader can accept my asserveration thta I would have resigned before I took part in such an uncermonial *march past*, witnessed by hundreds of policemen and bystanders.

The police force of Greater Bombay had reached the nadir of its pride and glory. I turned away sadly, and gave up my vigil at the window. I had not spoken to anybody about this incident, I would not have put it in print; Ribeiro has forced me to do it.

So where were the escorts of the Commissioner, and where was his car? Why did the Central Reserve Police arrive so late at the intersection? And where were the State Reserve Police? They were not on strike!

I learnt that the police drivers had made all the vehicles immobile by puncturing the tyres or letting out the air. The few cars with the officers had no drivers.

It did not need any police expertise to realise that in an operation of this kind, mobility was the primary factor for success. It was the Commissioner's duty to keep, at least, 50 trucks or buses ready in his office compound. He should have got drivers from other departments, or hired them. at a pinch. Some of the sub-inspectors and inspectors, who knew driving, could have driven the care and other vehicles.

I had known for some time, and it should have also been known to the Commissioner and his senior officers, that the police drivers were at the forefront of the strikers. Among the policemen, the lot of the driver is the unhappiest. He has to be on the *qui vive* every minute, and his hours of duty are irregular and long. He does not know when the Saheb will jump into his car and ask him to drive off to a place four minutes or four hours away. He has to gobble up whatever bad food he can get, on the run. He has to sit up, crammed behing the wheel in the hot sun, on some street, while his boss in some meeting. He cannot leave the wheel, because the boss might jump in at any moment. Many of these drivers have told me that they had suffered from piles, but couldn't get time off even for surgery.

They didn't mind all this, because it was, after all, in the line of duty, but when the boss went apartying on a Sunday (which was the poor driver's only day off) and came down the Lift of the building in the small hours, hardly able to stand because he had imbibed not wisely, but too well, then their cup of bitterness overflowed and they waited for a day of reckoning.

Whenever might have been the other steps taken to deal with the forthcoming mutiny, the mood of the drivers should have been taken into account, I again repeat that the question of preserving secrecy was secondary to that of providing a prompt and adequate reponse to any situation arising out of the 'incitement' by the lone Shevale or by any of his associates.

There is a portinent observation that I would like to make here about this 'super-cop', J F Ribeiro. A man covers his wife at his pleasure, and she has to submit willy-nilly, whether she is in the mood or not, because the male still claims it as his privilege. But there is one occasion when she has the right to expect-nay demand- that he cover her *physically* with has body, and that is when there is *physical* danger to her person.

From Ribeiro's own account, the petite Melba Rebeiro, had to face two such occasions: the first was in the Punjab, and the second in Romania. On both these occasions, the tall strapping super-cop was right beside her. On the frist occasion, when Ribeiro was walking with his wife in the Officers', Mess in Jalandhar, the terrorists opened fire from the wall according to his own account his reflex action was to fall flat on his stomach, leaving his wife to her own resources. She was shot in the leg.

On the second occasion, in Romania, when Ribeiro was walking with his wife near a park, the terrorists screeched to a halt behind them in a car, and opened fire. Again, according to Ribeiro's own account, he ran for the nearest house, and shut the door of the gate in the compound, after he was hit, leaving the unfortunate Mrs. Ribeiro to her own fate. We have the piteous spectacle of this poor woman banging on the door (gate) asking for assistance from her husband.

Ribeiro was not jusd a civilian ambassador- he was a trained senior ex-police officer. I wonder why he became so careless as not to carry even an automatic pistol with him! Be that as it may be, I am of the view that a man, who fails to protect his wife, if necessary at the cost of his own life, deserves to have a bullet put through his rapidly retreating posterior.

Further, I am persuaded that Shakespeare would have relished such a piquant situation and agreed with my sentiments on the subject, though, to be sure, he would have expressed them much better in iambic pentameter and immortal verse.

CHAPTER VII
KILLER AT BAY

The case of Raman Raghav, the serial killer of Bombay, will remain one of the most gruesome in the annals of crime. The only other killers, who could have been compared with him in ferocity and scope, were the Boston Strangler and Jack the Ripper. The Boston Strangler killed thirteen women between July 1962 and January 1964. He was never caught and prosecuted. A man named Albert de Salvo, a sex deviate and an inmate of the Bridgewater Asylum, made a 'confession' about these murders to Assistant Attorney General Bottomly, but he was never indicted for these crimes.

Jack the Ripper operated in London between August and November 1888. During this time he is said to have killed seven prostitutes in the Whitechapel District of London. He was never caught and his identity was never established. Several books were written about him and surmises made. Much later, W E Gladstone, former Prime Minister of the U K, was suspected of being Jack the Ripper. After Gladstone's death, his diaries revealed that he used to lead a double life. On the one hand, he was a straight-laced Puritan; on the other, he used to go to the Whitechapel area and visit prostitutes. He claimed in his diaries that he gave them Bibles, and prayed for their souls.

Raman Raghav killed twenty-one people in the suburbs of Bombay, and seriously injured an equal number, on his own admission. He was captured by the Bombay city police, and after an intensive investigation under my personal supervision, his case was sent up to the Sessions Court where he was sentenced to death. The sentence was later postponed by the High Court on the ground that he was incompetent to plead owing to insanity. He died in Yervada Prison. In the light of subsequent allegations made against the Bombay city police about their slipshod methods of work by the Sri Krishna Commission, a perusal of this chapter alone will show that it was not always so.

I was the Commissioner of Police of Bombay in 1968. In July and August, a series of strange murders had taken place in the western suburbs, which had baffled the police completely. Bombay is a longish island with the south end narrow and tapering, while the North spreads out into jungle and marsh (in those days). Though the density of population in Bombay city as a whole was higher than that of many other cities in the world, there were still areas in the north which were sparsely populated. During the monsoons, the hills and valleys were covered with thick grass and ankle-deep slush in which walking became difficult.

On the night of 5th July 1968, Abdul Karim, a 48-year old man was found lying dead on a *charpoy*. The man's head had been bashed in, and death was obviously homicidal. As Abdul Karim stayed in an isolated hut on the outskirts of Malad, a suburb of Bombay, no one had heard him cry out, nor had anyone seen the assailant. The police found that the hut had been ransacked, and Karim's relatives informed them that a wristwatch, a flashlight, an umbrella and a long coat were stolen. Besides these, a sum of Rs.262/= in cash which the deceased had got as his salary the previous day, had also been stolen.

While the officers of Malad police station were investigating this case, another murder took place on the morning of 19th July 1968 of one Yadav, a fifty four year old rent collector, who used to live alone in a room near a buffalo stable on the outskirts of Goregaon. A boy named Ismail, who worked in the stable, was passing by the deceased's hut in the morning. As it began to rain, Ismail took shelter on the veranda of the hut. Through the open door of the room, he saw Yadav on the *charpoy*, his head battered and bleeding, and blood dripping on the floor. The boy ran out and raised an alarm. The deceased's son, Hiralal, reported that a stove, an umbrella and a coat were missing.

Kumma Bharwad used to reside in a hut in Bhanjiwadi, off the Western Express Highway, in East Malad. His twenty-year-old wife, Roopa, had delivered a baby girl only a fortnight earlier. Kumma was so poor that he could not afford to buy a latch to the door of his one-room hut. At night, he secured it with a piece of string. Some three months before her delivery, Roopa had bought herself a luxury - a necklace made of black-and-yellow plastic beads worth a few *annas* at the most. After Kumma returned from his work as a labourer at night, they had their meagre meal consisting of *dal* and bread, and went to sleep. Kumma slept on one *charpoy*, while Roopa and the baby slept on another. At 2 AM, Roopa's sister-in-law, who stayed in the adjoining hut, came out to ease herself, when she heard the baby crying. She called out to Roopa to pacify the child, but got no answer. When she tapped on the door, to her surprise it swung open. The one small light in the room was burning, and Malubai saw Kumma and Roopa on their beds, their heads mangled and bleeding. The child also appeared to have been assaulted, and she was whimpering. Roopa and the child died on the way to the hospital. Kumma survived, but he could not remember anything about the attack.

I asked the city C I D to assist the local police. During their spot investigation, they found an umbrella and an iron jemmy lying on the grass outside the hut. The jemmy had fresh stains of blood on it (which later were found to be of human origin); it had obviously been the assailant's weapon. Jemmies were used by burglars the world over for prising open the bars of windows and breaking locks. This one had a peculiar shape, it resembled the cranking hsndles of old motor cars. It was, in fact, a fulcrum jemmy. The detectives found a few black and yellow beads on the floor, near Roopa's bed. Her neck had been seen to be bare. The murderer had torn the necklace off, thinking that the beads were of gold, then thrown it away.

On 15th August, the killer claimed another victim. He killed a twenty-one year old school teacher named Upadhyaya. The teacher used to give private tuitions in Hindi. He lived alone in a hut off the Western Express Highway in East Kandivli. The murderer had robbed him of a wristwatch, a student's compass box, two fountain pens, a magnifying glass, and a jar full of *ghee*.

The office of the Police Commissioner of Bombay is a massive Gothic structure built by the British in 1896. The Commissioner's room has a high ceiling that keeps the place cool, even in summer. In the adjoining large veranda, the Commissioner has his tea-conference with his deputies every afternoon. The institution of afternoon tea is as old as the office. Over tea and snacks I would meet my fourteen deputies, and discuss with them the important events of the day: crime, law and order and other occurrences.

"Is there then no clue to these strange murders in Malad and Goregaon?', I asked Scott, D C P Zone IV.

Scott was a stocky well -built man of 52, a seasoned officer who had risen from the ranks. (He often reminded me of the day, long back, when we were both seated in the annexe of the Government House, waiting for the investiture for our medals. He had been stabbed in the arm earlier in a riot.)

"No clue at all, Sir," he said. As you must have seen from my daily report, in the murder of the woman, Roopa, and her child, a fulcrum jemmy and an umbrella were recovered from the scene".

I nodded. "I suppose the killer saw Roopa's sister-in-law and ran in a hurry, leaving the articles behind.

"Exactly", said Scott. It's apparent that the killer has used the jemmy as the murder weapon in all these crimes. He would give one swift blow with the pointed end of the jemmy near his sleeping victims' ear, grab whatever petty articles and cash he could lay his hands on, and decamp as fast as he could. "

"And you think that it's the same person behind all these murders?"

"There seems to be no doubt, Sir", Kulkarni, the DCP CID intervened. "The modus operandi in all these cases is the same. He took out a small diary from his pocket and read,"In all these cases, the killer seems to have selected lonely huts on either side of the Western Express Highway. The victims have all been very poor people; the property stolen has been of very little value, as for example, pens, torches, coats, and umbrellas. The murderer has attacked the huts between the hours of one and four at night, when the inmates were fast asleep, and the injuries to the victims have all been caused in the parietal region of the head near the temple. We found the fulcrum jemmy, which had blood stains, and I agree with Scott that this was the weapon used in the first two cases, at any rate."

I said,"Couldn't you get fingerprints of the culprit?"

"Unfortunately, no, Sir," he said. There were hardly any objects with polished surfaces in the huts, and though the fingerprint expert tried hard, he was unable to develop any latent prints."

"What about your dog squad?"

"There too we've not been successful. It has been raining heavily these last few nights, and all traces have been obliterated. The umbrella was no doubt handled by the killer, but it was soaked in the rain, and the dogs were unable to pick up the scent."

"Well, where do we go from here, I asked?" I asked. "We cannot have a ruthless killer on the rampage, even if his victims are the poorest of the poor, can we?"

Ramamurthi, D C P Zone II, was saying something to his neighbour, and he looked up.

"I think I have a clue, Sir," he said. In 1965-66 we had a similar series of murders in my area in the eastern suburbs. That was, of course, much before you came here as C P. All the victims were poor hutment dwellers, staying in out of the way places, along the municipal water pipeline.. ."

"Is that what they call the duct line?" I interrupted.

"That's right, Sir. The duct line, " Ramamurthi said. "The modus operandi in all those cases was the same that we have here. The murderer always operated between one and four in the morning. He killed his victims in the same manner - one or two blows near the ear with a heavy weapon pointed at one end. In all, nine persons were killed and one injured. The injured man remembered nothing."

"Did the killer rob anything?" I asked.

"We didn't get any precise information on that. He must have taken things of small value. What else could he get from those poor unfortunates?"

"Was anyone arrested? If so, what happened to him?"

"As a matter of fact, we did arrest a man called Raman Raghav on suspicion. He had many aliases among which the principal ones were: Sindhi Dalvai, Veluswami, Thambi and Anna. Before we got hold of him, we had various theories about the murderer. At first we thought the man was a maniac or a devotee of some cult demanding human sacrifice. In March 1966, two plain clothes P C's, who were patrolling along the duct line saw this man moving near it. He wore long hair and a beard like that of a *sadhu.* They brought him to the police station, and while searching him, the Inspector found a pocket diary. He saw on some pages the words, *khatam, kilas* (finished), and against them there were some figures.

"What happened further? Did he disclose anything?" I asked, unable to contain my impatience.

Kulkarni interposed. "We traced his previous record from his fingerprints. He had nine previous convictions, mostly for burglary and theft. In 1951, he was convicted for five years in a case of dacoity with murder. He had five other accomplices, but they were let off. From that time, he decided to operate as a loner. We interrogated him thoroughly - in fact, Wakatkar, who is now in the C I D, was the Inspector in charge of Mulund police station then. We couldn't break him at all; he disclosed nothing.

"Could he have had some mental kink?" I asked. "You know, this business of being a devotee of some cult?"

"We thought of that, too," Ramamurthi said. He was kept under observation at the police hospital, and the police surgeon and other specialists tried all methods of making him talk - the truth serum and such, but it did not work."

"I suppose you had to let him go," I said. "What happened to him?"

The only thing we could do was to get him externed out of Bombay city. Two P C's were detailed to see him off. We don't know what happened to him afterwards."

"So it is possible that he might have sneaked in," I said. "Anyway I'd like to see the records and his photograph."
The next day I saw his photograph - front and profile, with and without his beard and long hair. A non-descript face, I thought, except for his eyes - a face you would see and ignore in a crowd. In the meantime, as he was a strong suspect, and the only one in the series of murders, I asked the C I D to send his *portrait parle* —his photographs and description - to all the police stations.

In the meantime, our killer struck again ... and again.

On the 27th of August, he attacked a young couple, Maruti Pawar (26) and his wife, Sushma (23), in their room in a *chawl* at the foot of the Borivli hill. The killer had entered the room by bending the bars of the window. Pawar and his wife were awake, and they shouted for help. They also tried to ward off his blows, but Sushma collapsed. Hearing their cries, the neighbours ran to the room, but the killer made good his escape through the window. He did not get any chance to take anything. Pawar and his wife, fortunately, survived, But they were unable to give any coherent details about the assault.

On the same night, the murderer killed Deva Bharwad. On the night of the 23rd he killed a woman named Shanta bai, and her two small children, Again on the night of the 24th he killed a grass vendor named Narayan Patil who lived in an isolated hut in Kandivli.

All these killings created a panic in the suburbs, and now began to get wide publicity in all the newspapers. Strange rumours also spread about the killer. Some said he was a maniac full of blood lust; others that he was a sadhu bent on propitiating some deity. After all, they said, was it not the thugs in the past, who used to strangle and rob innocent travellers to propitiate the goddess, Kali?

The police received reports about more than one bona fide sadhu, chased and beaten up in the suburbs by frenzied crowds under the impression that he must be the killer. Some people thought that the murderer had supernatural powers - that he could change himself into an animal at will and evade capture. The origin of this particular rumour was an incident where a woman was sleeping in a shed on the outskirts of Borivli. At night a fox entered the shed and bit her ear. She ran out screaming that the mad sadhu had attacked her. The neighbours searched her shed, but found no one inside. Someone saw the fox (now thoroughly frightened by the commotion) crouching on the roof of the shed. The crowd concluded that the fox was none other than the mad killer. They tried to catch it, but it managed to jump down from the back of the shed and disappeared into the brush.

A C I D officer was asked on the phone by a lady of consequence,"Is it true, officer, that the killer can change himself into a cat?"

He snapped back, "Madam, if the killer changes himself into a cat, I shall change myself into a dog, and chase him."

I was now besieged by frantic telephone calls, citizens' delegations, and newspaper reporters, all demanding instant action by the police. I could not forget how Sir Charles Warren, Commissioner of the Metropolitan (the police force of London) was forced to resign in 1881 because the police were unable to catch Jack the Ripper. And Jack's tally of victims was only seven, as compared to nineteen by our unknown killer.

After taking stock, I organized one of the biggest manhunts in the history of the Bombay police, or for that matter, in the history of any police in the world. I ordered a round-the-clock *beat* in the suburbs deploying two thousand officers and other ranks on the job. We also took the help of the Home Guards, and hundred of volunteers, who organized themselves into vigilantes. And I announced a reward of Rs.1000 for information leading to the arrest of the killer.

Among the investigation papers of the cases of 1966, the C I D found a list of Raman Raghav's old haunts. Plainclothes policemen were sent to all these places, where they showed his photos to the local residents and questioned them whether they had seen him before, and, more important, recently. One such place was a chawl known as 'Sharma Bhayya's chawl' in Poisar. The record showed that Raman Raghav had stayed there in a rented room in 1966. While the police were there, a young woman whose name was Manjulabai Dalvi, told them that she recognized the man from the photo. He used to be called 'Anna'. What was most important, she had met him at 11.30 in the morning of August 24th when she was returning home with a pitcher of water. She said to him,"Anna, where were you all these days, and what brings you here now?" He answered that he had come to pay Sharma Bhayya the rent he owed. She informed the C I D officer that when she met him, Anna was wearing a blue bush shirt, shorts, and was clean-shaven.

This was the most important lead that we had got so far. We now knew that our quarry was still moving within the locus of the crimes, and was likely to be found wearing the same attire. The Information was broadcast immediately to all the police stations in Bombay.

But, as if the cock a snook at the police, the killer struck again. At 6 on the morning of the 16th, Scott phoned me to say that the killer had accounted for two more persons sleeping in a hut at the buffalo stable of Dr. Mandlik at Chinchavli, Malad. When I reached the scene of the crime, I saw a crowd of several hundred people gathered outside the compound. I had to walk on a culvert on a nullah before I could enter the compound. The stables consisted of a main shed facing the nullah, with two small sheds at right angles at either end. The bed of the nullah must have originally carried a stream of fresh, clear water. In its place the nullah was full of buffalo-dung, dirty water and urine which was swept into it every day from the stables. The stench was overpowering. The hut in which the two persons were killed was at the nullah end. My officers were all there: Scott, Kulkarni, officers from the police station of Malad, and officers from the C I D

Kulkarni gave me a faint smile, and said,"At last, we've been able to get some good fingerprints from a stainless steel box. I am sending the box to the Finger Print Bureau, and we'll soon come to know if Raman Raghav is our killer or not".

"After eliminating the prints of the deceased," I said mechanically.

Not to be outdone, Scott said, "We have two eye-witnesses."

He brought before me the watchman of the stables, a man named Babu Shinde, and his son, Ramesh, a boy of 12 or 13. The stables housed 150 milch-buffaloes. In the middle of the shed was set a high table on which the watchman used to sit, so that he could view the entire shed, which was lit up with tube lights. Babu said that he used to sit up from 8 p.m. till 11 a.m. when his son took over from him. At 1 o'clock, when he woke up Ramesh, as usual, and Ramesh took a round of the stables to report 'all's well.' Ramesh came back and told him that he had seen a darkish man in the grass near the nullah. Both of them went to check, but seeing nothing they returned and sat on the table. After about 15 minutes, they heard the sound of a utensil falling, from the direction of the hut. In this hut, two brothers (hired hands in the stables) used to sleep. Their names were Lalchand and Dular. When they came near the door of the hut, they flashed a light and saw a man rushing out. He ran towards the nullah, and they lost sight of him.

I asked them, "Why didn't you try to catch them?"

They replied that they shouted '*chor, chor*' but nobody came out to help. When they went inside the hut, they found Lalchand and Dular lying in a pool of blood on their *charpoys*, their heads were mangled.

The officer in charge of the case told me that Lalchand and Dular had died before they reached the hospital, and that no dying-declaration could be taken from them.

When I reached my office after a quick bath and shave, I saw a large gathering of newspaper reporters in the anteroom. There was an excited hubbub, which stopped for a moment when I entered. All of them crowded around me.

"A statement," they cried in unison. "We want a statement!" They were shouting and gesticulating, and all of them seemed to be in an angry mood.

"I shall call you all in and certainly give you a statement." I said, brushing past them through the swing doors. As I sank into my swivel chair, ACP Basil Kane came inside and said, "A word with you, Sir, before you address them."

I looked at him enquiringly, "Yes, Kane?"

"The Director of the Finger Print Bureau has informed me that the prints on the stainless-steel box tally with those of Raman Raghav."

I sat up with a jerk."Is he quite sure?"

"He is positive, Sir," Kane said.

"O.K. Call the Press in," I said.

They all trooped in, and along with them, the officers of the C.I.D. I had never deliberately sought publicity with the Press (as more than one officer has). I found them, in general, fair. They were appreciative of the fact that I had for the first time, made a Press room with a telephone, in the CID office, where they had proper chairs, and were served tea and snacks before a Press briefing. If, on occasion, they were critical of our shortcomings, they were often appreciative of the good things we have done. On this occasion, I could not blame them entirely for their feelings against the police. After all, it could not be gainsaid that even after the killer had committed nine cold-blooded and brutal murders, the police had not been able to arrest him, or even establish his identity. For certain and every night there were scores of people, including women and children, keeping awake in fear and trepidation that hey might be next on the killer's list of victims.

"Commissioner," said a spokesman from the Press. "This is unprecedented. The entire suburbs are in a panic. Daily this monster is claiming his toll of victims; the police do nothing except register offences and record a few statements. It's no doubt true that only a few poor people are attacked, but do they not deserve protection as much as the rich? We want action. We demand action."

"Everyone deserves protection," I said. "The poor, equally with the rich. You know my views by now. I have nothing to do with the rich. I have put two thousand men on this job. We are doing our best..."

"Your best is not good enough, Sir", another speaker said. This man must not be allowed to go on the rampage."

"Is Raman Raghav really the killer?" a third asked.

"It's only the police who say so," another who was never too friendly with the police, said."Obviously, they're trying to hoodwink us to cover their incompetence."

I felt a hot flush rise from the back of my neck.

"We shall get him very soon," I said, with more confidence than I felt.

"How soon?' they chorused. We've heard this many times before."

"Gentlemen of the Press," I said. "One at a time, please. I give you my word we'll have the killer within the next 48 hours."

There was a general hubbub.

"What's the basis of your assurance?"

"Have you any clues of which we are not aware?"

"May we quote you?"

"Yes, you may quote me," I said wearily. Publish my statement by all means. And now, if you will excuse me, I am not prepared to answer any more questions. This conference is over."

The reporters rushed out to get their copy in the evening editions. Two of them came up to me and said," You have our sympathy and support. We know how difficult your job is. Good luck!"

After they had gone, I gave my officers a wry look. I said, "Of this, at least, we're sure. The killer is Raman Raghav, and none other. Let's go from there. He seems to be a man of low intelligence. He robs his victims of trifles for which he must be getting very little. So he goes on committing more murders. I am sure he is so poor, he must be wearing the same clothes described by Manjulabai: blue bush shirt, shorts and maroon shoes. And he must be coming downtown to sell these articles. The C I D must broadcast his description to our nineteen thousand officers and men. Surely, one of them is likely to notice him in the next 48 hours.!"

Kulkarni said he would attend to the matter personally.

The next morning (the 27th) I was in the middle of my breakfast when the phone rang; it was the control room The Inspector in charge told me in an impersonal voice that Raman Raghav was arrested that morning by sub-inspector Fialho of Dongri police station. This was followed soon after by the Inspector of Dongri confirming the arrest.

"Are you sure the man is Raman Raghav?" I asked the Inspector.

He said he was sure, but he would get confirmation soon when the Finger Print Bureau to which he had sent the suspect's fingerprints for comparison.

I did not wait to finish my breakfast. Dongri police station is in the centre of Bombay, not far from the Commissioner's office. When I went there, I found that the news of Raman Raghav's arrest had somehow leaked out, and about 50 people were gathered outside. I brushed past them, and entered the Inspector's room.
The officers brought Raman Raghav from the lock-up.

"Are you Raman Raghav? I asked. He said that he was Raman Raghav. His appearance was very much like his *portrait parle.* The only conspicuous part of his face were his eyes, which were unblinking. Sub-inspector Fialho told me how he caught Raman Raghav. He said he was walking on the Imamwada Road, a couple of furlongs from the police station. There were very few people moving about at that time in the morning. This man passed by him, and Fialho suddenly reacted. There was something familiar about the man - his blue shirt, shorts, maroon shoes.

"You there! What's your name and where are you going?" Fialho accosted him. Raman Raghav gave him a false name. His suspicions aroused, the sub-inspector caught him by the shoulder, and took him to the police station. There he was questioned further, when he admitted that his name was Raman Raghav. He did not appear to be unduly worried or frightened by the arrest or the interrogation. He had been in police custody before, and did not think he was arrested for the recent murders.

The officers at Dongri took a closer look at his clothes. There were dark stains on the shirt and shorts, which could be of blood. On a search of his person, the police recovered a pair of spectacles, a pair of scissors, an umbrella, a paper bag containing soap, garlic, tea powder and an *agarbatti* stand.

In the meantime ACP Kane and Inspector Wakatkar of the C I D had arrived. I asked them to take over at once the investigation of all the cases of Raman Raghav, and to remove him to the C I D lock-up at the rear of my office compound. I learnt at the police station that the Finger Print Bureau had identified the fingerprints of the suspect as those of Raman Raghav.

The news of Raman Raghav's arrest spread like wildfire throughout the city. Within a few hours about 10,000 people gathered at the police station, and then outside the C I D office. Huge crowds were to become a permanent feature during the trial of Raman Raghav, and the police had to make elaborate arrangements to control them every time the case was heard in the Courts.

I telephoned the Chief Minister and told him the good news. "Are you sure that he is Raman Raghav?" he asked. I replied that I was quite sure. When he congratulated me, I said," I am sure, Sir, that you would like to congratulate the officer who caught him." I gave the phone to Fialho, and the Chief Minister must have spoken well, because I saw that Fialho's face was beaming.

On returning to my office, I called another Press conference. This time the reaction of the Press was different. I did not, however want to hog the publicity. I gave the credit where it was due. I was the captain of the team - and it was a fine team!

Inspector Wakatkar sent Raman Raghav's clothes and his nail parings to the Forensic Science Laboratory for examination. He noticed mud in the seams of Raman Raghav's canvas shoes, and a substance that looked and smelt like dung from Dr. Mandlik's stables (the nullah nearby) to the Forensic laboratory also.

Raman Raghav at first refused to say anything to the C I D officers. I had said before that he had been arrested in connection with the murders on the pipeline and had disclosed nothing, as a result of which he had to be released. This had happened in 1966. But this time, the situation was different. In part due to the skilful interrogation by the officers from the C I D, and in part, to his own resolve, on the 29th August 19, Raman Raghav made a full confession admitting all his crimes.

What would make a hardened criminal confess? It may be that his conscience had at last awakened. It may be that he felt that enough is enough: As Raman Raghav said to me, he was ordered from 'above' to confess, just as (he said) that he was ordered by his *kanoon* (the supreme law from above) to commit the murders.

In India, the law with regard to confessions is different from that which prevails in the U K and the U S A. In India, a confession before a police officer (whatever be his rank) is not admissible in evidence, except in so far as it relates to the discovery of a fact - more specifically, about the production of stolen property. (In this context, it is worthy to note that even statements, made to the police by witnesses during the investigation, are not signed by the witnesses, as corroborative evidence. But these statements have to be given to the defence before the commencement of the trial and they can be used by the defence to contradict prosecution witnesses).

On the 29th of August, Raman Raghav made a statement to the C I D that he would show them where he had hidden the *ankhda* (the fulcrum jemmy). He also said he would show them where he had hidden various articles such as knives, stoves, umbrellas and coats that he had stolen during the murders.

He led the C I D officers to a grass field, off the Ahmedabad Road near the Aarey Milk Colony. In the field he had hidden all these articles under a thorny bush, and he took them all out.

On the 30th of August, he again took the C I D officers to Chichavli, to the house of a man called Michael D'Souza, from where he had borrowed a crowbar which was fashioned into a jemmy by a blacksmith. Michael produced from a drawer in a cupboard two fountain pens and a magnifying glass, which were part of the stolen property from the hut of Upadhyaya, the murdered school teacher. After that, Raman Raghav took them to the smithy of Lalchand Viswakarma, a blacksmith. Lalchand went inside his shop, and brought out the remaining part of the iron crowbar.

Later, the C I D interrogated Michael D'Souza at length. He said that he was a retired millhand. He had built a small chawl, and he and his daughter maintained themselves on the rent from the remaining rooms., and his daughter Violet's wages from a factory. He was a native of Tinneveli district, Madras State, from where he had come to Bombay 49 years back to earn his livelihood. He came to know Raman Raghav in 1951 when they were working together in the Sgreekrishna Mills at Malad. On the 11th of August, Thambi (the alias used by Raman Raghav with him) came to his room. Michael enquired where he had been for such a long time. He said that he had been working in Tinneveli. He had, however, brought his wife and children to Bombay, and wanted to build a hut for them, beyond the Chinchavli railway crossing. He said he had already bought the wood and other materials and wanted to borrow Michael's crowbar, and then Thambi left, promising to return it within three days.

On the 16th of August, Thambi again came to his room. Michael was sitting there with his daughter and a nephew, Melville. Thambi took out from the pocket of his shorts, two fountain pens and a magnifying glass.. He gave them to Michael. "We were drinking tea at that time," Michael said, so I offered him a cup. He said that he would not drink tea from my house, as we were Christians. He wanted to prepare it in my house, but I refused to let him do so. He got up to go when I reminded him about the crowbar. I said that three days had passed. He flared up at that. He said he would return it. "What will you do, if I don't?"

The police also questioned Viswakarma, the young blacksmith. He said that sometime in the middle of August, the accused had come to him with an octagonal - shaped crowbar. He said he wanted an instrument to be prepared of it of a particular shape; he wanted an arm one-and-a-half foot long, then a perpendicular twist of six inches at one end, and another twist in the opposite direction at the other. He also wanted one end to have a sharp point. The blacksmith made it for him in a couple of hours. While he was making it, he asked Raman Raghav why he wanted it of that shape. Raman Raghav said that he owned some sheep and he wanted it for tethering them and also for digging. He had kept the rest of the bar, which he produced before the police. The C I D sent the articles to the Forensic Laboratory for examination.

On 6th November, Inspector Wakatkar produced Raman Raghav before R M Devare, Presidency Magistrate of the 15th Court, Bombay. Raman Raghav told the magistrate that he wanted to make a confession. The Presidency Magistrate gave him time until the next day, so that he could reflect fully on the consequences of his decision. Raman Raghav was then taken into magisterial custody. The next day, the Magistrate asked all police officers to withdraw from the court. Raman Raghav was specifically asked if there were any police officers present. He said,"No". He then asked Raman Raghav if he had any complaint of ill treatment from the police. He had none. The magistrate also satisfied himself that there were no marks of violence on Raman Raghav's body.

Question: Do you wish to give your confession voluntarily?

Answer: Yes

Question: Has anybody asked you to make a confession?

Answer: No. I am doing it as I have an intuition to do so.

Question: Has anybody told you that if you make a confession, you will be dealt with leniently, or, that you will go scot-free?
Answer: No. Nobody has told me that.

Question: Do you know that you are not bound to make a confession?

Answer: Yes

Question: Do you know that your confession will be used in evidence against you?

Answer: Yes, I know it now.

Question: Do you still wish to make a confession?

Answer: Yes.

The magistrate then informed the accused that he was giving him twenty-four hours more for reflection. He also explained that he was being kept in magisterial custody, and not police custody.

On the 8th of November, Raman Raghav was again brought before the magistrate.

Question: "Did you consider and reflect on whether you should give the confession or not?"

Answer:" Yes".

The magistrate again gave him further time to reflect. He was brought before the magistrate, and the latter asked all the police to withdraw.

Question: "Do you understand that you are not bound to confess?"

Answer: "Yes, I want to confess.

Question:"Why do you want to confess?"

Answer: "I am ordered by the Almighty to confess, and hence I am confessing.

Question: "Do you know that your confession will be used in evidence against you?"

Answer:"Yes, I am prepared for the consequences."

Magistrate: "Now tell me what you have to say."

Raman Raghav: (Statement, originally given in Hindi, was translated into English as follows.)

"My real name is Sindhi Dalwai.I come from Agreshwar, Nellur, Tinneveli District, Madras State. I first came to Bombay in 1951 and worked as a millhand in Nava Bharat Mill for one and a half years. After that I joined another mill where I got a salary of Rs.125 per month. Three months later the police arrested me and put me in Byculla Jail. After my release, I joined three or four others, whom I met in the jail, and committed many thefts. I was sent to jail six or seven times for the thefts. I was also sent to prison for five years for committing a murder while stealing.

In 1966 I committed several murders while stealing, and for this, the police arrested me. I did not confess, and they released me after six months. I was then externed out of Bombay for two years, and went to Poona. I began to commit thefts in Poona, Dehu and Talegaon. At a teashop in Talegaon, I gave the order for a cup of tea. I found that the man had put too much water, and very little tea and milk. I decided to kill him. While I was going to his house for the purpose, a crowd gathered and caught me. They made out a false case of theft against me. I was sentenced to one and a half years by the Vadgaon Court."

Question: "What happened after one a half years?"

Answer: "I took a rail ticket to Karjat. From there I went on foot to Bhandup. In 1969 I went to Borivli. I began to commit thefts regularly from which I got amounts from One to Fifty Rupees. On the way to Dahisar, I came across a small hardware shop near the bridge. There I found a bar with a big handle. I took it to Jogeshwari and got it converted into an *ankhda*.

I saw a buffalo stable near a small village by the side of the Ahmedabad Road, near Malad. A bearded Muslim was sleeping on a cot there in a hut, the door of which was not latched. I gave the man a blow on the head with the point of the *ankhda*. The man died on the spot. I took his watch from his wrist. I also took from the hut a coat, an umbrella, a battery (torch). In the jungle I searched the pockets of his coat and found a hundred-rupee note, sixteen ten-rupee notes and some small change. I tore the coat into small pieces for use as handkerchiefs. I knew a Marwari pawnbroker in Malad. I deposited the cash with him, and used to take out small amounts when I needed them.

After two days, I went at dead of night to a chawl in Jogeshwari where a teacher used to stay. I gave him two or three blows with my ankhda, and he collapsed. I searched his house and took some cooked rice and vegetables. I also saw a bottle of ghee, which I took. I ate the food and went on.

"I saw another hut beside the road. I climbed from the rear of the hut and saw a man sleeping on a cot, and a woman with a child on another. I stood in the space between the cots. I gave the man two or three blows with the *ankhda*, and he died instantly. I killed the woman also. As the child started to cry I killed it. I snatched what I thought was a gold necklace from the woman's neck. The sound of the child crying had awakened the neighbours. I saw an old woman standing at the open door. She saw me and began screaming. I ran away leaving the *ankhda* and the umbrella, as I had no time to pick them up from where I put them.

"Later I went to the house of a Christian friend whose name is Michael. I asked him to lend me his iron crowbar for a few days and he gave it to me.

"The 'gold necklace' from the woman's neck had turned out to be made of plastic, so I had thrown it away. After three or four days, I saw a young man sleeping in a hut in a locality called Hanuman Nagar in Kandivli. I thought of killing him, but I did not get any chance of entering the hut. The next night I entered his hut by making a channel beside the door with the crowbar. I gave him two or three blows on the side of his head, and he collapsed. I took his wristwatch, a fountain pen, an instrument box and four one rupee notes. I pledged them with a Marwari, and got thirty rupees from him. I then went to Jogeshwari and got a blacksmith to fashion the crowbar into an *ankhda* according to my instructions.

"After four days, on my night prowls, I noticed a double-line *pucca chawl* at the foot of Borivli hill. The last room in the rear line was locked. I broke open the lock and went inside. Though I ransacked the room, I did not get anything worth stealing. In the next room I saw that a man, woman and child were sleeping. I had observed that people were residing in the adjoining rooms, So, as a precaution, I cut a string into small pieces and tied the latches from outside. I then broke open the window of the room where the three people (Pawar family) were sleeping. I gave the man three blows; the woman woke up and began screaming. I silenced her and the child with my *ankhda*. I heard the people running towards the room and good my escape through the window and up the hill.

After three or four days, I went to another hut and saw a man sleeping (Dava Bhadwad), and I finished him off with the *ankhda*. I ate some cooked rice and milk, which I found there. I found some pieces of silver and brass in a box. "

Raman Raghav also mentioned similar other killings, which have been described earlier. He then went on:"The next day I went to a buffalo stable near the Chinchavli rail crossing. I had cased the place some years ago, and I knew that cash of Rs.1000 used to be kept in the cupboard of the office. I tried to enter the compound by climbing over the rear wall, but I found that the height of the wall had been raised and I could not climb it. I found another way through the *nullah*, which flowed under an arch in the wall. The *nullah* was full of dung, so I took a stick of sugarcane from the field nearby, and immersed it in the water to see how deep it was. It was only two feet, so I waded through it into the compound. On my way to the office I saw two persons sleeping on *charpoys*. I thought they woulg awaken at any noise that I might make in rifling the cupboard, so I finished them off with my *ankhda*. One of them began to scream, so I gave him two blows. I saw a coat hanging on the wall. I went through the pockets and got some money. I did not get time to ransack the cupboard as people in the stable nearby had been alerted. I took my *ankhda* and ran back the way I came"

Raman Raghav said that he had become a loner because his accomplices had betrayed him in the dacoity. He chose the huts of poor people because they were isolated and there would be no eyewitnesses. He showed the shop of the Marwari with whom he had pledged some articles; the pawnbroker produced them before the police. Why did he take such trifling amounts for which he committed all the ghastly murders? He said he had to subsist from day to day, and theft had become for him his way of life.

There were at least six cases in which we had sufficient evidence to prosecute Raman Raghav, but we decided that we should send up to the Sessions Court the last case, namely, the murders of Lalchand and Dular in Dr. Mandlik's stables. This case was, therefore, sent up to the Sessions Court conducted before the Additional Sessions Judge, C T Dighe. The accused could not afford a lawyer, nor did he ask for one, but he was given one by the State, P V Pawar. That his procedure was not a mere formality became clear from the trial. At the outset of the trial, Pawar stated that from his talks with the accused, he felt that the man was insane. He said that he used to get a phone from God, and despatched the victims with his fountain pen, i,e., the *ankhda*.

The Sessions Judge ordered the police surgeon to keep the accused under observation, and give his report.Dr.Franklin, the police surgeon, kept Raman Raghav under observation for three weeks. He came to the following conclusion: 'the accused is not suffering from any infirmity of mind. He is not mentally retarded. His memory is sound. He possesses average intelligence. He has sufficient intelligence to understand the nature and object of the proceedings against him. He has faced other court trials in the past and is aware of the implications of this trial. He has enough intelligence to conduct his defence in a rational and reasonable manner. He is not certifiably insane and will be able to stand his own trial'.

The C I D marshalled their evidence before the court in meticulous detail. The important items in the evidence were the following:

1. The statements of the two eyewitnesses, watchman Babu Shinde and his son, Ramesh.

2. The evidence of Raman Raghav's fingerprints on the stainless steel box.

3. The production of the fulcrum jemmy used by the accused, and the finding of human bloodstains on it by the Chemical Analyser.

4. The statement and evidence of the Assistant Chemical Analyser, B.S.Nabar, that the fulcrum jemmy and the piece of iron crowbar (produced by the blacksmith Viswakarma) were of identical sectional dimensions and chemical composition. He had also found by spectrographic analysis, that the traces of dung on the maroon canvas shoes, and from the dung sample from the nullah, had the same physical characteristics.

5. The production of the coat by the accused, and its identification by some of the hired hands from Dr.Mandlik's stables.

6. The evidence of Michael D'Souza and his daughter, Violet, showing the source from which the accused had obtained the iron crowbar. Their evidence also showed his movements prior to the commission of the offence. (It may be noted that the fountain pens and the magnifying glass could not be produced as evidence in the trial as they formed part of the *corpus delicti* of another case.)

7. The evidence of the blacksmith, Lalchand Viswakarma, which showed where the accused had made the jemmy, and the production by him of the remaining part of the crowbar.

8. The evidence of Manjulabai showing the accused's movements prior to the offence.

9. The evidence of S N Shetty, owner of Jai Hanuman Restaurant, showing the accused's movements on the same night of the offence, in the vicinity of Dr. Mandlik's stables.

10. The confessional statement of the accused before the Presidency Magistrate.

After considering the evidence, and the arguments of the prosecuting and defence counsels, the Honourable Judge came to the conclusion that it was Raman Raghav who had killed Lalchand and Dular with the fulcrum jemmy.

The defense now took the stand that Raman Raghav was of unsound mind when he committed the murders, and that, as such, he could not be held responsible for them.

Section 84 of the Indian Penal Code reads: 'Nothing is an offence if it is done by a person who, at the time of doing it, by reason of unsoundness of mind, is incapable of knowing the nature of the act, or that what he is doing is either wrong or contrary to law'.

There is a difference between legal insanity and medical insanity. Any person who wants the benefit of this section must prove (i.e., the defense counsel must prove on his behalf) that at the time of committing the act, he was labouring under such a defect of reason as not to know the nature and quality of the act, or that what he was doing was wrong. Here the word wrong is to be understood in its legal sense, and not its moral sense. Raman Raghav's defense counsel argued that his movements in broad daylight with blood stained clothes, his committing brutal murders for petty gains showed that he was quite unaware of the nature of his acts.

The Judge discussed these arguments in great detail. Section 84 of the I.P.C. was based on what has come to be called the McNaughten Rule of English law. A man called McNaughten had shot a Mr. Drummond in 1843, mistaking him for Sir Robert Peel, then Prime Minister.He wanted to kill Peel because of a delusion that the latter was persecuting him. This rule did not admit of the plea or irresistible impulse and or partial responsibility. It was greatly criticised ever since the appearance of Isaac Ray's 'Treatise on the Medical Jurisprudence of Insanity'. The chief argument against the Rule was that it had not kept pace with developments in medicine. It was said that while medicine had come to recognize the mind as a whole, the McNaughten Rule smacked of the ancient and outdated doctrine of separate mental faculties, where the cognitive faculty was only one of the main divisions. A psychiatrist, Dr. Patkar, who had examined the accused, had come to the conclusion that he suffered from chronic, paranoid schizophrenia, of which the main symptom was a withdrawal from reality and frequent delusions.

The Hon'ble Judge, while rejecting Dr. Patkar's arguments, had said that the psychiatrist had made no attempt to shatter the delusions of the accused. Holding a belief was one thing, but remaining confirmed in it when attempts were made to destroy it, was another. If these delusions were systematized, they should have come out of the accused's mouth on earlier occasions also; the greed for money could hardly co-exist with the notion of battle. Lalchand and Dular were complete strangers, and by no stretch of the imagination could they be considered as people who persecuted the accused. The Judge also said that whenever the accused was asked about the order from *above*, he always gave the reply that he would speak about it *afterwards*. This led to the question whether all that the accused spoke was under the influence of schizophrenia, or whether there was a possibility of his taking advantage of the situation. (In this connection, it is worth recalling the cross-examination of the psychiatrist, Dr. Yellowlees, by the Attorney General, Sir Hartley Shawcross, in the British case against John George Haig. In his examination of the witness Shawcross had brought out the fact that most of the symptoms reported by the psychiatrist, arose from what he told him.

The Judge said that when sub-inspector, Fialho accosted the prisoner and asked him his name, he gave the Police sub-inspector a false name; his instinct to cover up was not in keeping with the behavior of a man who had committed a crime without knowing that what he did was wrong or contrary to law.

The Hon'ble Judge concluded:

"The case of the accused will remain unparalleled and unsurpassed in the history of crime for its heinousness, brutality, and *perversity*. I, therefore, find that he must be given the extreme penalty of death."

Though the prisoner had not appealed against the sentence, according to law, a sentence of death has to be confirmed by the High Court. Further, since he had no lawyer, their Lordships, the Judges, appointed an *amicus curia* to plead for him at Government cost.

At the advocate's request, a board of psychiatrists was appointed consisting of: Dr. J C Marfatia, Dr. V N Bagadia, and Dr. V R Deo. After examining the prisoner, the board came to the conclusion that he was suffering from chronic paranoid schizophrenia, and was certifiably insane. He knew the nature of his act, i.e., that he was killing human beings, but he did not know what he did was wrong or contrary to law. He firmly believed that he was obeying the *kanoon*. Hid unsoundness of mind had resulted in such a degree of defect of reason that he was incapable of cooperating with his defense counsel in the conduct of his trial and the proceeding before the Court.

After hearing the arguments of the counsel, Their Lordships came to the conclusion that the prisoner was clearly of unsound mind, and unable to make his defense. He completely lacked the capacity to understand the gravity of the crime or the seriousness of the death sentence. His personality had so deteriorated that his delusions and hallucinations wholly influenced him, and he was incapable of rational thinking and behavior.

Their Lordships ordered that the proceedings in the confirmation case be postponed. The State Government was directed to detain the prisoner in safe custody in Yeravada Central Prison.

The case of Raman Raghav is indubitably the most outstanding case investigated by the Bombay City Police. It showed splendid teamwork on the part of the ranks. While Fialho deserves full credit for his alertness in catching Raman Raghav, it should be noted that all ranks of the City Police had been alerted. For this reason I was confident that he would be caught within a very short time, and hence my statement at the press conference.

As for the investigation of the case, Inspector Wakatkar and his immediate superior, A C P Kane, would meet me practically every day in the evening, discuss developments, and obtain instructions. This was one case where I thought that (however busy I might be) I must personally supervise the investigation.

This chapter is based *on the first and most authentic account* of the investigation published by me in the 'Imprint' magazine of December 1972.

CHAPTER VIII

THE PROBLEM OF RIOT CONTROL

The most important problem facing the Police in India today is the problem of riot control. The causes of riots are many - some are spontaneous, others are deep-rooted. Not infrequently, politicians create the situations that lead to the riots. And the police are invariably blamed for using too much or too little force. The blame falls on some poor Reserve Police sub-inspector, while the officer in charge of the police station (appointed for his capacity to rake in the shekels), manages to remain in the background, as do his senior officers.

When I went into the witness box to give evidence before the Madon Commission of Enquiry, the presiding judge asked me (with facetious intent, no doubt),"Mr.Modak, it has been said that you are riot-prone. Is this true?" I answered,"Your Lordship, in answer to your query, let us consider only this riot of Bhiwandi. On 7th may, while my wife and I were having dinner with a friend, I got a telephone call from the Inspector General, A G Rajadhyaksha, at 8.30PM that serious rioting had broken out in Bhiwandi, and that the Home Secretary, L G Rajwade, had ordered that:

1). I should go there and deal with it, and that

2). I should stay there for a month and a half.

I had never visited Bhiwandi before, nor did I know anything about the background of the riot, which was, indeed, deep-rooted (as the sequel will show). How could I be responsible for attracting the riot?" (As the Inspector General, Rajadhyaksha, was *au fait* with all the events that caused the riot, he should have gone to deal with it, instead of maneuvering to send me).

Over the last fifty years, since Independence, I have not seen any substantial improvement in the methods of dealing with the major riots that have occured from time to time all over India. I see the same pattern repeated *ad infinitum*. Mobs are allowed to gather in their hundreds and thousands. However peaceful they may be at first, they soon become truculent, and then turn violent. They begin to throw missiles, which they have collected beforehand-or which they gather on the spot- stones, brickbats and bottles. The reaction of the police is also familiar. They are first drawn up in the regulation formation with the *lathi* sections in front, the tear gas squads in the middle, and the armed men in the rear. But all this becomes completely disorganized as the rioting progresses. None of these units has a clearly nominated commander in tight control of his men and responsible for their actions. As for the overall commander, the officer who should have been present on the spot, he generally takes shelter in the control room, controlling his men from as long a distance as he can possibly maintain. With the advent of commissioners of police (they seem now to be cheaper by dozen in Maharashtra), each one has become a super district magistrate (which was certainly not the intention of the Maharashtra State Police Commission in suggesting their appointments in Pune and Nagpur. I should know. I was the Member-Secretary, and these posts were created at my urging.)

The duties and functions of the armed policemen during riotous situations need special mention. It was laid down in the police manual eighty-five years ago that firearms should be used as a last resort. When firing has to be resorted to, orders were given to members of a squad or platoon by the commander with regard to the number of rounds, the kind of fire, and the person or persons on whom the firing was to be done. Later, when Reserve Police forces began to be used, it was laid down that each party should be under the orders of an officer from the police station (or district police force). They did not know anything about the local situation, nor about unarmed policing, and it was patently unfair to leave them on their own. These rules are now observed in the breach, and more often than not, these poor men are left to face the music. And armed men, both from the Reserve Police, as well as from the district police, are seen (sometimes on TV) facing the mob in ones and twos.

I feel that this is the proper place to make some comments on the use of the reserve police (whether from a State of from the Centre) in riot control, and in problems of law and order. The tendency seems to have developed for police officers in charge of districts and large cities to throw the entire burden for the maintenance of Law and Order on the reserve police. If the officer requires three companies for a particular purpose, for example to deal with a major agitation or a public meeting at be addressed by a VVIP, he will ask for seven, and get five. The implication is that if he is not given the number of men he wants he will not be responsible for any breakdown in the situation. On the other hand, the Director General (at the HQ) sees no reason why he should not send as many men as possible. Why should he face the blame for not sending enough men? It is the Government that will incur the financial loss, not he. The answer to this has appeared to me to be obvious. Why can the DG not send one of the stepneys in his HQ to go to the place concerned and satisfy himself that the numbers asked for are reallly necessary? And so it has come to pass that to give one glaring example at least thirty SRP companies have become, in effect, a virtual part of the police force of Mumbai City.

But the harmful effect of the misuse of the reserve police does not end here unfortunately. I know it for a fact that in Maharashtra, (and it must be the same elsewhere), the reserve police are being used round the clock without rest and respite. They are given no time for training, especially for musketry (firing) practice, which they have not done for years. I have seen them sometimes packed like sardines in a truck, waiting at a street corner in the hot sun. I have asked them for how long? For four and five hours, I have been told. They have not had baths for days together; they hardly have time to eat or to answer the call of nature. My blood boils when I remember a former home secretary compare their shabby turnout to that of the smart BSF. But a shabby turnout does not necessarily mean an undisciplined body of men. I would have liked him to have read Nigel Hamilton's definitive biography of Field Marshal Montgomery. His men were always shabbily turned out. I saw them (the Royal Warwickshires) at the rehearsal on the racecourse ground in Poona, for the Viceroy's Parade in 1934. They were, none the less, the best-trained men in the British Army. They were responsible for the turn in the tide of the War at Alam Halfa and at El Alamein.

As the D C P Headquarters in Bombay, I had to face one of the worst riots in the history of Bombay in 1956 - the riots that took place during the Samyukta Maharashtra agitation in Bombay. Many people have expressed the view (with hindsight, of course) that the Reorganization of the States on a linguistic basis was a great mistake.

Whether this view is correct or not, it was patent at the time that if Samyukta Maharashtra was sanctioned, Bombay had to be included in it. It was absurd to think of it as a separate City or State, or as part of some Greater Bombay State, which included Gujarat. However, this was what Morarji Desai insisted on, and got. And, as police officers, ours was not to reason why, or to take sides. As I have always seen it, my duty was to carry out orders, provided they were legal. If others did not agree with this credo, they should have had the guts to resign: no more, no less.I doubt if I could have handled these riots successfully, if I had not created the six Striking Forces that were mainly responsible for dealing successfully with them.

When I was an ASP in Satara in the forties, V S Bakhle was the Public Prosecutor. I was delighted to find that he had an excellent private library, which he replenished from time to time with the latest books; and he had wide tastes in reading. Since he allowed me free access to this treasure trove, I would take stacks of books on tour. Among these, I was greatly interested in the books of B H Liddell Hart on the revolution in warfare caused by the invention of the tank. Liddell Hart spoke about the deep strategic penetration of the armoured forces, racing ahead of the main infantry mass, and operating independently of it. I recalled this doctrine when I was D C P Headquarters in Bombay, and thought of applying it (in a very small way) to the police department. It led to the creation of the Six Striking Forces to deal with the Samyukta Maharashtra riots, which I saw looming on the horizon. Each Striking Force consisted of 100 men. It was completely mobile. In front was the command vehicle - either a Jeep or a small van. Behind it were two vans containing two platoons (thirty men each) with canes; they were thoroughly trained in my cane drill. And behind them was another van, which carried the Gas Squad, and two sections (of ten men each), armed with .410 muskets. Rifles were the standard weapons of the S R P F, which they had to carry. But I had found that the .303 rifle was not really needed when dealing with a mob in the city. It was calibrated up to 1300 yards, and even though it was a World War I weapon, it could be lethal at 1100 yards. The .303 bullet could rip through tin sheds, and even brick walls. A rifle had a magazine carrying 6 or 7 bullets and could make the user 'trigger-happy'. On the other hand, the musket was an old .303 rifle the bore of which had been made smooth, like that of a shotgun. It had a limited range of 100 yards and used ball cartridges., The musket had no magazine, so it had to be loaded every time when the user wanted to open fire.

Last but not the least, I had put officers in charge of these forces, not in order of seniority, but for their proven daring and initiative. I still remember three of them: sub-inspectors, Suraliwala, Temkar, and Shegunshe. They were three of the best.

These striking forces were placed at the disposal of officers who wanted them, and who could use them, but they were at best, a weapon, just as tanks were at best a weapon. Their effectiveness depended on the DCPs and ACPs who were expected to lead them - from the front, not the rear! When the riots were at their worst, on one occasion, I had given a DCP named Deshpande, two Striking Forces when he was at Lalbaug facing the rioters. It seems that he just sat back while the mob went on the rampage. I then got a phone call from him on the radio telephone, "Mr. Modak, you had better come here immediately. The mob has become violent, and if I take any action, allegations will be made against me". I went there, but before going, I said on the radiotelephone, "What about me, my dear Deshpande? Won't allegations be made against me? I am but a D C P, like you".

On taking thought, I came to the conclusion that the main problem of the police in facing mobs was to bear the first onslaught of missiles like stones, brickbats, bottles that were brought beforehand or collected on the spot. Once they did this, the initiative would be passed on to the police, who could then charge the rioters with canes, tear gas, or whatever. We used to try and face them with helmeted heads lowered, but I found the true answer in Kashmir. This lay in the proper use of shields. I have never claimed that they were my invention. I first heard of their use in Calcutta, and I sent for half a dozen, then 50, then 200, and last for 600.

This shield was semi-circular, and had a tubular steel frame, covered with expanded metal. It was three feet long and weighed exactly 3 kgs. If you took a crouching position, and held it properly, it could protect your body - well, almost! I have described elsewhere how I trained the Kashmir Armed Police in the use of these shields. In the beginning, they were a timid lot who were inclined to run at the slightest hint of trouble. There was only one way of teaching them, and that was by personal example. On the parade ground I assumed the apex of a V formation. Policemen in plainclothes in front took the part of the mob, and threw stones of all shapes and sizes at us. At first they were reluctant to throw any stones at their IG, but they soon overcame it when I announced a reward of Rs.10 to be given on the spot to anyone who hit me or my shield. Monitors were kept on both sides to ensure fair play.

One peculiarity we noticed about the stones was that the larger the stones, the shorter was their range, the higher their trajectory, and the slower their speed. It was the smaller ones -those that were a little smaller than cricket balls that came the fastest, and could hit the hardest. They could also sometimes take an unexpected curve. After my return from Jammu & Kashmir, when I took charge as the Commissioner of Police, Bombay in January 1968, I trained at least 3 Striking Forces, and gave my *personal* demonstration to all who were interested. Yes, it is true that I did not invite the Press or give special written invitation to my 14 D C P's. These latter, should have read the Police Notice; I do remember that some of them did, and witnessed it.

But the training in riot control that I taught did not end there. I developed a complete system of Indoor and Outdoor training (when I became the Inspector General in 1976) at the S R P F Headquarters Group I in Pune, with the help of S Choudhari, Commandant Group I, and R K Bayas, senior police prosecutor. This system was formulated in the shape of the 'Manual for the Handling of Civil disturbances, 1977' approved of and printed by the Government of Maharashtra.

When I last gave a personal demonstration in Pune, I was 56 years old. (So much for Ribeiro's allegation that I was frightened of a stone falling on the roof of his truck). I P S officers were urged to undergo this training; I could not force them to do so. I still feel that those below 40 should undergo the training, and that, if they do, they canot fail to become better policemen and policewomen .

My Manual has fallen into desuetude for reasons that are obscure. It certainly needs to be revised and brought up to date in the light of new knowledge and experience, but on scrutinizing it again recently, I was convinced that its basic principles are sound, and that it should become a fundamental part of the training of every police officer in India, first in his or her training school, and then in a refresher course, held from time to time. Further, I feel that it should be of great interest to all civil servants, politicians and citizens, interested in the maintenance of internal peace and order anywhere in the world. . I, therefore, make no apology for giving below a brief outline of its contents.

In the Introduction, I stated that a comprehensive course for the handling of civil disturbances was started at my instance, (when I was the Special IG) at the SRPF Group I in Pune on 29 June 1970. This course was based on a pilot course that I had run in Jammu and Kashmir in 1966-67. It had consisted of two parts: 1) Practical-Ooutdoor training in Shield Drill, and 2) Theoretical - tactics in dealing with mobs and legal aspects.

I, further stated in the Introduction that since the commencement of the Course in Pune in 1970, 58 such courses had been conducted, training altogether 1340 officers, of whom 277 were from other States in India. In addition, 41 Sib-Divisional Magistrates and Tehsildars were also given training in the theoretical and legal aspects of riot control.

The Manual was divided into five parts, the first part dealt with the legal provisions containing the rights of assemblies under the Constitution of India: what made assemblies unlawful, and the powers and duties of the police in dealing with them. Preventive and punitive measures under various enactments were next discussed. Statutes and Case Law were incorporated and brought up to date (i.e. till September 1975). The manner and importance of investigation into riot cases were discussed in great detail.

The second part treated subjects like mob psychology, crowd control and the different methods of handling different types of disturbances. A special chapter was included on the proper organization of Control Rooms.

The third part reviewed reports of important judicial inquiries from all over India and the observations of the Judges on the shortcomings of the police, and how the police could profit by learning from their mistakes.

The fourth part gave a detailed drill on the actual fieldwork of the shield platoons and companies, words of command etc.

The fifth part gave diagrams of field platoons and company formations, as well as schedules and necessary appendices.

I said in conclusion that the object of this training was to enable Law Enforcement Officers to prevent assemblies from becoming unlawful, and that, if this could not be done, to control them with the minimum use of force and the minimum loss of life and property. Containing as it did, the collective wisdom of Judges, Magistrates, and

Law Enforcement Officers covering a period of the last half-century, it could not but be of help to those who were required to face disturbances anywhere in the country.

The prelude to many of these riots used to be the '*bandhs*' in the cities (total stoppage of work) organized by political parties to show their muscle. Eventually, State governments began to feel that it was better to allow the '*bandhs*' rather than to try to break them.

One particular feature that I noticed during these '*bandhs*' was that school and college students would come out on the streets in large numbers and play cricket or football or kabbadi to their hearts' content - a sad commentary on the shortage of playing fields and greens in Mumbai and elsewhere. Every available inch of space is taken up by quick moneymakers through the not too scrupulous building fraternity, once again backed by politicians.

I would sometimes stop and ask these young people whether they preferred play to watching TV. 'Play, Oh definitely play', they one and all answered.

CHAPTER IX

THE POLICE AND SHAKESPEARE

In the middle of May 1956, I got a welcome reprieve from dealing with the furious rioting that had taken place in Bombay on the Samyukta Maharashtra issue. I was sent on deputation to the Police College in the United Kingdom for a refresher course.

In those days, the Police College was situated at a place called Ryton-on-Dunsmore in Warwickshire, four miles from Coventry, and fourteen from Stratford-on-Avon. It was housed in barracks that had been built for the Army during the war. The college gave refresher courses to senior officers from the different forces in the U K. There were 114 of them, including those from the Metropolitan (London) Police. Besides this, they also invited a certain number of officers from the Commonwealth forces: India, Malaysia and Africa.

They did not teach modern methods of investigation or any detailed police work. Instead, they dealt with broad aspects of police administration and control. One of the subjects to my delight, was a series of lectures on Shakespeare. My immediate reaction was, Why Shakespeare to seasoned old police officers? The instructor, who was an ex-Oxford Don, gave the reason. Till this time, the policy of the central and county authorities had been to give top police jobs such as those of the Police Commissioner of the Metropolitan, and chief constables of county forces, to people from outside, who had not risen from the ranks. But a decision had now been taken to give them to promotees from the departments. These officers had started their careers as police constables, the minimum qualifications for these posts being the O level - the equivalent of the Matriculation in India. It was felt that these officers lacked the background of a 'liberal education', considered the sine *qua non* of higher leadership. The term 'liberal education' embraced more than a nodding acquaintance with the humanities - subjects such as the classical languages, literature and history, as opposed to the science or technical proficiency. In peacetime, Bernard Law Montgomery, with his schoolboy diction, would never have risen, even in the Army, to a rank higher than that of Major General. As it happened, even at a crucial moment of the war in Africa, he was chosen at the last minute because Auchinlek's successor, Gott, was killed in an airplane crash.

In the limited time at their disposal, the Police College could, at the most, give only a glimpse of what they meant. This glimpse was an introduction to Shakespeare. Shakespeare represented a liberal education. He was not only the greatest poet and dramatist that England had produced, he was also the greatest writer that the world has known.And Shakespeare did not write or produce his plays for intellectuals and scholars. His plays appealed to people in all walks of life -'gamester, captain, knight, knight's servant, lady, woman of doubtful reputation, shops' foreman, brave sparks' (to quote Ben Johnson). His plays were not meant to be read in the scholar's closet; they were meant to be produced for money, and people got their money's worth, just as they do today, if they go to see them, and know a modicum of English.

A liberal education in India does not mean only a study of English writers! We have our own Kalidas and Tagore; in fact, we have a tremendous heritage of tradition and culture. We can study our own classical writers! However, this was England and we were studying Shakespeare.

The whole class knew that whenever the better known plays were discussed, I could recite extensively from the text. It was not the case that I had deliberately learnt the noble and uplifting passages by heart; I had, perhaps, read them over and over again (in odd places and at odd times), and they had just impressed themselves on my sensorium. The directing staff must have also observed, that whereas the officers from the other Commonwealth countries repaired every weekend to London to 'beat it up', I booked my accommodation and tickets at Stratford from the telephone at the reception centre.

Whatever be the reason, one day, the Don said to me," Mr. Modak, won't you give us a talk on Shakespeare? I am sure the whole college would be interested."

I agreed to give the talk, the gist of which is below (according to my recollection). I had made no notes, used no reference books. I said that for my B A degree, I had to study Macbeth and Twelfth Night. The professors seemed to concentrate on the scholarship displayed, on the sources of the Latin and Greek references, and on routine 'studies' of each character, which mainly consisted of a summary of what they did or said. They expected us to know what scholars like Bradley or Dowden had said on a particular topic. These learned gentlemen knew a great deal about human nature between the covers of a book, but very little about human nature in the raw, as we policemen and policewomen had come to know.

I really began my study of Shakespeare in the district of Satara, where I was first posted as an Assistant Superintendent of Police, after completing my training. It was not that I had plenty of time hanging on my hands; the situation was quite the contrary. Satara was at that time in the grip of the sabotage movement - from November 1942 to May 1945. Apart from routine dacoities and murders, train derailments, looting of treasuries and burning of railway stations were the order of the day. I was required to camp at the scenes of these crimes, many times in far away places, in villages, in *chavadis* (offices), *dharmasalas* (rooms for the poor), and sometimes under trees. After the day's work was done, and I had had my dinner, my mind would still be active, and sleep would not come to me easily. I wanted to read something as a distraction from the daily grind, but I could hardly take a stack of books with me. Then in my bride's belongings I discovered a compact volume of the plays of Shakespeare (which she had won as a prize). It proved to be a prize for me, too. I would take it with me everywhere, and lying on my campcot, delve into it with the aid of a kerosene lamp, far into the night. Sometimes I had to wait at a crossroads for hours for my car or a police bus. It didn't worry me at all. I would sit under the nearest shady tree, pull out my copy of Shakespeare and forget everything but the scenes and players who leapt before my eyes in living detail and rich colour. In my reading of Shakespeare, I ignored several things: I ignored the Greek and Latin references, I ignored the laborious puns and jokes, and I ignored the village banter. I had plenty of the last, around me for three years and a half.

I began to concentrate on the narrative, the development of the plot, and on the characters acting out their destinies in the confines of the plot. But above all, I concentrated on the blank verse, on words that seemed to me to be beautiful and majestic and enduring.

As I continued to read, I began to wonder why I felt that Shakespeare's greatest plays were his tragedies, (with the exception of Henry the Fifth, which was my favourite). The drama that they portrayed seemed to have some quality lacking in the other plays. Then I remembered 'Oedipus Rex', and the remarks that somebody had made about it. The writer said that the ancient Greek tragedians believed that every person, no matter how great, had some fatal flaw in his mental makeup (what they called a 'hamartia'), and that this flaw ultimately led to his downfall, and not the hand of fate. As portrayed by Sophocles, Oedipus was a completely honest man, but he was arrogant and hot-tempered. It was this hot temper that made him kill Laius in a traffic altercation on the outskirts of Corinth, not knowing that Laius was his own father. Only his arrogance made the blind prophet Teiresias tell him the truth, and only his hot temper made him ignore it. On reading the major tragedies of Shakespeare that I liked, it came to me that all his protagonists possessed these fatal flaws and contradictions in their characters, and that these contradictions led to tragedy.

At this time, two books came into my possession. The first was 'Narrative Technique' by T H Uzzel, and the second was 'How To Write A Play" by Lajos Egree. These were not books by scholars, but by craftsmen who wanted to teach the art of writing. At that time I had no intention of doing any writing. For one thing, I did not have the time. But these books taught me how to obtain a better appreciation of Shakespeare, and I began to read the book with a new insight.

Any work of fiction, be it a short story, play or a novel, must have drama to be meaningful and significant. And all great drama implies conflict - the conflict between man and man, the conflict between man and nature, and the conflict within a man's own nature, as in Hamlet. A story is, in fact, the dramatic revelation of character. Character can be fully revealed only in conflict. Is this also not true in real life? It is only when a man or a woman faces danger that his or her true qualities are revealed. I have seen plenty of tall, well-built police officers, full of brag and bounce, cower in the background when facing a violent mob. I have also seen some small, puny-looking man take the lead in pushing the mob back. And it is not only physical danger that a person has to encounter; it might be a dread disease, it might be a financial loss, it might be the death of a loved one.

But this revelation of character must be '*in the reflective delay*', otherwise the story is not a drama; it becomes only a melodrama. Let me give but two examples of the 'reflective' delay from Shakespeare.

In 'Measure for Measure', the Duke of Vienna goes on a supposed journey, leaving his trusted minister, Angelo, as the Lord Deputy. Angelo, who is a strict and puritanical man, decides to carry out the execution of Claudio, found guilty of fornication, a capital offence in the Vienna of those days. Claudio's sister, Isabella, a very beautiful girl, who is to join a convent, comes to plead on his behalf. As it often happens with men who try and suppress their natural instincts, Angelo's libido is aroused at the sight of the desirable Isabella, and he conceives the horrible idea of offering her Claudio's life in return for her chastity. As soon as Isabella has gone, he is torn by a raging conflict in his mind. He says,

What's this, what's this? Is this her fault or mine?
The tempter or the tempted, who sins most? Ha!
Not she; nor doth she tempt; but it is I
That lying by the violet in the Sun,
Do as the carrion does, not as the flower,
Corrupt with virtuous season'.

The second is from Macbeth;

Macbeth: I have done the deed, didst thou not hear the noise?

Lady Macbeth: I heard the owls scream and the crickets cry.
Did you not speak?

Macbeth: This is a sorry sight (Looking at his hands)

Lady Macbeth: A foolish thought to say a sorry sight.

Macbeth: (about the two guards)
One cried"God bless us" and "Amen" the other.
As they had seen me with these hangman's hands,
Listening to their fear, I could not say,"Amen".
...
But wherefore I could not pronounce "Amen?"
I had most need of blessing, and "Amen" stuck
In my throat.

Lady Macbeth: These deeds must not be thought
After these ways; so it will make us mad.

Macbeth: Methought I heard a voice cry,"Sleep no more!"
Macbeth does murder sleep, the innocent sleep'
That knits up the ravelled sleeve of care,
The death of each day's life, sore labour's bath,

Balm of hurt minds, great Nature's second course,
Chief nourisher of Life's feast-"

Macbeth was no Raman Raghav or Jack the Ripper.

The first quotation was an example of the reflective delay before the (contemplated) action: the second, after the action. But there can also be a limit to the reflective delay. In Dostoyevsky's 'Crime and Punishment', a poverty stricken student, Raskalnikov (rascal?) kills two old women with an axe for petty gain. His reflective delay takes over two hundred pages; it amounts to a morbid introspection for which there really *is not much cause.*

Egri says that every piece of dramatic writing, be it short story, play or novel, must have a premise or syllogism, which has to be demonstrated by the complete action of the writing. Thus the premise in 'Romeo and Juliet' is 'Great Love: defies even death'. In 'Macbeth', it is: 'Ruthless Ambition leads to its own Destruction'. In 'Othello', 'Jealousy destroys itself and the object of its love'. The premise is not necessarily a universal truth. It is true only for the particular situation of the play or novel in question.

These two tools of analysis made me savour to the full the qualities and purpose of not only Shakespeare's plays, but of all other fiction that I happened to read. Take again, 'Crime and Punishment'. What is the premise behind this novel? That crime does not pay? No one suspected Raskalnikov . He would have easily got away with the two murders, if he had not confessed. And what was the motivation for the confession? He was no Macbeth! And even Hamlet, a great practitioner of the reflective delay, would have got bored with all that snivelling the poor student did. One thing I have learnt is not to take any piece of 'creative fiction' at its face value, or the value placed on it by the literati.

By way of contrast, let us consider the long short story, 'The Strange Case of Dr. Jekyll and Mr.Hyde!' The greatly respected Dr. Jekyll discovers a drug that transforms him to Mr.Hyde, a man embodying all that is evil. The more he gets into the personality of Hyde, the more he likes the feeling of power, and the desire to satisfy his lust. But every time he does so, he has to take larger doses of the drug to get back to Jekyll. When, after committing a murder, he finds that he cannot get back, he kills himself. The premise of the story is that if a man indulges in evil actions, he will become evil.

This story came to Stevenson as a nightmare, but it embodies a great universal truth. There is good and evil in all of us, and we do not need to invent a drug to go to either pole of our being. Our thoughts are the real drug that decides what we shall become. The object of all spiritual disciplines is to control this whirling chase of thought that constantly goes through our minds when we are awake, and perhaps even when we are asleep in the form of dreams. J B Priestly calls it, the 'skull cinema'.

And all great fiction is a study of the struggle between good and evil (as the author has conceived of it). Sometimes the good is triumphant and sometimes the evil. The premise or theme shows the direction in which the story will go.

Ever since my study of Shakespeare in Satara, I have come to the conclusion that policemen and policewomen would become better in their professions by a study of Shakespeare. This study would enable them to understand human nature far better then a study of textbooks on social psychology or the sexual etiology of the neurosis.

But there is another reason why people should read and enjoy Shakespeare when they can. He described the routine action of the play in simple, straightforward prose, but when any deep emotional effect was to be achieved or any dramatic scene to be portrayed, he resorted to blank verse. It was lucky for him, and for the world, that the Earl of Surrey invented blank verse just before Shakespeare was born. While translating the Greek and Roman classics, the Earl of Surrey found that, in what is called 'poetry' - rhyming couplets - he would never have conveyed their emotion and depth.

Britain has now been reduced to its original size - more or less what it was at the time of Queen Elizabeth I. The British Empire (that was) reminds me of the Cheshire Cat in Lewis Caroll's fable. Nothing is left of it except its grin. The British are hanging on to it for dear life, as witness their membership of the Security Council, their membership of NATO, the Group of 8, and, of course, the ubiquitous BBC.

But in the long run, it is not the tangible things that always endure. I am persuaded that there are two things about the British that will not fade: the English language and Shakespeare. The English language has absorbed words, not only from the original Anglo-Saxon. Latin and Greek, but from many Indian languages - a glance through the latest edition of the Oxford Dictionary will prove this. What I most like about it is the number of synonyms and antonyms that exist in it to enable you to select *le moh juste* - the exact word. I do believe is simplicity, but I have gone to great lengths to obtain the right word. And the right word need not be polysyllabic, it can also be simple.

Certainly, we must develop our regional languages with their own rich traditions and literature! But English is no longer the language of our conquerors or a symbol of serfdom: to say so is to adopt a narrow point of view. Very recently, I learnt from a reliable source that in Pune city there are over 130 computer firms, and that Pune city alone makes export earnings of Rs.800 crores per year in software. This is due to the fact that we know English, and that the standard of English in Pune is very high. Would it be the part of wisdom to do our best to lose this advantage by suppressing and abolishing the study of English, even as a second language?

Books have always interested me. What kind of books? All kinds of books, all kinds of subjects. Bacon has said in his essay on Studies (familiar in my time to every schoolboy) that reading maketh a full man, conference (talk) a ready man, and writing an exact man. As to the first, I have been a voracious reader all my life: as to the second, we Indians are all fond of talking. As a nation we talk too much and much too fast. Contrary to the well-known adage, it is not the women alone who are inveterate gossips.

With regard to the third, 'writing', for a long time I had to restrict my writing to departmental work - reports, enquiries, manuals. In bureaucratic circles, since the days of the British, if an officer tried to publish any piece of creative writing, he was considered 'bookish', and unfit for the executive. Many of the best ICS officers (I have earlier given the example of Dennis Kincaid) were '*shunted*' to the judiciary. For a policeman, it would have been fatal. I had to wait before publishing anything, till I became too senior for anybody to cast his first stone at me on the score of my being 'theoretical'.

When I was eleven years old, my father was posted as the City Magistrate of Belgaum, one of the loveliest cities in which I have lived. We stayed in bungalow No. 97, next to the Alexandra Barracks in the cantonment. In the compound there were several mango and tamarind trees with long branches, over all of which I could climb with ease. I had discovered a comfortable perch, 'far from the madding crowd' (of my brothers and sisters) where I could sit and read my favourite books on

Sunday mornings. Plenty of green mangoes were all around me, and I would slice them, dip them in a mix of salt and chili powder, and munch while I read the books. As for the books, there were a limited number in a small glass-fronted bookcase in the drawing room. The three that I liked the most were Ivanhoe, Pride and Prejudice, and an English translation of Caesar's Commentaries on his Gallic wars - seven original volumes condensed into one. All through my life, I must have read 'Pride and Prejudice' eleven times. As Maugham says, the plot is perfect, and it holds your interest from page to page. I do not agree with him about the other novels of Jane Austen. Emma and Mansfield are boring, nothing much happens. As for 'Persuasion', Austen's most mature novel, I found the characters wooden and dull. Similarly, I cannot truly say that I liked Scott's other Waverley novels as much as Ivanhoe. Even in Ivanhoe, the delectable Rebecca was infinitely preferable to the wooden Lady Rowena. I would have ended it differently. As for Caesar's Commentaries, his limpid prose and his apparent candour delighted me. I say 'apparent', because later critics have held that Caesar wrote to justify himself, and every word was chosen with care. Even if this were true, we must give due credit to the greatest Roman commander of them all , for finding time to write the correct word,while leading his armies into battle.

Sometime earlier, my mother had bought a carton of books (among other household goods) from a Mrs. Harris, the widow of an American missionary, the Reverend Harris, who was the pastor of the Methodist Church down the road, where we went on Sunday evenings to worship, and the principal of the Beynon Smith High School where I used to study.

The Reverend Harris was a rotund, jolly man who liked to go on *shikar*(hunting) with his wife in the high forests of Karwar. One night we were all awakened by the sounds of motor car engines, and the shouts of people, and we rushed into the porch. A big crowd had assembled with *petromaxes* and lanterns. They told my father that in the truck outside, they had brought the dead body of the Reverend Harris. While hunting a bison in Yellapur, he had been gored by the wounded animal. His wife had shown great courage in coolly kneeling down and pouring seven bullets into the beast, which was killed.

Mrs. Harris soon left for the U S, and before going she had sold most of her household effects. The books from the cartons were placed in the glass bookcases. I seem to have inherited them, because nobody else ever read them. Among these books were a volume of speeches by great Americans Poor Richard's Almanack, Huckleberry Finn, O'Henry's Short Stories.

In those days, my maternal grandfather used to live with us. He was stone blind and used to read massive books in Braille, which some kind friend sent him. He had a Braille pocket watch, and a Braille typewriter, also given by some kind friends. He was a scholar in Persian, Arabic and Marathi. A convert to Christianity, he did his best to follow the Ten Commandments.

My grandfather was my guide, philosopher and friend. My father was busy with his work, and my mother was busy with her household chores. In particular, I used to consult my grandfather on my reading. He would make me read again and again the speeches by famous Americans. We were both great admirers of Abraham Lincoln and William Jennings Bryan. He was fond of my repeating the sayings of Poor Richard. I still remember the one about the cat, which could never catch rats because it wore gloves. I used to like Huckleberry Finn, but I was puzzled about the language and the grammar, so I read out some parts to my grandfather. After hearing a couple of pages, he said "*Beta* (child), it is obvious that the author is an illiterate person.. You'd better not read this book, you'll only spoil your English". In this instance, I did not follow his advice. Many years later, I read Hemingway's opinion of the book. He said that all modern American literature comes from one book by Mark Twain called 'Huckleberry Finn'.

I used to enjoy reading the short stories of O'Henry, but it seemed to me that the author had been imprisoned for cheating, and I again consulted my grandfather. After hearing me read the relevant portion, my grandfather said, "Beta, it is obvious that the writer was a criminal. If you read such books, you might develop criminal tendencies. I wonder why the Reverend Harris possessed such books. I am not surprised that he came to such an end!"

I said to my grandfather that in all fairness to the Reverend Harris, I found many of the pages uncut. Therefore, he could not have read these books, otherwise he would not have kept them. "Whatever that be", my grandfather said, " I have worked for Scottish missionaries who were solid Quakers, and I must say one thing for them; they had no hanky panky about them".

Bacon has said in his essay 'On Studies' that reading makes a full man, conference a ready man, and writing an exact man. As to the first, I certainly do not propose to discuss all the books I have read. I have been a voracious reader all my life. Bacon has also said in the same essay that some books are to be tasted some to be swallowed and a few to be chewed and digested. I intend to touch upon the last kind, because I sincerely believe that such books also constitute a part of one's 'liberal education'.

When I was studying in college in Poona, I had invested in four books, which were the equivalent of today's paperbacks. These were:

1) The Essays of Francis Bacon

2) The Socratic Discourses of Xenophon and Plato

3) The Orations od Demosthenes, and

4) Grey Wolf.

Do not let the titles intimidate you. Their contents were simple and clear; they have been my lifelong companions and are in good condition even today. As a comprehensive survey of the entire field of knowledge of his age, Bacon's Essays may be out of date, but as an account of what constitutes human nature, they will never fade. The contents of these essays present the bone and sinew of compact thought. And as for the manner of presentation, his epigrammatic style and use of antithesis still delight me.

The language of the Socratic Discourses is as simple as can be. He taught ordinary folk in the market yard to think through the meanings of the words they used, by asking questions and more questions on the answers they gave. And the most important aspect in asking questions is to ask the right question. As H Ellis said of Bacon,his pregnant maxim was that the right question was the half of knowledge. Truly, this is the basic method of all research. It is the basis of the art of cross-examination in courts. Hegelian philosophy was based on the thesis, antithesis and synthesis, but I do not think it was meant to supplant the system of formal logic, later enunciated by Aristotle, who was, after all, Plato's pupil. And I have always thought that Karl Marx's attempt to explain historical evolution by this process was rather far fetched. Yes, I have read the two massive volumes of 'Das Kapital' (in the English translation, of course).

I was surprised to discover that The Orations of Demosthenes did not contain any purple passages, or flights of fancy. They embodied carefully structured, persuasive arguments. And if they smacked of the midnight oil, isn't it a pity that some of our 'great' political orators do not take more care in the preparation of their speeches.? In having to make security arrangements for public meetings of VIP's of all political shades, I have had perforce to listen to the rambling disconnected outpourings of these 'towering' leaders; they were certainly 'towering' because they spoke from rostrums fifteen feet high. But as far as the content of their speeches was concerned, it was, more often than not, trite, repetitive and boring.

Grey Wolf was a different kind of book. It was the life of Mustafa Kemal, the founder of modern Turkey. He was a great soldier, and a great patriot, but his whole life was one long struggle against reaction and orthodoxy. Unlike Enver Pasha, he was no courtier, he was always outspoken and blunt, sometimes to the point of rudeness. Most important of all, Kemal Attaturk was clear-eyed, and knew the limits of his power and position. The Western nations thought that once he made Turkey independent and free, he would launch on a course of expansion and conquest; they were in for a surprise. He said,"Thus far, and no further!" He refused the Caliphate, and was entirely, completely secular. To deal with the recent earthquake, Turkey needed a Mustafa Kemal.

Every one reads crime novels, and I suppose, police officers are no exception. Before I began to write two crime novels, I decided to make a detailed study of the genre. However, I got browned off, reading novels of how the local police (in the UK) having failed to solve a puzzling case of murder, called in the services of the great private detective, or the 'expert' Inspector from 'Scotland Yard'. As for the former, they exist only in the fertile imagination of the writers (and readers). The 'expert' from The Metropolitan (Scotland Yard) would never have been allowed in the county limits and if he had, he could not have done much without local knowledge.

Even so, I was somewhat intrigued by the style of Dashiell Hammet. I read with interest The Glass Key, The Maltese Falcon and Red Harvest. Hammet's detective belonged to the 'tough guy' school, who used to smoke incessantly, and speak through clenched teeth in staccato sentences. But his writing seemed to have more depth. In time I came to realize that all these writers of the staccato school derived their inspiration from Ernest Hemingway. True, he did not write usually about crime, but his terse style was copied by hundreds of writers throughout the world. I, therefore, read and studied all the novels and short stories written by Hemingway. 'The Old Man and the Sea' got him the Nobel Prize, but I think that 'A Moveable Feast' is the second great statement in American Literature.

While learning the craft of writing in a garret, as an expatriate in Paris after World War I, Hemingway told himself that the first and most important thing for him to learn was how to write one 'true' sentence. Write the truest sentence you know, he told himself. It must be a simple declarative sentence without any ornamentation of any kind. It must reflect his own personal experience. He felt that the emotion he wanted to convey would, somehow, filter through the reported facts. The simple sentence and the simple word would help him recreate the actual experience in all its immediacy five years hence, or thirty-five years later. The result was that a vividness and vigour informed all his prose which has been equalled by very few writers.

In order to get things exactly right and memorable, Hemingway went where the action was. He thought that war was the best subject of all. He was wounded as an ambulance driver in Italy in World War I, and he wrote his 'Farewell to Arms' based on his experience there. Later, he went to Spain during the Civil War as a correspondent, and wrote 'For Whom the Bell Tolls'. Then in peacetime, he found action in bullfights, catching marlin in the deep sea, and killing lions in Africa. But the point that he was trying to make was that a man showed his true nature only when facing danger. I do not think that anyone can dispute such a view.

I have a feeling that Hemingway would have liked to write about some of the experiences that, willy-nilly came my way. There can be no question that he would have made a much better job of depicting them than I have done. Anyway, we both seem to have had one thing in common: we both seem to have been impressed with Ecclesiastes, or the Preacher. And my writing, such as it is, has been greatly influenced by Hemingway.

We are much too deeply involved in life, the mere living. Or, as Wordsworth put it, the world is too much with us. Late and soon, getting and spending, we lay waste our powers.

We seek temporary relief from our cares and worries by indulging in gambling on the racetracks or in cards, or in late partying (for those who can afford it). Or, we watch third rate movies and read third rate 'blockbusters' that titillate our senses by vicarious sex or violence.

Wordsworth advocates long and steady gazing at the sea in order to evoke its poetic overtones. Today there seems to be an increasing number of stargazers with amateur telescopes. Maybe, by gazing at the stars, they realize the smallness of man, the shape of things entire.

Why not spend part of our spare time, and everybody has some spare time, in reading good books, which are now available in paperback at the same price, as the others mentioned above? Once we get the taste for them, we will surely derive, deep down, a consolation, a satisfaction, a sense of fulfilment never known before.

Bookshops are flooded today with books, not many of which can be classified as 'Literature'. The question then arises, what is true Literature, and what is its true object? If literature is to serve it purpose, it cannot be confined to the dimly lit rooms of bibliophiles, nor to the sparsely filled halls of professors in ancient halls of learning.

Great literature must be able to move the average reader, at least as much as fairy tales for the very young, or explicit, but modern versions of Sodom and Gomorrah. As I have said before, Shakespeare wrote for the common man or woman who did not miss a bawdy joke (of those times). And so did Chaucer for that matter. And he was for realism in whatever he wrote, be it sad, or be it ugly. But he was able, by the magic of his art to transmute all the sadness and ugliness into beauty. That is what the modern writer should aspire to do, in some measure, if he wants his books to give people some help in the art of living and loving their neighbours as themselves.

CHAPTER X

POT POURRI

I. POLICE WELFARE

In the Gilbert and Sullivan Opera, 'The Pirates Of Penzance', the police sergeant sings a song about the hard lot of a policeman. Among the different branches of the police forces in India, the lot of the Armed Police has always been the hardest. These policemen are different from the Reserve Police. They get no special pay and, per force, have to undergo long hours of work. An armed guard of, let us say, one head constable and three constables, is required according to the rules to be relieved for 24 hours after 24 hours of guard duty. In practice, however, they are not relieved for weeks or even months. All that is done is to give them one extra man. The guard commander then arranges a little relief for them to go in turn to their homes for food or a bath.

The strength of the armed police at a district headquarters is limited. The sanctioned guards are very few, and a small strength is left as an emergency company. However, the impression among the general public and the politicians is that the police have unlimited manpower. This is because they see large bodies of policemen when some VIP rolls by. There is no separate distinction between the uniformed staff and the plainclothes staff, as prevails in Western countries, The men are pulled out of other duties to man the police *bandobast* which is laid on for this or that purpose.

It is no secret that unarmed men (at the police stations, etc.) manage not only to keep body and soul together, but often increase the circumference of the former. The armed men cannot do this. In frustration, many of them resort to drink, and then the lot of their families becomes unenviable.

During the time I was in service, the Government had not allotted any money for a welfare fund for the police families, now is it alloted today. While in Kolhapur, I had arranged a Ranji Trophy cricket match, from the profits of which I had set up a welfare fund for the police families. (The money was collected by selling tickets at the Box Office. No kind of pressure was brought on any rich or influential persons to buy the tickets. This reprehensible practice, which now seems to be in vogue, was banned by Government orders). My wife has always taken a great interest in welfare activities, and we opened a dispensary with a paid nurse, where volunteer doctors would examine the wives and children of the policemen and treat them for their ailments. We bought sewing machines with which the wives would learn to make garments, and arranged for their sale.

We continued these welfare activities until my retirement. When I was transferred to Bombay as DCP (Headquarters), we started two mobile dispensaries, and opened a small hospital for the armed HQ in Worli. We continued these activities even in Jammu and Kashmir. I had obtained used woolen garments in good condition sent from Bombay by Mrs.Cherian, the wife of the Governor, and my wife came with me to the most distant police stations in Gurez and Leh, and distributed these garments to the policemen and their families. This might be one reason why policemen would come to me long after my retirement, and volunteer information about what was going on at their level.

CHAPTER X

POT POURRI

II. A CASE FROM THE VIGILANCE BRANCH AND THE RESCUE OF 1400 WOMEN

The Vigilance Branch of the CID in Bombay dealt with prostitution, gambling, drug abuse and juvenile delinquency. When I was the CP of Bombay, the Anti-Corruption Bureau had made an enquiry against a sub-inspector of the Vigilance Branch, named Mehta, for amassing Rs.11 lakhs - a princely amount for a PSI in 1968. They had established that he had a partnership in three brothels. Making money was bad enough, but for a police officer, whose job was catching prostitutes, to run brothels was intolerable. I was greatly disturbed, and at the end of the departmental enquiry, asked him to show cause why he should not be dismissed.

This officer had been a security officer to a VVIP, before his posting to the Branch. The amount of pressure brought on me to let him go was unbelievable. I sacked him, but this did not make me popular with those in authority.

The case of PSI Mehta, however, got me interested in the problem of rehabilitation of the unfortunate women who are forced into prostitution for one reason or another. In my talks with police officers and social workers, I discovered one fact. Most of these 'fallen' women did not want to be rehabilitated, They preferred to go back to their trade, since they felt that they had nothing more to lose.

But, I also discovered another peculiar fact. Many girls and young women from all parts of the country used to run away from their homes because of ill-treatment from their parents, or husbands, or because of some mistake they had made or, mainly, because of sheer poverty. They would board trains or buses, often without tickets, and land up at

Victoria Terminus and Bombay Central Railway Stations, or at major bus stops. Once there they did not know what to do and would walk up and down the stations. This is where the 'madams' from brothels, dressed like kindly grandmothers would be waiting for them. They would be promised jobs or shelter for the night. Sometimes well-dressed ponces would promise them jobs as film extras. Once they were enticed inside the brothels their fates were sealed. They would be repeatedly raped till they agreed to lead the life that was in store for them.

Something could surely be done to save these poor women! I kept policemen and policewomen in plain clothes at the important railway stations and bus stops. My wife was then the President of the YWCA of Bombay. At the YWCA we made a reception centre for these women. At this centre, the wives of senior police officers and volunteers and social workers from the Maharashtra State Women's Council, Association for Social Health and others would come there and talk to these women and take down their histories at length. The women who were thus rescued were from various states in India, mainly from Andhra, Karnataka, Tamil Nadu, and sometimes even from Nepal. The police contacted their relatives, and often these women were received back. Sometimes, they were sent under police escort to the State CID's for their further conveyance to their native village. When these women had no place to return to, the ladies arranged employment for them. I continued this scheme on a larger scale when I became the IG of Maharashtra. Charity should begin at home. My wife fancied one only woman. She brought her home as a domestic. In due time she got her married to our young man-servant. The marriage was performed by civil register in the YWCA. The daughter of this couple has been brought up as a member of our family and is shortly to sit for her final B.Com. After her graduation we intend to send her for the MBA, or some equivalent post-graduate course. In this way, we had rescued over 1400 girls who were from places all over the country. I learnt, however, that the scheme fell into desuetude after my retirement.

CHAPTER X

POT POURRI

III. THE PROBLEM OF CORRUPTION

When I took charge of the Anti-Corruption Branch, it was a part of the Office of the Inspector General. I soon convinced the Government that to be at all effective, it had to be independent of the IG (on principle), and work directly under the Government. The Anti-Corruption Bureau was thus created, and I was appointed its first Director. I held the appointment, off and on, for eight years. The Prevention of Corruption Act, with which we worked, was the same as that was used by the CBI. They were concerned with public servants in Central employment, while we dealt with those in the State employ.

The largest number of cases that we initiated was against the police, not because the police were more corrupt, but because we knew their *modus oprandi* better. At my suggestion, the Government appointed officers from the Revenue, PWD and Sales Tax as Deputy Directors to help me.

In the beginning, we made a large number of 'trap' cases. Currency notes were wiped with anthracene powder, which subsequently showed up on the hands of the culprits under the blue of the ultra violet lamp. Bribe takers became wise to this, and the bigger ones would take the money only from middlemen whom it was difficult to catch. We then began to make out cases of disproportionate assets. It was difficult to prove these cases in a court of law, so we used to report them for departmental action. Because of the large number of cases, the Government had appointed special officers to conduct them. Unfortunately, these officers were all retired gentlemen, and we found that in most of the cases the culprits were let off.

It became difficult to prove corruption cases against senior police officers. I remember one such officer whose wife was not only attractive, but highly educated. She once complained to me that her husband was very secretive about his accounts. She did not even know what his salary was. All this when she was a wage-earner herself-teaching in a college. I did not have the heart, to tell her that perhaps he did not want to destroy her illusions.

One important case of disproportionate assets that we did send up to the court was that against L B Dudhane, then Chairman of the Maharashtra State Electricity Board. The newly appointed Chief Minister, S B Chavan, had asked me to make a preliminary enquiry. I made my enquiry and submitted my report to him on 24th March 1975. I said there was much evidence against Dudhane, that I should be allowed to register the offence and make the open enquiry immediately. I got the sanction on 29th March. We knew Dudhane had stashed a large amount of cash and jewelry in the locker of a bank on Madame Cama Road. Unfortunately, he got enough time to remove it, and when we raided the bank, we found Mother Hubbard's cupboard bare. However, he did not have enough time to remove the documents from his house, or he did not expect the Anti-Corruption Bureau to raid his house (because of his close friendship with the former Chief Minister), and we seized these documents. Dudhane was convicted in the special court, but later acquitted on appeal.

My enquiry enabled my officers and me to get a close look at the working of the Maharashtra State Electricity Board. What we saw was not a pleasant sight. My 'humble' opinion is that all Electricity Boards should be privatized, the sooner the better.

It is my considered opinion that if the police are corrupt, and the volume of corruption is increasing, other departments like the PWD, Forests, Regional Transport Authorities are even more corrupt. I am, therefore, a little puzzled at the arguments advanced even by some judicial enquiry commissions, that the work of the police is more visible, so they must be, like Caesar's wife, 'above suspicion'. In the first place, I have never understood why Caesar's wife was expected to be above suspicion. Was Julius, the original Caesar, himself above suspicion? It was no secret that he had made a vast fortune during his campaigns in Gaul and Spain. It was the accepted thing during the period, for politicians sent out as army leaders on conquest, to make large fortunes. I do not know how they did it in those days, but in the case of Caesar, at least, it was not done at the cost of good government.

In the second place, if corruption is all pervasive, if it infects every limb of society, how can honesty ever survive? In his play,'Troilus and Cressida', Shakespeare has tackled this subject, and he has come to the conclusion that it cannot. I think what he says is as relevant today as it was when he wrote the play, or rather, at the time when the play was supposed to have taken place.

The scene of action of the play is the Trojan war. Helen may be the most beautiful and alluring woman in the world, but her conversation with her companions shows that she has a dirty mind, and her love for Paris is an illicit love.

Honesty and courage are represented by Hector, the eldest son of King Priam, the cleanest and bravest among the warriors on-both-the sides. On the other hand, Achilles, half man and half god, the hero on the Greek side, is at heart a coward, and is capable of any kind of treachery. Innocent and pure love seems to exist between Troilus, the youngest son of Priam and Cressida, a young and beautiful maiden.

Achilles is enraged with Hector because the latter has killed (inadvertently) his catamite, Patroclus. But he is afraid to meet Hector, face to face, in single combat, and when an encounter does take place, sportingly, Hector lets him off as Achilles pleads that he is not in a mood to fight. Later, when Hector is walking unarmed, Achilles has him attacked by his myrmidons. When Hector tells him that he is unarmed, and reminds him of his previous encounter, Achilles taunts him and says that he (Hector) was a fool to have trusted him.

By some cruel quirk of fate, Cressida is inveigled into entering the Greek camp. There she meets Diomedes, arrogant, macho, and self-confident. She allows herself to be seduced by him. Troilus and Ulysses watch this scene hiding behind a bush. Troilus had followed her, but Ulysses has spotted him and has given him safe conduct through the Greek lines on the promise that he will not speak. Cressida allows herself to be seduced; she is not raped. Shakespeare wants to say that when the whole atmosphere is corrupted, honesty and innocence cannot survive.

I like reading Shakespeare even today because what he says is so true to life. Times can change; people can change; but human nature remains the same throughout.

If officers of higher rank cannot resist temptation, how much can an inspector of police do so? When I was IG, an inspector who had worked under me in the Anti-Corruption Bureau, requested me to post him in Pune. He said he wanted to repair his old *wada*, get his daughter married, and attend to some other domestic matters, as he was to retire within a year and a half. This inspector would have been happy with any posting in Pune. He had, however, done outstanding work in the Anti-Corruption Bureau, and I deliberately posted him to the Traffic Branch of the state police. The STB was known as one of the greatest avenues of corruption, but I thought to myself that here was an officer who would show that he was made of a different mould.

Some time later, my wife told me on two or three occasions that this officer was pestering her to allow him to build an upper floor to my house in Pune. He claimed that he would do it very cheaply, I said to her, that however cheap he might make it, we could not afford it, and I could not allow a police officer to build any part of my house. There the matter ended.

After my retirement, this officer, 'PI' (Police Inspector) (who had also retired) came to see me.

Scene: My drawing room.

PI: "Sir, I have come to thank you from the bottom of my heart for posting me to Pune in the STB."

Self: "Well, I hope you have repaired your wada, and got your daughter married."

PI: "That, of course, but I have not come to thank you for that."

Self: "Then what do you want to thank me for? I don't understand."

PI: "Sir, in the STB, I have made enough money to last my family for three generations. That's why I want to thank you."

Self: (At that late stage, recriminations were scarcely in order)."That was not my intention in posting you to the STB."

PI: "It might not have been, but it would have been foolish of me to have gone against the System." Then after a pause, 'I asked madam and

I pleaded with her to let me build the second floor of your house. Why didn't you let me? Surely it was clear that I would have borne the expenses!"

Self: "I suppose I was a fool?"

PI: (With both hands cupped before me) " Sir, the words have come out of your mouth, not mine! Is it necessary for me to say anything?"

There was at least one thing in favour of this man. He was honest about his dishonesty.

When I worked under the first Swadeshi Government, the watchword was 'Moral'. Politicians would lecture to us, mere mercenaries, how greatly moral their standards were (compared to ours): 'Moral' ENDS and 'Moral' MEANS. Gradually, before we knew how it happened, the word 'moral' was substituted by the word 'political', and some of us came to learn (the hard way) that 'political' ends justified any means. And did the British have very high standards of morality? Lord Morley wrote in his book ' On Compromise', that on principles (of morality) we must never compromise. And yet, as Secretary of State for India, he (along with Lord Minto, Viceroy) initiated the Morley-Minto reforms, which created separate communal electorates. Lady Minto was, at least, relieved. She wrote to a friend back home that she thanked God that as a result of the Reforms Act (1909), the British would be able to remain in India for several years more.

CHAPTER X

POT POURRI

IV. ON LAND GRABS FOR THE POLICE

There has always been a shortage of land for the ever-expanding police force of Maharashtra. We felt this lack particularly for the reserve police battalions and the training schools for the constabulary. In 1957 I was appointed on promotion to the newly created post of DIG Training and Headquarters (the reserve police). D S Joshi was then the Home Secretary. He called me one day and said that the land on which St.Peter's School stood in Khandala had reverted to the Government, and several departments were competing for it. If the police were interested, he would try and get it allotted to us. He wanted me to inspect it and let him know.

Without losing a moment, I got into my car and drove straight to Khandala. I had asked the SP Pune Rural to meet me there. We saw the land on the slopes of the hill. It had imposing school buildings, including 125 dormitories with tiled bathrooms, a big church, and a beautiful breakfast room in pale green tiles (for the Nuns) which had a magnificent view of the valley below. I saw that some workers from a demolition company had started to remove the tiles on the school buildings. I asked them to stop at once, and ordered the SP, Braganza to post an armed guard on the premises to prevent any further demolition till I got the place for the police.

On my return, I met Joshi and told him that the allotment of the land to the police would be a godsend. At my suggestion, the IG wrote the same day to the Government and asked for the land for a training school for constables. In a meeting of the senior police officers, I was ridiculed for my proposal for the school at Khandala. Nagarwala said that for several months it would rain so hard that the recruits would never be able to drill, and would be wasting their time. They advanced numerous reasons why we should not take the land, rather than why we should take it. However, the IG, M M Chaudasama, overruled them. I had convinced him of the simple fact that if land was offered to us anywhere free (by the Government) we should take it. We were bound to find some use for it, sooner or later. The land was allotted to us shortly thereafter. In the meantime, Joshi phoned me again. He said," Didn't you say that you had put an armed guard to prevent demolition of the school buildings in Khandala?"

I said I had.

Joshi said, "The Chief Engineer has just phoned me. He says that he had stopped on the way to see the place; the wreckers have done great damage to all the structures, and there was no police guard that he could see. "

I went again to Khandala. It was a terrible sight that met my eyes. The dormitories had all been demolished and the sanitary fittings were lying around broken. The roof of the church had been knocked down and the statues inside were lying in pieces. Above all, the breakfast room had gone and there was no guard within sight. I had given the SP, Braganza, a simple oral order to post a guard of one and three, and he had forgotten all about it. I only gave him a scolding, which he probably nursed throughout his career. I had not read Guderian then. If I had, I would have first given him a written order, smiled at him (a la Surendra Nath), and made a report against him to the IG.

The old drill manual says that the object of drill is to teach men to obey orders and to do it in the correct way. This was not an isolated incident of the failure of a young IPS officer to carry out a simple order. How many examples must I give? How can our young IPS officers make their men obey orders if they fail to do so themselves? If you scold them or pull them up, they resent it as a lifelong insult.

At about the same time, Joshi told me that a huge plot of land in Wanowrie called the 'Eve's Estate' was available. It had belonged to Sir Victor Sassoon, and he had named it after his young American wife. During the war it had housed a field hospital for the Army, and had now been acquired by the State Government. I went and inspected the land. It consisted of hundreds of acres of the finest land at the foot of Ramtekadi, behind the Army School of Physical Training. It housed numerous barracks of all shapes and sizes. This was not the case for posting a guard of one and three or a platoon, or even a company. We needed to put one or more battalions there at once. And they were available ready to be put.

The plan to create a reserve police battalion for Bombay was first mooted towards the end of the British Rule. A battalion was established at Purandar Fort, and Dodwell, Superintendent of Police, was made the commandant. The state reserve police force and its creation under a separate Act was done by K J Nanavatty, who became the commandant of the first group, consisting of a thousand men. Two such groups were placed at Sambre, outside Belgaum. For want of accommodation, they continued to remain there even after the reorganization of States.

I proposed to the IG, Chudasama, that these two groups should be moved to 'Eve's Estate' which the Government had given us. I said that unless we did it immediately, the premises would appear to be unoccupied, and we would lose that most valuable and extensive piece of real estate. Chudasama called me next day and said that he had consulted Nanavatty (then the DIG CID, but considered an expert on SRP matters, and anything connected with the armed police). Nanavatty had flatly told him that it would take at least six months to transfer the first battalion and another six months for the second. It would take at least two months to get the first railway train.

I reminded the IG respectfully that I was the DIG in charge of the Reserve Police. What, exactly, had Nanavatty to do with the matter?

'I consulted him because of his expertise,' Chudasama said. 'After all, he was the creator of the SRPF'.

'Sir,' I said. 'No one can deny the fact that Nanavatty was the creator of the SRPF. But what has that to do with moving the battalions here?'

' You don't seem to appreciate the difficulties involved,' the IG said. 'Nanavatty says we shall have to hire special trains. To get the Railways to give them will, itself, take months.'

I said," Sir, the commandant of Group I , Col. Jadhav, is a seasoned ex-Army officer. May I call him by wireless? You could , at least, ask him what he has to say,"

Chudasama could not but agree to this reasonable suggestion, and Jadhav arrived next day. When I mooted the proposal to him, he was overjoyed. He said," Sir, this is a deliverance. The Karnataka State has been requisitioning my companies and those of the second battalion for all sorts of duties in the interior. We are given no time for drill or recuperation. Even to bring our companies for duty each time to our State is a cumbersome job."

"How long will it take you to bring the battalion to Pune, and how long to get a railway train? " I asked him.

"I can move my battalion within a month, he said." As for the train, I can get it within ten days. I happen to have very good relations with the Divisional Superintendent. Please, please let us do it."

I took him to the IG. Within twenty days Jadhav brought his battalion, lock, stock and barrel to Pune, and installed it on 'Eve's Estate'. The commandant, Group II, Shinde, brought his battalion after another fortnight.

Some people in the police have forgotten, or do not know about the sequence of events. I have put it here for the record.

When I became the Commissioner of Police of Bombay, I inherited a bulky file concerning some land at Marol. The file was concerned with the acquisition of a fairly large plot of land for the police department at Marol in the suburbs of Bombay. There are many ways of quick disposal of files. One is to read only the last page and push it on to somebody else. A look at the last five or six pages of this file showed me that the plot involved was of 90 acres, a size not dreamt of by the police, in Bombay city. I called the DCP Headquarters, MG Katre, and the office superintendent. They said that there were many difficulties in getting the plot. The Tehsildar was not in favour of handing it over. Professor Choksey of Tatas owned a bungalow right in the middle of it and had a road leading to it which cut it in half. There was a piggery also in the middle, and the owner had gone to court to fight for his claim on his part of the land.

I asked the DCP HQ if he had seen the plot. He had not. Had an ACP seen it? Apparently not. Had the police station inspector seen it? A telephone call revealed that he had not. Then who had seen it? Some PSI, who was transferred to another police station a month back. I told the DCP HQ that it was absolutely impossible for me to know the correct position unless I studied the file. I took it home and spent several hours on the next Sunday, reading it from the first page to the last: 146 pages in all.

I was ready on Monday. I called the DCP HQ, Katre, and asked him to do the following things for Wednesday:

1). Arrange for my visit, along with him, to the site of the land at Marol.

2). Request the *Tahsildar* to be present

3). Arrange for my meeting with Professor Choksey in his house at Marol.

On Wednesday we visited the site. It was a large, extensive plot with an empty shed where a ginning mill had been operating. The land sloped down towards a fringe of coconut trees on one side. Choksey's bungalow was situated on a hillock in the middle with a narrow asphalt road leading to it from the main road. And the piggery was situated at a corner at one end. The *Tahsildar* had come with maps, papers, and tapes. I said to him, " I am told that you have raised some objections about handing over the land to us. May I know what they are?"

He said," What objections, Sir? On the contrary, I have been urging your department to take over the land. I have even managed to have the ginning mill removed from here. No higher officer has ever come to discuss the matter with me. They send only PSI's and head constables."

"What about Choksey's house right in the middle, and the piggery? " I asked him.

"As for the piggery", he said," the civil case may go on in the court for a number of years. It's at one end, and the owner fenced it in. What does it matter if it remains there? In any case the pigs won't be anxious at all to encounter the police. And as for Professor Choksey, you are going to talk to him. There are huge plots on either side of the road." He urged me to take over the possession of the land at once. "I have kept out the squatters with great difficulty, Sir" he said. " I asked for help from your department for preserving their own land, but they did not give me any."

I met Professor Choksey. " I shall be very happy if the police came here", he said to my surprise. "The illicit brewers come at night near those coconut trees, and once or twice they have threatened me. I have owned this plot for years. How will it affect the police? There's enough land on both sides for you to have taken the two plots separately."

I asked Katre to put a platoon in the ginning shed immediately, to go and see himself that it was in place, and to report that he had done so. I have found again and again that such elementary instructions, (in writing at times) to IPS officers of the rank of SP are necessary. We took possession of the land that very day.

One can draw a few valuable lessons from this episode. Files are sometimes living things (depending on the subject), and they should be treated with respect. It was discovered that even, the Dead Sea Scrolls had something important to reveal. If they involve personal visits and inspections, these must never be ignored. Last of all, officers in the police department often think wrongly, that people are against them. Very often, these very people want to help them. Public Relations for the police do not mean *personal publicity*, as more than one super cop seems to think and practice. Such officers often misuse the goodwill that exists for the department, for their own selfish purposes. When I was the Commissioner of Police of Bombay, I had an Assistant Commissioner in the CID called Basil Kane. He was a fairly good investigator, but his forte was not in his detective skills. It was in his public relations. There was practically nobody in any walk of life, that he did not know, and he exerted great influence with many of them. He was willing to help people, and they, in turn, were anxious and willing to help him. He had very good relations with the Press, but I never found him doing any publicity for himself. We could do with more officers of his mould, rather than with those who possess only brag and bounce, and happen to be photogenic.

CHAPTER X

POT POURRI

V. OF ACTING, ACTORS AND SUCH

Historians of the future will not fail to mention that in the Twentieth Century, one of the greatest influences on society (in any part of the world) has been the cinema, and its child born of later years - the Television screen.

We read a great deal in the media of the outstanding benefits that exposure to TV has had on the education of the young in different parts of the world. But, as I see it, the films that both the screens show are mostly on sex and violence - explicit sex and mindless violence. This portrayal is even extended to cartoons and the so-called 'funnies'. In the West, because of their pre-occupation with the pursuit of money, or just pleasure, parents have found it convenient to leave their children 'safely' glued to the TV screens at home. They might have been left safe from physical harm, but the deleterious effects of these films containing scenes of murder, mayhem and explicit sex have been incalculable and all-pervasive. The plastic years of childhood are most susceptible to their evil influence. The recent result in the United States has been the shoot-outs by teenagers who seem to have easy access to guns, and who, perhaps have not grasped at the difference between lethal weapons and the toys with which they had played only a short while ago.

The effect of the TV revolution is not confined only to Western countries; it has now come to stay (more particularly) in India, where TV sets are becoming an essential article even in *jhuggies*, and *chawls*.

'Bollywood' has now replaced Hollywood as the producer of the largest number of films in the world. It is no secret that these are mostly financed by the likes of Dawood Ibrahim and Arun Gavli. The characteristics of these films have remained the same in the last forty years. It's the same *masala*, to use an expression common to film magazines and Sunday newspaper supplements. The faces may be different, the locales may be different, but the voices in the songs are the same. And the actors and actresses perform the same gyrations and the same antics that their grandfathers and grandmothers did long ago. Children and grandchildren inherit their roles, just as they do in the political firmament. You turn on the switch and they greet you with the same.

> 'Quips and cranks and wanton wiles,
> Nods and becks and wreathed smiles...'

Had Milton been present, he might have been glad that he was not in a position to see them.

The Board of Film Censors is unable or unwilling to exercise any control. Even little cuts are resisted tooth and nail by the interested parties in the name of the right to freedom of expression. And is it not surprising that there is not even a single police officer on the entire Censor Board?

This fascination for movies and actors is, unfortunately, not confined only to the young. It pervades all ages and all sections of society. People are inclined to confuse acting with doing, and when it comes to gods, actors are often identified with the gods they portray on the movie screen. This adoration of actors has now intruded into politics. Film actors have become Chief Ministers and Governors. With their vast wealth (mostly ill gotten) there is nothing they cannot aspire to be. The recent elections have shown the sorry spectacle of all political parties making use of actors to draw crowds, since their leaders can no longer do it themselves. In ancient times, Roman Emperors provided spectacles to the 'hoi polloi' in the form of 'circuses' in the arena. Today, actors and actresses provide these 'circuses' in Bharat, that is India. Unfortunately, escape from harsh reality is a permanent facet of life throughout the pages of history.

This influence of the movie world is not confined only to India. It has been in evidence in the land where movies began, the United States. One outstanding example is that of Ronald Reagan, a B grade movie actor, who became Governor of California, and twice, the President of the United States. Reagan had the most essential qualification of a politician in the US. He had the gift of the gab, which he had finely honed as president of the actors' guild. It is said that in many respects he remained an actor even in the White House. 'He read his carefully prepared speeches and cue cards *with conviction.*' His biographer has said that he was an actor in the White House and out of it. In India, our politicians must also have the gift of the gab, but, they hardly, if ever, give prepared speeches, and so need no preparation and no cue cards. The reason should have become obvious to my readers: most of them speak before they think.

CHAPTER XI

THE BREAKDOWN OF LAW AND ORDER AND THE PROBLEM OF POLICE LEADERSHIP

I. THE KILLING FIELDS - AN OVERVIEW

Bihar is, Of course, a case study by itself. Law and Order have ceased to function in large parts of the State for more than twenty years. And it was L P Singh, (no less a person), who told me in 1996 that Bihar was the best administered State in India! (L P Singh was a former Chief Secretary of Bihar). In Bihar, private armed gangs hired by landlords have operated freely murdering tenants or other enemies, attacking the police, or each other. Bihar, the richest State in terms of natural resources, has become the poorest.[1] *Naxalites*, in turn, attack these gangs of the landlords with impunity. And through it all, the police are helpless spectators, if not altogether moribund.

In the Northeast, ultras derail trains, loot treasuries, throw bombs at police patrols, and kidnap likely prospects for ransom. Hardly any of them are caught. The worst feature of these attacks is the constant threnody that you hear from the innocent victims of these assaults, echoing from one end and their relatives of the country to the other, on and on, without a stop. And, what is the reaction of the rulers to all this? They issue statements and appoint Commissions of Enquiry.

One would have thought that Karnataka was a well- run State, but even here the lord of the jungles is Veerapan, the infamous sandalwood smuggler who has never been 'nabbed'. He must have the backing of many forest officials, forest contractors, and, of course, the police.

The latest episode in the serial drama of Veerappan has unfolded quite recently, bearing out my gloomiest forebodings. On the 30th of

1. In terms of the economy and the administration

July,2000, Veerappan kidnapped the actor, Rajkumar, from his farm house on the outskirts of Veerappan's jungle. Why the aging 'matinee idol' chose to build his house there, and not in Bangalore, is another mystery. To express their anger at this outgage, Rajkumar's fans in Bangalore city went on a rampage, burning buses and other vehicles, ransacking shops, and forcibly declaring a *Bandh*—a closure of all business activity, schools and colleges for ten days.

The chief ministers of Karnataka and Tamil Nadu then went into a huddle and decided to send an emissary, a journalist, who was on friendly terms with Veerappan. In all, this man has made about four trips in a vehicle with all his bag and baggage. Among other things Veerappan has demanded the release of 121 detenus from Karnataka (his henchmen), and 5 other terrorists from Tamil Nadu. Apparently, he has not demanded any ransom money-probably he has so much. The CMs were happy to concede all his demands, but, as (at the time of writing), the Supreme Court gave a stay order, they have had to pause. They were not a bit abashed by the remark of the President of India, K R Narayanan, in his independence speech, (referring to Veerappan) that it was time that the civil society and the lawful goverment asserted their authority and primacy over the dare-devil heroes of crime and banditry.

Veerappan is said to have committed 130 murdersm, killed several hundred elephants for their tusks, and cut and sold enough sandalwood from the forest to make several fortunes. From the fact that he seems to be hob-nobbing with extremist gangs, it would appear that he is aiming at his own political 'rehabilitation', and a subsequent political career, And, why not, if the former Bandit Queen, Phulan Devi can become a respectable member of Parliament?

But the worst case is that of Jammu and Kashmir. The ascendancy of the militants has not been an overnight miracle. Step by step, they have gained a fatal stronghold over the Muslim population through many devious ways. One of them is fear. Another is by removing as many Hindus as possible (Kashmiri Pandits) from the valley, to show that Kashmir is in fact, if not in law, a Muslim State. I have described before how this was the result of the policies and attitudes of D P Dhar and his cohorts.

Recently, they have repeatedly attacked not only police headquarters, but also those of the Army. In particular after the Kargil war, they want to demonstrate that it is their writ that runs in the Valley, and not that of the Government of India.

According to The Indian Express of 14 November 1999, the Chief of Staff of 15 Corps, Major General Mukherjee, told media persons,"We cannot prevent such attacks. We can only instil in them (the militants) the fear that they cannot get away alive from such attacks."

From the fact that these attacks have been continued, it would appear that the requisite fear has not been instilled in the militants, and that their suicide squads are ready, and able to launch them at will.

The basic truth is (I admit I am repeating it) that we have no *intelligence* worth the name about the activities of the terrorists operating in the Valley itself, let alone outside.

The time-honoured method of apprehending terrorists, or anti-social elements of any kind, has been that of setting up informers from within their ranks, and of getting information about their local contacts and supporters. If the reason given by Intelligence Agencies is that these people are 'foreigners' and it is not possible for them to get an contacts, my reply is that the terrorists inside the country do not work in a vacuum. It is as plain as a pikestaff that they have strong support in the Valley. Further, this support is not confined to the villagers on the border any more. It is in the principal cities of Kashmir, particularly in Srinagar itself. It is also equally plain that the terrorists have infiltrated into the Government services, like the Police, Revenue, PWD, and that this infiltration is not confined only to the lower echelons.

The inevitable question is: why have the Intelligence Agencies not been able to establish sources among these people? The Intelligence agencies which are mainly involved in the work of Intelligence gathering in Jammu & Kashmir are: 1) The State CID, 2) The Intelligence Bureau, 3) Military Intelligence, and 4) RAW.

As I understand it, the work of Military Intelligence is to gather information about enemy troop movements[1] inside and outside our borders.[2] The Pakistan army and irregulars had occupied places and positions within our own border in the Kargil area. It was surely the primary duty of Military Intelligence to have prevented this, however cold or long the winter, or at least to have known about it. They cannot pass the buck on to the IB or RAW, or the State CID in the matter. But

1. On the battle front (in times of war), and
2. (in times of peace).

it is not their duty, as I see it, to secure the kind of intelligence that I have referred to above, which could have been available, not only on the mountains of Kargil, or the jungles of Gurez, but in the offices and shops of Srinagar, or in its labyrinthine *gullies*.

And if 'foreigners' from Pakistan or Afghanistan are involved, it was the duty of RAW to get this information. Illustrious officers from RAW have hankered after the prize postings in the U S A, or the U K, but as for the countries on our border which matter the most, these have either been neglected or RAW is still quite *raw* in getting from them any intelligence worthwhile. The most recent and the most flagrant example is that of the senior officer from RAW, posted in Nepal, boarding the Indian Airlines Flight IC814 at Kathmandu, not knowing that he was going to have hijackers for company. *Fee Fi Fo Fum.*

It has become patent that despite the vast sums of money spent on these two Central Government Intelligence Agencies, their output of work has hardly been commensurate with the expenditure on their upkeep. Despite the voluminous paper work that they do, they have not been able to deliver the goods during the thirty years that have gone since I was unceremoniously thrown out of Jammu & Kashmir.

I have always had a close rapport with the Armed Police, wherever I have been posted. They have responded to my demands and expectations with loyalty and alacrity. One reason why I have not had the same feeling about the unarmed police could be their comparative ineptitude and readiness to turn a dishonest penny whenever they could. Perhaps their opportunities to do this are far greater than those of the armed police.

During my short tenure of a year and a half in J & K, I had developed this rapport with the Kashmir Armed Police too. I began to get the impression that with their families and roots in the Valley, they could become the nucleus of a constant flow of information. If I had remained in Kashmir, I would have created such sources, regardless of Surendra Nath, or any of the local officers.

Within a short time of my departure from Kashmir, this same band of loyal armed policemen became mutinous and unmanageable. A bomb exploded right inside the office room of the I G, injuring him badly. The armed policemen became openly mutinous, and barred themselves inside the K A P Headquarters. The Army had to be called in and a tank used to make a breach in the wall.

I do not blame the K A P for this sad state of affairs. I blame the senior police officers in charge; I blame the senior I A S officers in charge of the police; I blame the politicians in charge of the I A S, and the police.

I felt then and I feel now, that the time when I was in J & K, and the years immediately following, were the years when Kashmir could have become part of the Indian Union, not only in fact, but also in spirit. As Shakespeare has put it:

> "There is a tide in the affairs of men, which taken at the flood,
> Leads on to Fortune. Omitted, all the voyage of their life is bound
> In shallows and in miseries...And we must take the current
> When it serves, or lose our ventures."

At the cost of repitition I say that had I been allowed to remain there for five years, and had that *Vetal**been pulled from off my back, then, I venture to aver that in my humble capacity of IG, I would have changed the shape of things in the State of Jammu & Kashmir for ever and aye.

Before sanctioning the order to remove me from Kashmir, the Prime Minister, Mrs. Gandhi, never sent for me nor ever asked me what I had to say in the matter.[1] If she had done so, I would have told her all that I have written above. Perhaps, I was too small a man and an outsider to boot, as compared to that master of political intrigue and maneuver, that Kasmiri expert on Kashmir, D P Dhar. Eventually, she did send him out on some diplomatic assignment. But I do not entirely blame Dhar for all that happened. I blame those high and mighty members of the I C S, the I A S and the I P for their supine attitude towards Dhar and the Kashmir problem. Why did they not go to her and give her their frank opinion? What is the worst that could have happened to them? A transfer? And they did not call me even once and ask me what I had ro say before my removal. After all, was I not specially selected as an apolitical man to overhaul the police structure?

One valuable lesson I did learn from my ouster. If anything was said or written about a subordinate with a prior good record, before taking any action, I always gave him a chance to state his side of the case I even gave this chance to officers with bad records.

* VETAL (Vay-Taal) the demon who, according to legend, would jump from a tree on to King Vikramaditya's back, and offer him gratuitous advice.

1. She must have known that I had been specially selected for this job.

CHAPTER XI

II. ADMINISTRATIVE (POLICE) INADEQUACIES

As against the above dismal picture, let us consider the position of the police force of Mumbai city, which is said to be the equal of Scotland Yard - whatever that means, but no more. During the communal riots of December 1992 - January 1993, not only was the police force of the city paralysed, but even the State administration had ceased to function for at least ten days. The police complained that they did not have a sufficient number of 'columns' at their disposal. Now, I do not quite know what, exactly, the then police commissioner, S V Bapat, meant by the word 'column'. According to the drill manual, the definition of the word 'column' is 'a body of troops one behind the other on parallel successive alignments.

A column can consist of a squad, a platoon, a company, a battalion, or even more. Let us take it that in his evidence before the Sri Krishna Commission, by the word 'column' the police commissioner meant a force of company strength. To begin with, how many companies of the SRPF did the commissioner have? I had only seven companies during the course of the Shiv Sena riots. Even though I had asked for more, they did not arrive in time. I did not ask for any aid from the Army even for a Flag March. During the Samyukta Maharashtra riots of 1956 in Bombay city (when I was DCP HQ) we did not call the Army. With due respect to the Army, what more can they do than the Armed Police? In dealing with mobs, they cannot bring to bear any more formidable weapon than the rifle. Further, to open fire, they want written orders of a magistrate *on every single occasion.* Last of all, I am firmly of the view that that the Army should not be used to quell riots. And in this particular matter, I agree with the view of those who say that the Criminal Procedure Code is out of date; it was enacted at a time when there were no reserve police battalions, and the strength of the provincial police was inadequate. When large-scale disturbances took place, the civil authorities had no alternative but to call the Army.

Now it may be argued that the Mumbai Riots of 1992-93 were an exceptional occurrence. The normal pattern of policing that prevails in the metropolis is very effective. What then is the normal pattern of policing in Mumbai over the last fifteen years? Extortion and kidnapping seem to be the order of the day. Dawood Ibrahim's gang and Arun Gavli's gang are only two of the gangs that rule the roost in Mumbai city. The only answer that the police seem to have is in encounters, true or faked. That this is not enough is clear from the fact that these and other gangs still continue to operate with impunity.

The basic modus operandi, used by the police since time immemorial, is of introducing informers into their ranks. The object of this never-ending exercise is to collect information, not rake in the shekels. It can only be done at the level of the constabulary, but under the strict supervision of capable senior officers with a sense of dedication and total integrity. Admittedly, all this is not thew work of a day, but whoever said that successful police work was based on only a little running around, combined with plenty of publicity on the part of a 'super cop' or two?

The records will show that the police commissionerates of Pune and Nagpur were established on the recommendations of the Maharashtra State Police Commission of which I was the member-secretary. They were instituted at *my* instance against a great deal of opposition . In the note that I had prepared on the subject, which was incorporated in the report of the Commission (which also I had drafted) I gave the following reasons for their creation. In brief, I said that in the growing metropolitan cities of Pune and Nagpur, there were special problems concerning urban crime, traffic control, festivals, control of not infrequent riots, all of which needed the constant supervision of a police officer, who combined in his person the functions of a District Magistrate and Superintendent of Police. This officer could only be a Police Commissioner like the ones in Bombay or Calcutta or Madras. While the administrative control of the Commissioner would be with the IG of Police, he would work directly under the Government in matters of law and order.

The Government of Maharashtra approved of this recommendation, and while I was the DIG of Pune Range, I was asked to submit a detailed proposal for the formation of the police commissionerate for Pune city.

These two commissionerates became the prototype for many commissionerates, not only in Maharashtra, but also in other States. Even while I was in Pune, officers from these States used to visit Pune for information about the new police pattern.

After my retirement, I came to settle in Pune in 1984. Pune is the place where I spent my boyhood. As of this day of writing, there have been fifteen police commissioners in Pune. Why has there been such a large turnover, Subramanium, the then Governor of Maharashtra asked at a police function? Whatever be the reason for the rapid turnover the question that I cannot forbear from asking now is this: has the creation of the police commissionerate been justified? I do not want to cast aspersions on this or that police officer, but I cannot truly assert that the policing of Pune city has shown any marked improvement over the previous pattern.

Let me say, first of all, that the intention of creating this post was never to give 'job satisfaction' to the senior officers of the police department,(that many of them are hanking after), but to give the department what amounted to, a golden opportunity to serve the public better. This the police could hardly be said to have done in Pune. As of this day of writing, dacoits attack houses, not only on the outskirts of Pune city, but even in the heart of Pune, in Koregaon Park, where I live. They are not armed with sophisticated weapons (in this modern age), but carry swords, axes and knives.

Since I have settled in Pune, burglars have dropped their visiting cards three times on my house. On the first occasion, I saw one of them standing inside the wicket gate. Forgetting my age, I foolishly gave chase, but he got away. On the second occasion, I heard the slight sound of something falling on the patio, and went up to discover that the thieves have filed away the steel frame of the broad window. I call them thieves, because they ran away. Had I confronted them, the section of the offence might have been changed to a robbery, or a dacoity. But I think the bottom of police prestige in Pune was reached when the editor of some rag, his family and friends, came in a bus to the police commissioner's house, brushed the armed sentry aside, entered the house, tore up the telephone line, broke up the furniture, and frightened his old parents out of their wits.

When S V Bhave was the police commissioner, he was very satisfied with the detection done by his staff. I told him that in the area where I lived, there have been one-and-a-half dozen break-ins with thefts, none of which was detected, he admitted that this was so, but said that the detection in the rest of the city was very good.

As for traffic control, there is none to speak of in Pune city. I have been driving my old Fiat (as I cannot afford a driver) and I should know. The policemen on point duty are probably the laziest in the world. After half an hour's point duty, the poor police constable is tired an prefers to stand on the side and watch the traffic go by. I move around in the Camp area, and I have hardly seen any officer of and above the rank of sub-inspector supervising the traffic. Auto rickshaw drivers and drivers of two wheelers weave in and out of traffic, endangering the safety of others as well as of themselves. Traffic jams are a frequent occurrence. I can testify that during these instances when I have been caught in them, no policemen, let alone higher officers, have ever arrived to sort them out.

I am tired of hearing the old chestnut about the staff being inadequate. Hardly any patrolling is done at night, because, we are told, the staff is inadequate. When I was chairman of the police advisory panel, I had got directly sanctioned from the Government within four months, the posts of 3000 policemen, (one thousand each for Mumbai, Pune and Nagpur) for the Beat System. The members of my panel and I had worked out the details of the beats in the three cities. What has happened to these posts? I have reason the believe that the beat system was never implemented. On the contrary, the then home secretary, Salvi, and the IG, Nagarkar, were furious with me fro getting it sanctioned 'without their consent'. Let it be noted that according to the wishes of the Chief Minister, and as laid out in the GR, the panel worked directly under the orders of the Chief Minister, and not of the Home Department or the Chief Secretary.

Senior police officers are wont to hold endless conferences with their subordinates and the Press over endless cups of tea on the 'falling crime graph'. Verily, it is indeed falling, but I am not able to agree that the reason is improved methods of detection, et al. In the old days, the police took (at least at a lower level) what was called 'blood money'. They screwed it out of the thieves and robbers by the use of the third degree.

All that changed with the advent of Prohibition and *matka* gambling. Neither the Prohibition law nor the law against gambling was enforceable. I should know about the former, because I was in charge of Prohibition Intelligence while director of the anti-corruption bureau, for several years. Briefly, the raw material for the illicit brew was, dirt-cheap. All that was required was rotten jaggery, a drum, and some empty kerosene tins. Whatever the number of stills, as soon as these were seized, others sprang up on the vast coastline of Bombay and its suburbs - in fact, in any open space. It was not possible to prove conscious possession, as required by law. And smuggling of foreign liquor from Dubai and other places (along with gold and other contraband) became a flourishing trade. Smugglers still used the old Arab *dhows*, which were practically unsinkable, but now their sails were removed and they were powered by engines that could make them show every time a clean pair of heels to both customs and police launches.

It is not the case that the position was not explained to those in authority, but by that time, Prohibition had become an article of faith with rulers like Morarji Desai, who thought that all that was required for its 'success' was a tough stance with the police. Corruption followed the pattern of the experience in the United States, If regular packets of *payola* were placed on the tables of the officers, how many would resist pocketing them and at what level? It will now be clear why the normal crime graph showed a continuous downward trend.

But the worst feature of this emerging scenario was not only that new mafia gangs were established, but, as in the U S, they began to diversify into other fields like the cinema and the building trade, never known for straightforward and honest dealing in the first place.

I admit that for the past several years I have been out of touch with the working of the police administration. I am, therefore, unable to understand why this new generation of gangsters has to resort to kidnapping, robbery and murder. Perhaps the liquor trade and gambling are no longer the lucrative fields they once were.

There is a great deal of discussion these days in the Press and elsewhere about the continued lack of the use of scientific methods by the police in the detection and investigation of crime. Now when such methods are available, why don't the police use them? Perhaps, the examination of fingerprints has become old-fashioned these days with the use of DNA tests of blood. However, it is a moot point how far scientific methods alone can help in police investigation. Recently I read an article in an American weekly magazine, which discussed the pattern of crime in six of the principal cities of the United States. The article said that the conviction in crimes of violence in these cities was less than two percent. It is therefore the duty of a police organization, like the much-vaunted CBI, to make a detailed examination of the problem, and suggest to the States' police how they could make greater use of science in 'nabbing' offenders, and 'nailing' them down, (to use the two words most favoured by TV announcers).

Scientific methods can be no substitute for the nitty gritty of police investigation. This includes the proper registration of offences, the collection of evidence, the recording of statements and other minutiae. At this instant, I recall the work of a sub inspector called Dange, who was in charge of Islampur police station in the 1940's, when I was an ASP in Satara. He was a stocky middle-aged man who was always cleanly dressed in a *dhoti*, shirt and coat and a grey cap frimly fixed on his head. He had risen from the ranks, and passed the qualifying examination for PSI, but he had never been to the police training school, and did not know any English. However, what Dange did not know about police investigation was not worth knowing. The way he pursued an investigation was an education in itself, and his case papers (always in Marathi) were a pleasure to read. From the Sessions Court, Dange got only encomiums in case after case. I suggested to the SP, Hobson, that Dange's was a fit case for a police medal, but he did not follow it up.

Mumbai city has one of the finest police forces in India (for that matter, in the world). I know whereof I speak. I was the Police Commissioner in 1969-70. Let me site two examples of police investigation in Mumbai during my time. The first I have already given, that of Raman Raghav. I have deliberately described at length to show how thoroughly such cases were pursued not a step was missed, not a stone was left unturned. The second is the presentation in the Coroner's Court of the 56 deaths caused by police firing in the course of the Shiv Sena riots. The Coroner's Court is the only Court where the jury system prevails. These cases were investigated under the personal supervision of R S Kulkarni, Deputy Commissioner, CID. The police firing was justified in each one of them, a Herculean operation by any standards. I was, therefore, greatly distressed to read the remarks of Justice Sri Krishna on the routine investigation of the police into the cases during the Mumbai riots of December 1992 - January 1993. He said the investigations were lackadaisical and arbitrary. The serious nature of the cognizable crime was suppressed in order to give a rosy picture. Lack of care was noticed in recording FIR's, statements of witnesses, identification parades. The judge goes on record to say, that the cultivation of sources, long and short term, was inactive, and crucial intelligence reports did not reach the higher officers in time. What a state of affairs that a judge has to comment on the lack of police sources and Intelligence!

Justice Sri Krishna has made remarks even on the physical fitness of police officers. A particular ACP was unable to climb the Kasaiwadi Hill (presumably due to his bulk). The officer urged him not to risk it either, but the judge climbed the hill nevertheless, leaving the officer behind. He has rightly observed that a minimum standard of physical fitness should be a must for every police officer.

I doubt that there can be any one who would dispute the truth behind this observation. Physical fitness, whatever be the rank of the officer, is a must for a policeman, as much as it is for a military man. This impels me to make an aside at this stage. The Alitalia incident happened immediately after the crash of the plane, sometime in 1962 on top of a hill called Devandya in the village of Nimgiri in Pune district. All the 96 passengers and crew were killed, and the police were required to go to the site of the accident and bring the dead bodies and valuables down. The operation was in charge of the DIG, Pune Range, who happened to have more avoirdupois than was strictly necessary in a police officer. He remained at the bottom of the hill in the village nearby. The IG, K J Nanavatty, later told me with a guffaw that the DIG had said that if he were made to climb the hill, one more dead body would have to be brought down. I did not raise the subject, Nanavatty had. I said to him that the DIG was not on the verge of retirement; he had fourteen more years to go. Would any of the constables or head constables in the party have been excused on the same grounds? Though this officer was later found fit to be the IG of Maharashtra for over seven years, he was certainly not fit to be a sentinel of the Sahyadris, *for even one single day*.

The major criticism against the police by the politicos, lawyers, social workers has been that they were the deliberate creation of the British Raj by means of a semi-military organization meant to suppress the freedom movement, and that, further, this organization is now an anachronism in this year of Grace. They say that even after fifty years of freedom, the police still do not realize that they are the servants of the people; they are as unpopular as they were during the days of the British.

Let us first consider the issue of their alleged unpopularity. When I was a member of the 'Police High-Power Committee' in 1986-87, I had occasion to visit Ahmednagar district, and talk to the SP and his senior officers. They told me that out of the 63 officers in the district of and above the rank of PSI, 61 were appointees posted to particular police stations at the behest of the politicians. The SP was unable to move them anywhere. It did not take me long to discover that this was the position all over the State.

Since these politicians were the elected representatives of the people, how could this overwhelming majority of police officers be said to be 'unpopular'? In many cases, the most corrupt police officers were posted to the most important police stations, at the insistence of the politicians.

In 1970, the post of Special IG was created in Maharashtra, and I was kicked 'upstairs' and appointed to it. Th e subject of posting of police officers, of and below the rank of Inspector, was allotted to me (in the division of work). The very next day, I got a call from the P A to Minister for Home, that the Minister desired that six officers (he gave the names) should be posted to particular districts, and to particular police stations in those districts. I told the PA that I was unable to accept such oral orders supposed to be given through a PA. Could he put me on to the Minister? I would like to speak to him. The minister did not come on the phone, but the same afternoon I got separate orders for each of these postings signed by the Minister. Thereafter, I used to get a dozen or more orders every other day.

Now an order signed by a Minister has to be carried out, provided it is legal. I had, therefore, no choice but to carry them out. I mentioned in the orders, that the Government desired the postings, to make it clear that the IG was not a willing party to them.

At the next senior officers' conference, the officers all raised their voices in protest against these orders. They said that the most corrupt police officers were being posted to the most important police stations, many of which were communally sensitive. They said that whenever riots broke out, and other law and order problems arose, these officers (posted by the Government) were the first to make themselves scarce.

They were the ones who burked serious crime and gave a bad name to the police force. I asked them to put their complaints in writing, which they did.

I took up the issue with the home secretary, R D Pradhan. He discussed it with the Minister for Home, and told me that it was decided that I should select twenty of the worst cases, and that he, the IG, Rajadyaksha, and I should go to the Minister and discuss the matter with him. We three went to see the Minister in his chambers. I was armed with the files and confidential records of the twenty officers. However, when I began to discuss each case, we were told by the home minister that this minister or that, this MP or that had asked for the officer and his posting. (these were 20 out of 160 cases). After the revelation there was complete silence. Neither the home secretary nor the IG had a word to say (why did they come then?). At last, I said, What is your decision, Sir?" The home minister said that he would have to consult the ministers concerned. I said, at last,"Is this a matter then for a cabinet decision?" I shall draw a curtain on what transpired thereafter. The meeting broke up and the home secretary left without a word. As for the IG, instead of commiserating with me, he was jumping with joy at the police officers' conference from where we had come. And Ribeiro has the effrontery to say that I was afraid of, a home minister, or any minister. *Fee fi fo fum*!

At about this time, an officer who had been a Reader Inspector to Majeedullah (when he was DIG, Pune Range) told me about the following incident. He had just taken over the job of Reader to the DIG, when he got several phones and chits from MP's , MLA's and other politicians about the same thing, that is, asking that particular officers should be posted to particular places, He took these names to the DIG, and asked him what he should do. Majeedullah replied to him in Urdu, "Beta, thou shoulds't not bring these requests to me. Give them what they want. We should not interfere in such matters. Just put up the orders for my signature." Majeedullah had come recently from Hyderabad on the reorganization of States. Apparently, this must have been the practice there. It soon became the practice in Maharashtra with spineless officers at the helm of the police department.

CHAPTER XI

III. IS THIS A SOLUTION ?

The 'National' police commission has propounded the solution that the drawbacks in the working of the police department can only be removed by giving it '*functional autonomy*'. According to them, the complete separation of the executive from the judiciary has ensured that automatic checks exist in investigation and criminal procedures. They have advocated that the control exercised by the District Magistrate should be removed, and an officer to be designated the 'district officer', should only have powers of co-ordination of all activities in the district, including those of the police. They want a statutory commission , called the 'security commission', consisting of the Chief Minister of the State, the Leader of the Opposition, some retired judges and others only to have powers of appeal and review.

In the first place, I would like to ask this question to the national police commission and like-minded people: In which democratic country in the world have the police been given '*functional autonomy*'? In the UK, the police commissioners of the two Metropolitan (London) police forces function directly under the Home Secretary. The country and borough forces are under the respective borough and county councils. In the United States, the city police work under their mayors, and county forces under their respective elective bodies. In the Maharashtra State Police Commission, we asked various members of public bodies and individuals whether they would agree to the removal of the control of the District Magistrate. Their unanimous answer was that the police would have to be placed under the *zilla parishads* or municipal corporations. I remember that many of the newspapers (generally critical of the police) came out with this headline "For God's sake, don't make a 'municipality' of the police."

But won't the supervision of the senior officers of the police department be enough? Surely with the creation of the posts of so many supervisory officers of the rank of DG, IG, DIG, the supervision should be foolproof? If the Central Government is prepared to provide the facilities for a quick tour of about fifty police stations in the country, of an independent group of men and women, I am prepared to show them what kind of supervision really exists at the police station level, or for that matter, at higher levels. Nor, it will be seen, have the 'automatic controls' provided by the separation of the executive and the judiciary made much difference.

By suggesting the creation of a Security Commission, which would include both the Chief Minister and the Leader of the Opposition, perhaps the NPC thought the police could play off one against the other. The result will, however, be very ambigous. The police will be subjected to enormous pressure from both the groups, and might break up into factions.

A brief review of the history of the police in India is necessary at this stage. Before the advent of the British, there was no organized police force either in Moghul India or in the Maratha States. In the capitals or in the other important cities, there used to be a *kotwal* at the head of a rudimentary police force. One of the main functions of these *ghasirams* was to pay their respects every morning to the King. I discovered that this routine still existed in Mumbai when I took charge as the CP. I saw that most of the time spent by these senior police officers, in particular, the DIG CID and the DCP CID was in idle chit chat with the Chief Minister while he was shaving. I resumed the practice of meeting the Chief Minister (home) only as laid down in the orders or, if I had anything particular to discuss.

The national police commission has stated that the British introduced the system of policing through trial and error. I agree, it was not by design. After many changes, they finally adopted the Metropolitan system in the Presidency towns of Bombay, Calcutta and Madras. The system was meant for large cities, hence the word 'metropolitan'. It could not by its very nature, have been applied to the mofussil. In the reports of the police commissions of 1861 and 1902, mention has particularly been made of the high-handed behaviour of the *darogas*, as the police station officers of the rural areas were called in those days. The police forces for each district were separate, and were controlled by the Deputy Commissioner, Collector, or by whatever name the district magistrate was called. The two reports as well as the efforts of the District Magistrates to keep a tight control over the activities of the police, do not show a desire on the part of the British to give the police more powers for enforcing their dominance over the people.

At about this time, the Indian Penal Code was drafted by T B Macaulay and the Evidence Act by Sir James Stephen. Far from giving the police any executive powers, or 'autonomous' powers, these Laws have curbed the exercise of authority by the police who have always chafed under their restrictions. Now if these two Acts are considered old-fashioned and out of date by the police or by anybody on their behalf, would there be any person among defence lawyers, politicians, or the educated public, who would be willing to allow their alteration by one jot or tittle, so as to give the police more powers?

When Sir Charles Napier conquered Sind, he saw that the metropolitan system or policing could not be applies to the vast tracts of territory in that province; he felt that some different system was needed for the internal organization of the police. He, therefore, decided to adapt the pattern of policing of the Royal Irish Constabulary which was semi-military in character, but not under the military. And he made it clear that he did not intend to 'militarise' the police by undoing the system.

Napier was eccentric in some respects. After conquering Sind, he sent a single-worded telegram to the Board of Directors of The East India Company, 'PACCAVI' (meaning, 'I have sinned'.). The members of the Board were puzzled, until one of them remembered Julius Caesar' s 'Veni, Vedi, Vici', after his decisive victory at the battle of Zella, in Gaul.

In spite of Napier's eccentricities, the British thought that some of his ideas were good. Sir George Clerk, then Governor of Bombay adopted this one, after visiting Sind in 1843.

Whatever be its internal organization, the police force was firmly 'under the command and control' of the civil authority. It was not given any 'autonomous powers', which the national police commission are now seeking to give it. As for the overall control of the statutory commission, as suggested by the NPC, it will only be for purposes of appeal and review, a situation with which neither any Chief Minister nor Leader of the Opposition will be satisfied. In practice they will both start interfering with the detailed work of the police, and the police will have to try to please both, or they will break up its two or more gropus or factions in every district and metropolitan area.

The moot question is this. Even if the proposals of the NPC are accepted, as 'altogether fitting and proper', would the States of the Indian Union be willing to incorporate them in suitable amendements to the Constitution?

The establishment of the Federation of India was not a historical process as was the case with the United States of America. The Amercian

Colonies had been working independently, under the Crown. After gaining Independence from the Crown, they agreed on 15 Nov. 1787 to form a Confederation of all the 13 Colonies. When the arragement was found unworkable, they accepted a new Constitution as the Philadelphia Convention on 17 Sep. 1787 in accordance with which they formed the (Federation of) the United States of America. But there was no such historical process in India. By the Government of India Act of 1935, the British created the fiction of seperate States Federating into the Indian Union - the Provinces of British India, and the Princely States.

In this Act the Government did give real power to the States - especially, control over the police. Perhaps they thought - and even reactioneries like Churchill might have thought, that Indians would be so involved with the nitty-gritty of governing in the States, that they might later agree to the Dominion Status within the British Empire.

For the present discussion, it might be pertinent to note that the Indian Constitution has incorporated almost all the provisions of the GOI Act of 1935, insofar as they pertain to the States of the Union. When the Congress took over power in the Provinces (later, States), the Home (police) portfolio was given to one of the ministers, as just one of the subjects, e.g. Kidwai held Home in UP, and Munshi in Bombay. Soon, however, these politicians discovered that real power lay with control over the police, and not with Revenue -- control over Collectors/ DMs. They have since, made full use of this power, as we have seen. The CM has always held home.

I, therefore, revert to my original poser. Once they realize the implications of the proposals, will these politicians (of any hue) be willing to handover the powers to the police (autonomy), or will they be even willing to share them with the (leader of) the opposition? As American teenagers would say, 'No Way!'

Further, it may be worthy of note that as (we see) the authority of the central government is becoming weaker by the day, the States aer hankering after *more* power, not less.

To my way of thinking, what is practical and possible is the curtailment of the powers of the States to transfer and promote senior officers, say of the rank of IG and above. It might be possible to make them agree that the selection and posting of these officers should be done by some central authority like the UPSC, which should also have the power to transfer them freely to other States, apart from within their own.

CHAPTER XI

IV. DISTRICT MAGISTRATE VERSUS SUPERINTENDENT OF POLICE

District Magistrates are also revenue collectors. In fact, that was the original function taken over from the indigenous rulers by The East India Company. In some States thay are called 'Deputy Commissioners', in others, like Maharashtra, 'Collectors'. In the same manner, Superintendents of Police were called District Superintendents of Police in some States like Bombay.

The relation between the District Magistrate and the Superintendent of Police has bedeviled the district administration since long. The police have chafed under the control of the District Magistrate. They have claimed that in the historical past it might have been necessary to place the police under the control of an officer having judicial powers. Now that the District Magistrate is a Magistrate only in name, he and his officers no longer try cases, as they once did; why is it necessary, they argue, for another district officer to exercise control over the police?

Let me make one fact clear at the outset. Insofar as the large cities are concerned, my view is that the police commissionerates are necessary. If they have not functioned properly, the fault lies with the selection of wrong personnel to man these posts, and the lack of proper supervision by the Home Secretary and the DG of police. After giving deep thought to the subject, I feel that officers should be carefully selected for these posts, irrespective of seniority, and they should be given special pay as an encouragement to give of their best.

The question of control of the District Magistrate over the Police, and the extent of his control has two aspects to it. In the first place, it is a question of principle; in the second, it is a question of practice. In the not infrequent disputes between the District Magistrate and the Superintendent of police, it was not always the police who were in the right and the District Magistrate who was in the wrong. I shall deal with the second issue first by giving some examples within my knowledge. In the district of Ratnagiri (before the bifurcation), this relationship assumed comical proportions when the DM and the SP were asked to share the palace of King Theebaw for their residence. Though the palace was vast, it had no garage and only one porch. The r9ight to park his car in the porch became a subject of bitter dispute between the DM and the SP.

In the course of my career, I have met some 'good' DMs and some who were not 'so good'. I have already given the examples of two of the first kind, D N Capoor of Thane and Sondhi of Jammu. Let me give a third, that of G L Seth, ICS, who was DM for the short time that I was SP in Sholapur. One morning I was standing in the main *chowk* dealing with a communal riot, when Seth suddenly came up and stood beside me. He said,"Modak, I have come to help you and not hinder you. Tell me how I can do it. If you want me to sit in the *chowkey* nearby, I shall do that, and if you want me to go back to my office and sit there, I am willing to do that also."

I said,"Thank you, Seth! What more can an SP ask of his DM? Do you go and sit in your office. I have had your SDM beside me all along, and he can give me any orders (for the use of force) that might become necessary. I don't think that will be necessary. This is a piddling riot as riots go."

I had not asked Seth to come and stand beside me. I did not need his presence beside me. But he had come on his own; *that* was the great thing. In my experience when facing riots, very few District Magistrates had ever done, so. They no longer had the excuse that DM's had in pre-independence days, that they were also Judicial officers. They had no more judicial powers than Commissioners of Police in cities. Now, since a D M often rubs into the police department the fact that he is in command and control of the police force of the district, it is incumbent on him to personally order the use of the force that he considers necessary in a particular situation. And the State Government concerned should take action against him when he has failed in this important part of his duties.

Seth was not only one of the most brilliant and hardworking DMs I have met. He was always affable and helpful. I, therefore, felt very much let down when I learnt that subsequently a very junior SP had quarreled with him over some Club matter.

When I was special IG, I was asked to make an enquiry into the conduct of the police with a B.Ed students' riot in Malegaon, Nashik. I could clearly see that the handling of the riot by the SP and his Additional SP was maladroit and clumsy. Yet they were blaming a young IAS officer named Kelkar, the District Magistrate, for not 'co-operating' with them. When I sent my Deputy Superintendent to Kelkar to ask him when I could record his statement, he said," I have discussed the matter with the Special IG, and he knows my views. As for my statement, I must support the police, must I not? Please tell the Special IG that he might type out my statement as he wills. He need not take the trouble of recording it in person. I am prepared to sign whatever statement he wants," This much for the alleged lack of co-operation on the part of the DM!

But not all DMs are so helpful. When I was posted to Kaira district in Gujarat in 1948, my first DM was T M Chaudhary, an officer who had been previously superseded by the Government. Probably he wanted to show (the Government and me) how tough he was. There are always complaints against the police (as against the personnel of other departments), not all of which are true. Whenever Chaudhary got a complaint (usually anonymous) against the police, he would send it to me with the remark that the police were useless., guilty and that I should take drastic action against them. I took no notice of these remarks the first few times, but when they were made on every unsigned letter, I protested strongly against his condemning my police without even an enquiry. I said, further, that I found most of the complaints without any substance, but if he was not satisfied with my reports he could make the enquiry himself.

Those were the days of unrest on the borders of Pakistan, but Muslims in the small town of Kaira, hundreds of miles away, could not have posed any threat to the Government. The DM's house was an old Peshwai building on the banks of the river. In a shanty nearby there was a colony of some poor Muslims who had been residing there since long. They were known to the police as a harmless lot.

Chaudhary wanted me to make a report for their detention under The Preventive Detention Act of at least ten of these 'criminals'. I told him that they were *not* criminals, nor did they have any political affiliations. Further, he had been given a 24-hour armed guard at his residence for his 'safety'. (Some previous SP had given him the guard contrary to the police manual rules in order to curry favour with him). I refused to make the report.

Chaudhary took his revenge shortly thereafter. While Kaira was the HQ of the disatrict, the hub of all activity was in the city of Nadiad, eleven miles away. I was required to go there frequently, and the only place in which I could stay and was entitled to stay, was the Inspection Bungalow. Chaudhary had reserved both the suites on a permanent basis, and the other district officers, including myself, had to fend for ourselves.

After the reorganization of States, we had taken over the State of Cambay. The state Guest House had been converted into the Inspection Bungalow. It had half a dozen suites to my knowledge. Chaudhary issued an order that only officers of and above the rank of District Magistrate could stay there. This was obviously done to belittle me. I had to move the Government to get it changed, but it took a long time.

Chaudhary was soon transferred and a man called Kharker took his place. He was a thin man with a toothbrush moustache and a balding pate. When going out, he wore khaki shorts with grey stockings, black coat, and a white sola topee. He had risen from the ranks and had reached the pinnacle of his ambition. On our first meeting, he said he would 'co-operate with me', and I was happy. I assured him that I would go more than half way.

One morning in November I was working in my office, when my orderly announced that the 'Collector Saheb' was standing on the veranda outside. I went out and saw Kharker in his usual attire. Though it was a cold winter morning, beads of sweat were on his face. I ushered him into my office and made him sit down. He was visibly shaking. I said," Mr. Kharker, what is the matter? Please take this cup of tea". I asked my orderly to pour out a cup from my thermos.

At last he spoke. He said he was driving to Nadiad (with his driver at the wheel) when a small boy suddenly ran across and was hit by the car. He was on the outskirts of Nadiad, and a big crowd soon collected. A police sub-inspector passing by came to his help and extricated him and his car from the crowd. He also took the child to the Mission Hospital.

I called my Home Inspector, Kamdar, and asked him to put the Nadiad inspector on the phone. The Mission Hospital was one of the best in Gujarat, and the PSI said that the child was being treated there.

Kharker said that it was the newspaper publicity that he was worried about. "Even if the worst happens, and the child dies, what could you have done?" I said. "After all, it's your driver who is responsible."

In the meantime Kamdar passed me a note. The driver had told him that the Collector Saheb was driving the car and not he. The Collector did not have a licence, not even a temporary one. He didn't know driving, and had insisted on taking the wheel.

I went out to the veranda and had a long talk with Kamdar. "Can you manage the difficult Press, et cetera in Nadiad? I asked him. "You must also speak to the Inspector, Nadiad. We have to protect our DM."

He said he thought he could do so; he was a very resourceful man.I went inside and gave Kharker another cup of tea and sympathy. I also phoned the Superintendent at the Hospital, Dr. Aldrich - a famous surgeon himself, and requested him to take personal interest in the injured boy.

The episode was dealt with 'satisfactorily', but I had nary a word of thanks from Kharker.

A month later I got a phone from the DM's office, saying that he wanted to see me urgently. When I met him I found that the matter was not all that urgent. It was an application from somebody for a revolver licence. As was the practice, it had been sent to the police for verification of the applicant's character and status. The police station officer had reported that the applicant was a history sheeter (a person with a criminal record), giving details. I had, therefore, not recommended the application.

The DM's office wanted to grant the licence (for reasons best known to themselves).

I explained the position to Kharker patiently. He then rang the bell and sent for his deputy *chitnis* (the senior clerk who dealt with police subjects) and said," Mr. Modak, I agree with your views, but here my deputy chitnis and there are you. If you can convince him, I shall nothing further to say."He then leaned back in his chair, as his shoulders shook with silent laughter.

I said,"Mr. Kharker, You can sanction the grant of the licence in spite of my effort, if you don't agree with it. My job (if at all there is one) is to convince *you* and not your deputy *chitnis*. If you are prepared to change places with him, I shall try to convince him." That was that.

Some time later, the Range DIG had come to inspect my district. He said,"Modak I met Kharker this morning. He says that you are not co-operating with him."

"Does he. Indeed?" I said. I then narrated the above incidents to him.

Soon thereafter, I was transferred to Belgaum, and later to Kolhapur. After the merger of the States, Kolhapur had been reorganized as a new district. The Collector's office and residence were established in the palace, where Colonel Edwardes, the political Resident used to stay. The SP usually gets second best in such cases, but here (so far as his office was concerned), he got third best.

As I have described before, my HQ was located in an excellent place, with my bungalow next to it, but my office was on the outskirts of the city in a slum area. It was originally a middle school building with poky little rooms on two floors, and long narrow verandas running on both the floors. There was a small porch in the centre, in front of the ground floor. For the first two or three days,I would get down there from my car, and go up the rickety wooden staircase to my office room facing the north. The building had no fence, and towards the north end, a public latrine had been installed. The unpleasant odour from it was overpowering, and to avoid it I would get down from my car on the side, and walk the length of the veranda to the staircase. I had to keep my office door closed all the time, because whenever there was a crosswind, (which was often) a blast of the unpleasant scent assailed my nostrils. I asked my staff how my predecessor, Roach, had managed to survive the ordeal over two years. The answer was that he had not. He never went to the office, but managed his work from the cubbyhole in his bungalow.

One morning I had gone down the side of the building as usual from my car, and was walking along the veranda, when I espied an iron cot in one of thre rooms with somebody half-reclining on it. I was surprised and entered the room, and I saw a familiar thin figure in a singlet sitting up on the bed. It was none other than Kharker with a sheepish grin on his face. I said. "Mr. Kharker, what on earth are you doing here?" Kharker seemed to have taken the vow of silence, because he spoke only with nods of his head - up and down for 'yes' and sideways for'no'. The head -clerk, a man called Bhise, (as far as I can remember) then came forward and said that Kharker was his brother-in-law, and he had allowed him to stay there for a couple of days.

"But why here?" I asked. "Why not in your flat? How can he stay here?"

The head clerk informed me that his family was in Pune, and that he himself lived in one small room somewhere.

I said,"Mr. Kharker, you were my Collector once. How can I let you stay in this horrible place? Please accept the hospitality of my house. I shall phone my wife just now. Give her half an hour, and she will have the guest room prepared for you. I'm sure she'll be happy to give you the kind of food you want."

Kharker nodded his head sideways, to say "No".

I said,"Then let me reserve a room for you in the Circuit House," and when I saw the look of alarm on his face (at the expense), I said,"Don't worry about the charges, I shall be happy to pay them." Then I got a brain wave and said,"Won't you co-operate Mr. Kharker?" He nodded his head sideways again. My head clerk, Bhise, drew me aside and whispered,"Sir, please allow him to stay here. We'll manage."

This time I nodded my head up and down and left. For the next three or four days, I would drive right up to the porch, braving the steady, relentless smell from the North, till the orderly gave me the all clear.

Many years later I learnt that some kindly DM had given a few of the empty rooms in his vast office for the SP's use, and the SP had shifted his office there. Out of curiosity I asked what had happened to the school building. They said it was given back to a High School.

"But the stink? I asked. "Didn't they mind the stink?"

I was told that they did not. They were delighted to move in, the teachers and the pupils, because they had previously occupied some hutments near a garbage dump.

Who does not know about the 'Steel Frame' that ruled India in the name of the British Raj. They were originally a small body of brilliant men from 'Oxbridge', who came into the Indian Civil Service the ICS) through a stiff competitive examination. Boys of thirty ruled the vast tracts of land that formed the districts in India. Some of them found time to write learned treatises on the customs of he 'natives', or on the history anf geography of the sub-continent . Of course the police were there in the background as a necessary adjunct, but they were always kept on a tight leash. Later, the higher officers of the police also had a competitive examination though it was not so stiff.

With the advent of Independence, these examinations continued in India for the newly christened Indian Administrative Service (IAS) and the Indian Police Service (IPS). Since the vacancies could not be made up by examination alone, emergency recruitment was resorted to for both the services. For the IAS in particular, the main source was the ex-officers from the Army, who had been themselves emergency commissioned officers. They had been selected from among schoolteachers, storekeepers and clerks. The military uniform seems to have given them some special status (not accorded to the police uniform) , though a large number of them had served in the Supply Corps, and not many had done any actual fighting.

I remember one such officer, a former school and college friend of mine called Ogale. He had become a Major in the Supply Corps, and I used to meet him every so often on the Satara Road. His job was to escort empty convoys from Delhi to Madras and back. A few of these convoys consisted of British troops. The idea seems to have een to maintain a kind of Flag March from the north of the country to the south, showing the presence of the British Army *in being* (a phrase made memorable by Auchinlek).

These persons with their limited intellectual background suddenly found themselves catapulted into positions of importance in the bureaucracy. I personally, did not mind this (it was their luck), but what I resented was their assumption of of intellectual and academic superiority over mere policemen. They seemed to think that the mantle of the ICS of old had automatically descended on them. I had at that time given a series of talks on the radio (this was before the advent of TV) on 'Shakespeare and the Common Man'. Shortly thereafter I had published my first novel. When I presented a copy to the then Home Secretary, far from giving me even a formal word of thanks, he made a sour face and threw it aside. A very senior bureaucrat told me that he had written a peculiar remark against me. He said," It seems almost as if he is jealous of your books and talks". As for my old friend, S L Ogale, his attitude towards me changed completely the day he got into the IAS.

I would now like to revert back to the first item that I had mentioned in this issue of the DM and the SP, namely the question of principle. The national police commission has mentioned a number of unnecessary restrictions placed by the different States on the position of the SP vis-a- vis the DM. It would be pointless for me to repeat them except to say that they should be removed forthwith. But on principle, the police cannot be left in autonomous control in a democracy. The district police officers cannot be sure that even they would get fair play from their superiors, particularly if such a superior has the brains and mentality of a louse. Excuse me! I know whereof I speak.

In principle, however, it is my considered view that for matters of law and order, the control of the District Magistrate will have to continue. If this is accepted, the DM will have to be allowed to offer his remarks on the work of the SP pertaining only to law and order, but giving the SP the right of reply to the Government. Further, I see no reason why the DM should initiate the SP's annual confidential record. In some States the practice already exists wherein the DIG initiates the Annual Confidential Report, while the DM offers his remarks, separately on the work of the SP pertaining to Law and Order only.

CHAPTER XI

V. OF SALUTES AND SALUTATION

This happened one morning in March of 1945 in Satara. The Congress party had withdrawn its agitation, and the Government had released all political prisoners. This was followed by elections to the Provincial Assemblies. The Congress was returned with a very big majority in Bombay and had formed the Provincial Government. The new Home and Revenue Minister, Morarji Desai, was on his first visit to Satara. He was staying in the house of the district Congress President, Sathe, and a large number of people had come to call on him, including the district officers.

I climbed up the narrow wooden staircase to a room upstairs where all the callers were assembled. The Minister was in the room next door, and we went to pay our respects, one by one. When we returned from the room, refreshments were being offered to us from a table. While I was sipping my tea, I found myself standing beside Dewan Bahadur Mutha. He had replaced his huge silk turban and long silk coat with *khaddar* and a white cap.

I used to meet D B Mutha at the club sometimes. He was normally an affable man and would regale me with accounts of how he had climbed the social ladder, step by step with the titles of Rao Saheb, Rao Bahadur and Dewan Bahadur. He had also told me once, that he was now aiming for a knighthood.

He sidled up to me with a sly grin and said," So the ASP who used to kick and shoot those Congresswalas has now to grovel before them and salute them, eh? And how does he like it?"

I said,"I have never kicked anybody in my life, Dewan Bahadur. Surely you know that? And I have never shot at any Congressmen who went to jail like goats into a cattle pound. But if any shooting was done it was to protect people like you from the bastinado. Have you forgotten how you once begged me to give you a guard during your visit to some friends at Ashta?"

Mutha had become red in the face. " The Collector ordered you," he spluttered. "I asked him".

"The Collector never spoke to me," I said. "And why did you thank me so profusely afterwards? As for groveling before the Home Minister, I have never groveled before anybody in my life, and never will, so help me."

"You have to salute him, all right," he sneered. "You are a mercenary".

"I admit I am a mercenary," I said. "All of us are, the ICS and the IPS, every single one of us. But I have never been a *bagalbacha** of the British, like some Dewan Bahadurs, I have known. And, by the way, have you decided to turn in all your titles? I should wait, if I were you, to see which way the wind blows."

This time his face had become purple. "I'll go and complain to the Home Minister right now," he spluttered.

"Why don't you, Dewan Bahadur?" I said, Let's both go to him and complain. You complain first, and I'll complain afterwards."

Mutha did not take me up on my offer. He turned his back on me and moved away.

The old Infantry Training Manual, Volume I, has defined saluting thus: 'It is a military method of greeting a superior, not a servile act. It is the outward sign of the inward spirit of discipline and respect for superiors. The general tone and feeling in a regiment is indicated much in the manner in which the men salute and the officers return the salute as by any other action.'

In short, a salute demeans neither the person who gives it, nor the person who takes it.

When I was SP of Kolhapur in 1951, B V Keskar, Deputy Minister of State for External Affairs in the Union Ministry had come on a visit

* Stooge, literally, child in the armpit.

to the city and was camping in the Circuit House. I had given him an armed police guard, and every morning when he came out, the guard would turn out and present arms. During the rest of the day, the sentry would give him the butt salute if he passed by. I noticed, however, that Keskar would deliberately turn his back on the guard, and begin talking to his visitors. I, therefore, withdrew the guard. The Collector asked me why I had removed the guard. He said that the Minister was very angry and he was going to complain to the Chief Minister. I explained why I had removed the guard. I said,"These policemen are ex-servicemen. They have fought in many wars, and are descendents of the warriors of Shivaji. They cannot tolerate this insult, nor can I. Let him complain to anybody, but do give him this piece of advice: If he ignores an honour guard during one of his visits to a foreign country, he might find a bullet in his back."

Keskar was a silly man. He had called a public meeting in a theatre in the city and explained to the assembled people India's foreign policy. After the meeting was over, he called the journalists on the dais and started talking to them about foreign policy matters, which seemed to me to be of a secret nature. He suddenly realized what he was doing, when he found them taking down notes industriously. He stopped in the middle and said," I don't want you to take down anything that I say. I wanted only to have a chitchat with you."

One of them got up and said,"Sir, you may have time for idle chitchat, we don't." They all collected their papers and trooped out, leaving the exposition of India's foreign policy the worse for wear.

There is a distinct difference between a military salute and a salutation. The Oxford Dictionary describes a salutation as a 'word or gesture of greeting, an expression of respect.' Complete prostration before a king or a superior was said (by European historians) to be a peculiarly oriental custom. In Marathi, it is called *sashtang namaskar*-touching of the 'eight' limbs on the floor with the hands extended. The ancient Greeks called it 'prosykinesis'. It was the regular custom in the Persian Court, and when Alexander returned to Babylon after his expedition to India, he tried to establish it in his court. There was such a strong reaction among his generals and Macedonian troops that he quickly withdrew the order. It was not introduced in Europe till the time of the Roman Emperor, Diocletian (AD 284-306).

It seems to me that though the practice was discontinued long ago, the mental attitude of complete prostration continues till this day - in the Government, in business, in all walks of life. It is basically a hangover from feudalism - servility towards your superiors, expectation of the same servility from your subordinates. And I beg to differ that it is only an oriental custom. In his published diaries on Churchill, Lord Moran describes a scene that took place on 30 December 1951 on RMS Queen Mary, on the voyage to America. Lord Moran had been personal physician to Winston Churchill during World War II and Lord Ismay, then General Sir Hastings Ismay, was his chief of staff (in Churchill's capacity as defence minister). They were all sitting down to dinner. Moran says that ten years had passed since they had traveled thus on the Queen Mary, yet that night they might have been again back during the War. Churchill was, as usual, continuing with his dull monologue, while opposite him sat 'Pug' Ismay. He was still listening to Churchill with his mouth open as if he did not want to miss a single syllable, uttering the same throaty gurgle, overwhelmed, as he seemed to be with those same trite 'words of wisdom'. "Pug' anyway had not changed , though everything else seemed different. Toadyism, or servility, or call it what you will, seems to be a 'global phenomenon.'

I remember one Chief Secretary, in particular, who could have been the exact double of 'Pug' Ismay, his behaviour before the chief minister was sickening. Retired DGs of police getting jobs as 'security chiefs' to some industrial house or the other are a peculiarly unblushing, unpleasant lot. In return for a fat salary, a car and a driver, they are prepared to sell their souls to the devil. Opening doors for their'bosses, getting passports for their maid-servants is all grist to their mill. After my retirement, I may have had to live in genteel poverty, driving my 1963 Fiat, but I have had this small satisfaction in my life: I have never genuflected before anybody, save my God.

Let it be noted further, that these sycophants are the ones who shout the loudest about 'political interference'. They are prepared, at all times, to go more than half-way, not only to meet the demands of their political masters, but to anticipate these demands. And the few who oppose this abject surrender are dubbed as 'tactless', 'stupid', 'foolish'.

After my return from Kashmir, a former IG of West Bengal, an IP officer, chanced to meet a friend of mine in the civil service. He told my friend that he was certain that I never became an IG, because I was found unfit. Several years before this talk, I had visited Calcutta when this gentleman was the Commissioner of Police. As a matter of courtesy, I called on him in his house. He deliberately phoned the Chief Minister, S S Ray, in my presence, and had a long talk with him in which he addressed the Chief Minister as 'Siddharta'. (Actually, Ray's intimates call him 'Manuda'). The point here is this. However close his personal relationship with the CM, was it proper for a CP to address him familiarly thus in the, presence of a stranger? And what a cheap way of impressing anybody. I would never have expected this from a fellow member of a former covenanted service. This officer was a great success with the Congress government' he was also very 'successful' with the Communist government that followed. He would have been successful with any kind of government. I have only this to say: such officers have no right to talk of 'political interference'.

Sometimes the adulation of those in power takes strange forms. Morarji Desai had just become Finance Minister and he was to go abroad (for the first time) on only a seven-day visit. A crowd of thousands had gathered at the Santa Cruz airport; I was the CP and had to make the police arrangements. The number of people who had come to garland him was legion. A stage had been put up at one end of the departure hall, and a man stood behind a microphone announcing the names of the institutions and individuals that gave the garlands. My colleague next to me said *sotto voce*"What a waste of flowers! They would have sufficed for all the temples in *Mumba Devi*!"

Morarji then went to the VIP lounge, where he rested for a while. As he was emerging to go to the tarmac, the wife of a senior ICS officer threw herself in front of him, and screamed," Bapuji, Don't go. I'll be left all alone!"

"How much alone, dammit? " my colleague said between his teeth. "Her husband is right behind her."

I said," May be, she thinks he is another *Sant Tukaram**going to *Vaikunth* on his borrowed steed."

A lady of silks and satins, now clad in homespun, pure white, must have heard me. She glared at me. I glared back at her.

* Sant Tukaram was the poet saint of Maharashtra. Legend has it that he went to *Vaikunth* (Heaven) on a *garud* (eagle) lent to him by *Indra*.

CHAPTER XI

VI. ON SOME PROBLEMS OF POLICE ORGANIZATION

I believe that I have given enough reasons to show that the present organization of the police in India will have to continue: if it is decentralized, the police force will lose its cohesiveness and solidarity. A break up of the force might, paradoxically, might lead to a break up of the unity of the Indian Federation itself. I would urge, however, that in order to reduce political interference, the selection and promotion to the posts of the rank of Inspector General and above should rest with the Union Public Service Commission, and that changes should be made in the law to ensure its acceptance.

Uniforms and a bit of marching up and down do not make for discipline and efficiency. These depend on training, of which the main constituents are Drill and PT. The two can be at variance, as the following incidents that took place in Pune in January 1934 will show. Nigel Hamilton has narrated it in his definitive biography of Montgomery, titled 'Monty'. It took place early in the morning on the racecourse at Pune. The GOC of the Southern Command was, General Sir George Jeffreys, who had written volume I of the Infantry Training Manual (on drill) when he was on the directing staff at Camberley. Jeffreys was obsessed with ceremonial drill. We too had to learn these movements at the Police Training School, and I remember how Staines, the drill instructor would take great pleasure in getting the ASP commanding the company, 'boxed in.' At the end of the Manual, there were any number of diagrams showing the complicated movements of which Frederick the Great would have approved. But they seemed a trifle unnecessary either for the Army or the Police. During my outdoor drill examination, the DIG who had forgotten everything about the drill, asked Staines, the HDI, to make me perform some complicated movements. He was unable to catch me out on any of them; eventually, when I wrote the police drill manual, I added some more at the back.

Lt. Col. B L Montgomery had arrived in Poona from Cairo on Christmas Eve. His battalion, the Royal Warwickshires, was in the line at the Racecourse that day. Monty was a fanatic on training, and was, probably, one of the greatest peacetime trainers the British Army has had, but he did not set much store by ceremonial drill. The first thing Jeffreys told Monty, even before he could present arms, was that he was seven paces too far to the left of the centre of his unit. All he had to do was to turn his horse seven paces to the right; instead, he ordered the whole battalion to side step the number of paces to the left.

Lieutenant Holdich[1] perhaps does not remember the reason for the rehearsal: I do, because I was there. It was a rehearsal of a parade at which the then Viceroy, Lord Willingdon, was to attend. My father was the Additional District Magistrate of Poona and he had been asked to liaise with the Army. I had then entered college. It was a holiday, and he took me in the car to see the parade at close quarters. I do not, of course, pretend to know the details of this incident, but what I did notice was that the most of the mounted officers could hardly walk after the parade was over. Could a bit of cantering be such an arduous job, I wondered? In the coming years at the PTS, and in Kolhapur, I did not find it so. Perhaps, those Army officers lacked practice. Perhaps they had a premonition that the horses were not going to be of much use in the next war, even though Jeffreys would have galloped ahead of his division, digging in his spurs, flashing his sword, as he egged his men to face the German armour. This image is not fanciful. It is what exactly happened to the Polish Cavalry when they faced Guderian's tanks.

Spit and polish may not be all that important, but surely, they are a must in an army or police *training institution*. Many years ago, when I was IG, I was invited to give a lecture at the Indian Police Academy in Hyderabad. At the Academy they were all very kind and hospitable, but I was taken aback when I was received at the station by a young assistant commandant, in smart uniform, but with large chunks of hair sprouting from the sides and back of his cap. His head of extra hair and his stance led me to believe that he was doing his best to imitate Shashi Kapoor in turn doing his best to imitate a police inspector. My discomfort was further increased when, during the entire course of my lecture, I had to see the Deputy Commandant (an officer of DIG's rank), sitting on the front seat, wearing his whistle lanyard with the back to the front.

1. Who has mentioned this incident (in Nigel Hamilton's biography of Monty).

In the Police Training School during mess nights, we used to play the game of finding fault with each other's uniform.That night the IPA invited me for dinner in their magnificent Mess dining room with its wall-to-wall carpeting in dark yellow. Somehow, I did not like playing this game with my hosts.

Once when I was camping in Baroda for some Anti-Corruption Bureau case, the IG, Kamte, asked me to see him. He was on the parade ground watching the SRPF group. After I had finished my discussions, he said broodingly," We follow these Army manuals in drill, but what we need is a police drill manual with modifications for the police."

I said,"The two acknowledged experts could be asked to write it."

He said,"Nanavatty and Nagarwala? I have asked them in turn. They each kept the project with themselves for a number of years without writing a line. Listen, why don't you write it?"

I replied,"Sir, I am no expert."

He said,"I have seen you drill and I have inspected your parade. You are the only officer who has been able to answer my numerous questions on drill. I know you can do it. How about it?'

I replied that I would consider it an honour to be asked to write the Manual and that too while I was in the Anti Corruption Bureau, which had nothing to do with drill.

Kamte asked,"How long would it take you?

I replied,"A year and a half at the most."

He said,"Done!"

He called his steno and dictated the order for me to write the manual.

I submitted the drill manual within the stipulated time. Kamte had retired, and Chudasama was the IG. This was the first Manual of Police Drill printed in India.

I have already dwelt on the subject of inspections of police units.

The object of these inspections is not merely to find fault with the working of the police station, district or whatever. The main object is to give the poor constable or subordinate officer a chance to meet his *mabaap*, the IG, DG or whoever, and to present his difficulties, to ventilate his grievances. I am persuaded that these interviews are one of the best methods of keeping a force contented, of preventing a mutinous atmosphere.

If a census is taken in any State, it will be found that in spite of the great increase in the number of top police posts, many units have not been inspected for years, some not at all. One such unit was the police wireless headquarters in Pune. I was probably the first IG who has ever inspected it.

An important item during inspection was to interview all the officers of and above the rank of PSI. While I was doing this, an officer named Chaitanya (of Inspector's rank) came before me. He seemed very knowledgeable about his work, but he had a protruding stomach. The DIG had written that he was too fat, and therefore unable to climb up the mountains where the booster stations had to be fixed. As all bright young people know, the VHF (Very High Frequency) waves can operate only on the line of sight.

I read out to the officer the remark that the DIG had made about him. He heard it, and said quietly," Sir, the DIG is sitting in the next room. Could you kindly call him and ask him which mountain I had failed to climb?"

I called the DIG. He named a certain mountain on the road to Ahmednagar. Chaitanya said," Sir, I have not climbed the mountain just once. I have installed the pylon there with the help of my subordinates. I have had to stay at the top for a month as per the DIG's order to ensure its working. We all shared one raoti (small police tent) which would often collapse because of high winds. And I had to go down and climb twice a week to thje village to buy our victuals. It's the DIG who has never gone up the hill, or even seen the pylon after it was working."

I asked the DIG whether this was true. The DIG had to admit that it was. I wrote on the man's ACR that I had questioned the officer and the DIG and found that the latter's remark was unjustified and should be treated as cancelled. I wrote also that in spite of this officer's protuberance he was fit for promotion.

I asked Chaitanya," As a matter of curiosity - why can't you get rid of this - ah- - roundness in front.?"

He said," Sir, I have tried everything. The doctor says that it is due to some hormonal deficiency. I promise to try harder." Somehow, he reminded me of Pisal.

CHAPTER XI

VII. DEPLOYMENT OF FORCES

Of all the problems that I have faced during my 37 years in the police, I have found the problem of deployment the most vital and the most tricky. In warfare, success or failure can depend on the proper deployment of the forces available. Emerson says this of Napoleon:

'The art of war was the game in which he exerted his arithmetic. It consisted, according to him, in having always more forces than the enemy, on the point where the enemy is attacked, or where he attacks.'

The principle, whether in peace or in war with any large body of uniformed men is the same: to make the best use of the manpower available. Do the police do this always, or most of the time? On the TV pictures of the recent flood havoc caused by the super-cyclone in Orissa, I was not able to espy any super sops or even any ordinary cops at work. The Army, Navy and Air Force were there, but what about the police? When hungry mobs attacked food convoys, there was not a single policeman in sight to try and maintain order. And if a woman reporter from a private TV channel could visit remote flood-affected areas, why could not the State police? As is usual, when everything was over, we saw a plethora of police 'brass hats' strutting about like pouter pigeons and behaving as if they were always there.

We now learn that the policemen are suffering from stress. Some are definitely suffering from stress, but many are not, especially in the higher ranks.

Every morning, when the Superintendent of Police or the Commissioner begins his office work, the statement (by whatever name it is called) of deployment is put up before him. It shows him how the police strength of the HQ armed and unarmed is deployed for the day. Armed guards are required for various duties: for treasuries, for escorts of prisoners in the courts, or out of station to other courts, and for multifarious other duties. In addition, a special armed reserve is kept for emergency duties.

It is the duty of a police officer in charge of a unit to scrutinize the statement. I wonder how many do so! It is only when an officer does this regularly, that he has a right to speak of shortage of man power.

A sentry has always to be alert. We have daily reports in the newspapers of this or thar guard being overpowered by extremists in remote places, or in places not so remote, like Srinagar city itself. The duty of the sentry is one of the most arduous that an army or police *jawan* has to face; for this reason it was provided long ago that an armed guard should be relieved every twenty four hours, and given twenty four hours' rest. This never happens in practice. The powers that be think there is an unlimited reservoir of force in every headquarters. The Intelligence Bureau puts all sorts of people in the 'Z' category.[1] The State government is expected to provide SPG guards for them - how they do it is their own business. They, in turn, ask the local police officer to provide guards for this or that purpose. No extra strength is sanctioned. When the guard is continued for some time, the State government assumes that the local police have enough strength and do not need any more. And even when it is sanctioned, it takes at least six to eight months before the recruits are ready for duty.

I have already emphasized how the reserve police are being deployed continuously without any rest or respite. For this, the police department is itself responsible. Why can the DG not send one of his stepneys to the city or district concerned and verify whether the requisitioned force is really necessary?

It is all a question of proper deployment.

During riots and civil calamities, or some special occasions, proper deployment assumes great importance. In Mumbai, for years, a clerk named Deodhar was in charge of deployment, especially during riots. He used to be asked for help even after his retirement.

The subject of deployment is not in the curriculum of the police training institutions in India. It should be. But this is not a subject that can only be learned from lectures. Every probationer in the IPS should be given two months training as an understudy in large cities, so that he,

1. Security Guards have now become a Status Symbol, the number of men in the Guard, more so.

or she, realizes its importance. By some quirk of fate some officers and other ranks have continuous and arduous duties all the time, while others get all the cushy jobs. I saw this in the Army when I was in Jammu and Kashmir. I used to visit the most remote places where BSF and CRP guards were posted. These were under the operational control of the Army. I came to know many of the army officers well. I found they had spent most of their service on the frontiers.

"Why could you not get in turn cantonment postings in the rear?" I asked them. They said they had no godfather to help them get such postings. It will be clear why some policemen suffer from stress, others not at all.

The question of supervision is allied to the question of proper deployment. In the State of Maharashtra, at one time there used to be one IG. Now there are five officers of DG's rank - four additional DGs and over one dozen IGs. This is the situation in every State in India. The police departments are now beginning to resemble the old Nepalese Army that had as many 'commanding generals' as privates. No doubt the strength of the police forces has increased a great deal, but even so, has the efficiency of the force increased in equal measure with the increase in higher posts? I doubt it very much.

In an uniformed body of men, some people talk of the 'chain of command'. How can there be any worthwhile chain of command with so many commanders?

Serious riots, great calamities and the like are times for the exercise of extreme vigilance and care. Some senior officer must be designated with the full responsibility and the power to deal with them. He need not be the DG himself. If it is so desired let the DG, who is generally a political appointee, by all means orbit round the Chief Minister (or other VIP), administering to him the soothing syrup of flattery, or indulging in chit chat (with adequate pauses for chortling and gurgling, a la Pug Ismay,) provided that the control of the operation to another officer is clearly demarcated.

In the old days, the British used to make us prepare detailed plans for different emergencies like communal riots, train disasters, epidemics, et al. The Range DIGs would examine them very thoroughly during their inspections, and ensure that they were brought up to date. And we were made to take rehearsals, so that if the time actually came for their use, every man did his duty without let or hindrance. Why could this system not be revived? In the training that I gave for mob control to the SRPF in Pune, I had provided detailed maps of the areas in most of the important cities in Maharashtra, where such riots had occurred and were likely to occur. Such maps should be ready in every important city and district. Thorough planning and preparation are advisable in many aspects of police work for riots, earthquakes, train disasters, floods, they are a must.

As for the kind of officer chosen to face the music, the most important quality that he should have is the quality of leadership.

And this brings me to the ingredients of effective police leadership at all times, but particularly, during emergencies - leadership of an uniformed, disciplined body of men waiting to be led by somebody with courage, confidence and control.

CHAPTER XI

VIII. ABLE AND DISCIPLINED LEADERSHIP

In a recent book on Leadership, written by a former DG of Police, four different types of leadership have been portrayed, each of which has to be applied when the leader is confronted with a different situation. This officer has spent a large part of his service in the Intelligence Bureau and perhaps, he found their application useful in the Bureau. However, through the years, the Intelligence Bureau has been known to have built mountains (of paperwork) on molehills of information. Even its most ardent admirers will have to concede that its record of success has been less than spectacular.

I do not claim to be conversant with the business world, but I doubt, whether, in practice, different styles of leadership can be worn or discarded like shirts, on different occasions. In dealing with a uniformed, disciplined body of men, I would prefer the definition of leadership given in the old drill manual:

Leadership depends on simple and straightforward human qualities. A leader, above all, must have the confidence of his men. He will gain their confidence by commanding their respect - respect for his determined and ready acceptance of responsibility; for the clearness and simplicity of his orders and the firm manner in which he insists that they shall be carried out; for his thorough knowledge of his profession; for his sense of justice; for his commonsense; for his keenness, energy and habit of forethought; for his sense of humour; for his indifference to personal danger and the readiness with which he shares his men's hardships; and for the obvious pride which he takes in his command. Most important saf all, by his own example, he must inculcate in his men the qualities of self-control, self-respect, patriotism, loyalty, pride of being an Indian, and a high sense of honour.

When senior police officers go on parade, they do not actually participate in close-order drill. But even if they do, drill and PT are not enough to develop the *espirit de corps* that must exist at all times between a Leader and his men. The Oxford dictionary defines this spirit as 'the loyalty and devotion uniting the members of a group.'

How does one develop it then? In all armies and police forces, socializing with other ranks is discouraged and rightly so. The only known way to foster the spirit is by playing games with the men: hockey, football or volleyball. The British police had made the playing of games by young officers, and even those not so young, compulsory. I continued this practice regularly when I was Superintendent of Police, and sometimes, when I was a DIG. As a SP, I made it a point to distribute volleyball sets to every police station. There was always a little space near a police station. During Inspections, I would play every evening with the policemen and the local youths (whom I encouraged to join in the game).

When you play games with your men, a strange thing seems to happen. They cease to be faceless pawns on a chessboard: they become individuals, each with his own distinct personality. You find that a camaraderie has developed between you and your men which will carry over when yon lead them in riot control, or when facing floods or earthquakes - that is, if you do happen lead your men.

How is it with our young IPS officers - men and women- today? Do senior police officers maintain that they have no time? If they reduce the time they spend in futile conferences with their subordinates or endless discussion with local politicians and other bigwigs, they will find the time,

Politicians and the news media are fond of saying that this or that situation has been put 'on a war footing', though they may have the vaguest notion of what a war entails. The recent affair at Kargil has in a sense brought war on our doorsteps through the TV and other news media. But it is a fact of life that, since long, people have a great admiration for the uniform (the army, not the police), even though the officers wearing it are often not genuine warriors, but only the'also rans', yclept the Supply Corps.

But in the discussion on Leadership, let us, by all means, consider the subject of war and battles. War is the ultimate crucible that tests men's souls, as well as their bodies. It has been shown again and again, that the great captains of history have had all the qualities that make for leadership - qualities that would have come to the surface in any field of human endeavour. I am, therefore, giving the example of one such man, Heinz Guderian, who revolutionized the art of war during the Second World War. His breakthrough on the River Meuse and dash to the Channel coast behind the British army, which was deep inside Belgium, is, by any standards, one of the most decisive campaigns of history.

Someone might object,' Why a German? Why a follower of Hitler?' If Hitler had taken Guderian's advice on warfare, the result of the war would have been different. We are all glad that he did not, because the consequences of that monster ruling the world are too dreadful to contemplate.

But after the lapse of so many years, historians and western analysts of the science of war are no longer inclined to lay the blame for Hitler's aggression on the German Generals, and least of all on Guderian, who was not even arraigned before the Nuremberg tribunal. He was not a Nazi, he was a professional soldier par excellence, and he was a patriot. Moreover, he was one of the few generals who could dare speak his mind fearlessly to Hitler. Hitler would not let him pursue his advance on Moscow when it could have been successful. Later, in winter, he wanted Guderian to advance and encircle Moscow from the rear. He refused to carry out the order and Hitler sacked him.

Guderian's is the unique example in military history of a man who studied and mastered the new doctrine of mobility, was responsible for the production of the tank and the training of the men who would use it, and led the forces he had created in the blitzkrieg that took place in Poland, France and Russia.

Guderian's autobiography, 'Panzer Leader', is one of my favourite books - I never tire of reading it. It can never pall on me nor grow stale. In many ways, it reminds me of Caesar's commentaries on his campaigns in Gaul. It has the same immediacy of unfolding action, the same logical analysis of events, the same candour. I am, therefore, giving below an outline of some of the outstanding events in his life, because they constitute in my opinion, the sine qua non of Leadership in peacetime pursuits, as much as in war.

From 1901 to 1903 Guderian studied in the principal cadet school in Berlin, where he learnt, among other things, the rigid features of

Prussian discipline. But one outstanding feature of the training was that the candidates were allowed to express their opinions freely to the point of execution of an order. However brusque Morarji might have been, he allowed an officer to express his views freely up to a degree. Y B Chavan continued this practice. However, I found out the difference when I went North. You were treated all right so long as you agreed with whatever your superior officers, or your political masters, said. But if you openly disagreed with them, woe betide you!

Guderian was frank (and perhaps hot-tempered by nature). This brought him into open conflict with the General Staff, who began to regard him as an obstacle and a mere technician.

In 1908 Guderian became a *leutnant* in the 10th Hanoverian Jaegar battalion (the light infantry). While there, he got an opportunity to specialize in either artillery or signaling. He chose the latter because they taught the brand new wireless telegraphy, and he, instinctively, saw a great future in it.

During World War II, he was in one of the signaling units. In those days wireless sets were cumbersome affairs carried on horseback. Instead of the central control contacting the units and laying down a signaling discipline, the reverse was done, with the resultant jamming of the channels. Guderian realized that if proper use had been made of wireless even during World War I, the results of the ensuing battles in his sector could have been very different.

The importance of wireless telegraphy and telephony does not seem to have been realized by the Allies even in World War II. The headquarters of the French Commander-in-Chief, General Maurice Gamelin, was situated at the Chateau de Vincennes, close to the 'pleasures of Paris', and at least 200 miles from the Front. Gamelin had no radio communications 'for security reasons'. The telephone system was so bad that despatch riders had to be sent with the messages on motor cycles. They took 48 hours to reach the Front!

Montgomery has said in his Memoirs that Eisenhower's headquarters was on the *western slopes* of Cherbourg, 400 miles away from Normandy. He has described how, after the Battle of Normandy, he sent a very important wireless signal to Eisenhower giving his views on the manner n which further advances into Germany should be conducted. He received Eisenhower's reply in two parts, the second coming first after a lapse of two days. The telephone system also did not seem to work.

When riots are tearing a city to pieces, senior police officers love to exercise remote control: as remote as possible.Long after my retirement, I was once called to the Police Training College at Nasik, to give a lecture to the cadets. On going down to the Hall for the lecture, I learnt that a big riot was taking place in the city. The Vice-Principal informed me that the Principal A S Inamdar, could not come because the DG had given him urgent duties in connection with the riots. The Principal had the rank of a DIG, and as the Range DIG had gone on tour to some district, the Principal was asked to take his place till the former's return. "It's quite in order, it's the right thing to do," I told the Vice-Principal. After my lecture the officers told me that the Principal had invited me for a cup of tea in his office. I saw him sitting there in mufti (Plain clothes). I was surprised and said so. I said I thought he had gone to the city on bandobast. He replied that the DG had asked him to keep a watching brief. So the Principal was neither here (in the lecture) or there (facing the riot).

I was staying in the Police Mess, in one of the rooms on the first floor. Having nothing to do in the evening, I stood on the balcony and heard the comings and goings below. The IG (Law and Order) arrived in the evening. He ought to have gone straight to the control room in the city before even arriving at the Mess. I heard any number of telephone calls and bustle and activity. But the IG waited till the Range DIG had returned from his tour and reported to him. My enquiries revealed that it was only then, one and a half hours after his arrival, that the IG (Law and Order) went to the city with the DIG.

A very serious riot had occurred in Ahmedabad much earlier when I was the DIG Anti Corruption. The Home Secretary had told me that the then IG had not visited Ahmedabad in two months, till at last the Government had to write to him. I said," Is that all the Government did to him? Why should he have visited the scene of the riot at all?"

But coming back to Guderian, during World War I, he had to march through Ardennes forest with his cumbersome wireless pack. He kept his eyes and ears open, noting everything. Later in 1918, he had to attend some staff course in Sedan, which was then under the Germans. There too, he observed everything. These two factors were to be of the greatest importance in the battle for the West in World War II.

Do we observe everything that we see as a matter of course? In the words of Kipling, do we, live the unforgiving minute with sixty seconds worth of distance run?

In battle, the most obvious way to defeat an opponent is to attack him face to.face. This can be costly, and if he is stronger than you, fatal. All military experts seem to agree that for a frontal attack, you must have a superiority of three to one. The preferred method is to catch him unawares, and attack him in the rear, his weakest point. In classical times, battles were fought to achieve this aim in two ways. The first one was called the Cannae maneuver, by means of two pincers, one at either flank. It was so named after the battle of Cannae fought by Hannibal against the Roman consul, Varro. The second was called the Arbela (Guagamala) maneuver named after the battle of Arbela fought by Alexander the Great against King Darius III. It lay in finding a weak spot on the front and driving a wedge through it. Cavalry were used for charges in these highly mobile battles.

With the advent of breach-loading guns, such maneuvers were no longer possible, and armies went underground into trenches, which sometimes extended the length of the whole frontier. During World War I, hundreds and thousands of troops were thrown into attacks following heavy artillery barrages, as at Ypres and Passchendaele, with very little success.

Towards the end of the War, the stalemate was broken by the British invention of the Tank. It was only partially successful at Cambrai, as it was used only to spearhead the attack by the Infantry.

After the War, P C S Hobbart and J F C Fuller developed the theory of the independent use of armour. Fuller and B H Liddell Hart wrote books on the subject of deep strategic penetration of the armoured forces, racing ahead of the main infantry mass, and operating independently of it. The orthodox military establishment was against it, and efforts of these pioneers were stopped by the then CGS who answered to the name of Sir Archibald Montgomery-Masingberd. The orthodox army leaders felt that the rapidly advancing tanks would expose their vulnerable flanks to enemy artillery and get destroyed in the process.

In the meantime, in January 1829, Guderian found himself back to his original 10th Jaegar battalion at Goslar as a company commander. He was greatly disappointed: he wanted to join the newly created

Inspectorate of Transport with its emphasis on mechanization. Perhaps some jealous person deliberately maneuvered his posting. But as Kenneth Macksey says, Guderian did not allow this setback to cloud his vision and faith in the future. For two years he plunged himself into training an infantry company. This was the basic level of the army, where one could teach and learn the fundamentals of war. At that time Germany lay prone its victors. What could the lone commander of a company do to change things? But Guderian behaved as if he was preparing his company for war. He drove his men hard, but drove himself harder. He did not ask his men to take any risks, which he himself was not willing to take. And he established that close bond between the common soldier and himself and that was to last throughout his career.

I do not know how many police officers call their men together before some important *bandabast*, and explain to them what they have to do, and why they have to do it. This surely is also is an essential duty on the part of a leader.

In early 1922, Guderian was posted to the Inspectorate of Transport, and it was there that he found his metier. By the Treaty of Versailles, Germany was forbidden to use or manufacture Tanks, bur nothing forbade the study of the new weapon. He put in he next ten years in intense study and practice. The British were the pioneers in the history of Tank warfare, but their literature on the subject was available only in English. Guderian was not averse to learning from the enemy anything that was useful and necessary. He specially learnt English and French, translated the works of J F C Fuller and others into German, and circulated copies of his books (at his own cost) to his subordinates. He, himself, wrote and published 'Achtung Panzer', which became a classic.

Further, he conducted exercises on tank dummies of canvas placed on motor cycles. School children used to poke the dummies with their pencils and shriek with laughter, till one day they found real steel inside the canvas. On 17th April 1922, the Germans had signed the Treaty of Rapallo with the Soviets, which included military collaboration. Guderian had parts of tanks secretly built by firms, such as Daimler-Benz, and assembled them on the banks of the River Kama inside Russia where he conducted secret exercises.

Above all, Guderian developed radiotelephony to be used for communication on the tanks. Radio control was central to the new doctrine of strategic penetration of tanks concentrated and rapidly deployed behind the enemy front. Hobart had carried out his demonstration on the Salisbury Plain in 1927 without radio control. Guderian showed what a difference it made with the developed radio technology.

Since 1954 the VHF (very high frequency) telephony has played an increasingly important part in police communications. In 1956, after I had completed the Refresher Course at the Police College in the UK, I had visited several police forces in the UK to see their working. At the Police College, the cognoscenti had asked me not to miss seeing the Lancashire Police, which they considered the most progressive among all the police forces in the UK. At Preston, the Chief Constable, Sir Eric St.Johnston, and his officers gave me a warm welcome. They showed me their VHF system, and explained that they were the pioneers in installing it. They claimed that in 1934, the RAF had taken it from them, studied it and installed it in their planes. VHF played a vital part in the Battle of Britain: it was because of VHF that the limited number of fighter planes with the RAF were able to be at the right place at the right time to confront the Luftwaffe.

And Guderian preached the doctrine of the commander of a tank unit '*leading from the front*'. My opinion is that this applies to the police as much as to the Army. My practice has been all throughout my career to lead from the front, whether I was facing a riotous mob or an obstreperous superior. And unless police officers of all ranks do this, the police forces of India, despite their vast numbers and multiple high-ranking leaders, will remain third-rate, no better than the ones I used to observe in the old princely States of the Deccan.

In his doctrine of the rapid exploitation of the breakthrough, Guderian was not worried about his exposed flanks: he argued that speed should make up for any such vulnerability. The object of the advance was to destroy the nerve centre of the enemy, to drive inside so fast that there would be no enemy troops or armour to oppose them. General Von Kleist has stated how, when he was half way to the sea, a member of his staff brought an intercept from the French radio that the commander of the 6th Army on the Meuse had been sacked and General Geraud appointed in his place. As he was reading it, the door opened and a handsome French General was ushered in. He introduced himself with the words,"I am General Geraud."

After his victory in Poland, Hitler decided to attack on the Western front. The Germans were going to put into operation a modified version of the Schlieffen Plan, but the details fell into the hands of the enemy, as an officer, carrying a copy of the Plan. overflew into Belgian territory in his plane (owing to bad weather). Most people have read how, at almost the eleventh hour, Hitler adopted General Manstein's new plan to attack with armour through the forests of the Ardennes (an Arbela maneuver), Manstein asked Guderian for his opinion. Guderian was not only the acknowledged tank expert, but he had been there, as I have mentioned earlier. He assured Manstein that it could be done.

The Allies had 4200 tanks, as compared with 2800 with the Germans. Not only did they have more tanks, but also the French tanks, like the Somua S35 and the heavy Char B, were far superior. They carried twice the armour of the Pz IV's and their 47- mm gun was better than the 37- mm gun on the German tanks. At the *schwerpunkt* (the decisive point) the breakthrough in Sedan, Guderian had only 1260 tanks. But the Allied tanks had no radiotelephones, and they were distributed all over the front in 'penny packets', to assist the infantry.

Guderian led the brilliant attack with his three panzer divisions. The point worthy of note is that it was nor a slap-dash affair. Earlier he had conducted 'Map Exercises' explaining to each commander his precise role. He could not conduct any field exercises because of lack of fuel and ammunition.

I have deliberately given the example of Guderian and Warfare, not to parade my knowledge, but because I have found him to be the best example of many of the views I have propounded in this book. And if Guderian was willing to learn from foreigners (and his enemies) why can't we learn from him? As to the Art of Warfare, I do feel that many of the lessons the large police forces (which obtain in India) can learn from it are more apposite than those from businessmen, economists and calculators.

Written orders were given to each unit commander. When a change of some plan became necessary at the River Meuse, Guderian remembered that an alternative Map Exercise existed, took out the orders and reissued new ones. The fact that never ceased to astonish me is that this entirely new kind of invasion was no slap-dash affair. It was thoroughly rehearsed, even with written orders given to the most forward sub-unit commanders. The lesson that the police should learn is that rehearsals (map exercises or sand models, call them what you will) are a must for the police if they want to face unexpected events with efficiency and despatch.

Guderian always acted on the assumption that whatever we do, should be a surprise to the enemy and not to ourselves. And he firmly believed in the principle of maintaining balance at all times and under all circumstances. We have seen in our discussion of unarmed combat, that when an attacker lunges forward to hit, he is momentarily off balance. He must regain his balance as quickly as possible in order to defend himself. And this may involve a step back. As Lenin would have said, 'One step backward, two steps forward'. Guderian was always mentally prepared (as Macksey put it), to back pedal if necessary. Mentally, he was as flexible to retrograde panzer movements, as progressive ones (as he showed in Russia).

A country must, of course fight for every inch of its frontier, but if an all- out war is on, it might become necessary to take up strong defensive positions in the rear, if only to launch a strong counter-offensive. When I was SP of Kolhapur in 1951-52, General S P P Thorat had come to Kolhapur, his native place. He needed help in some small matter, and I offered to call on him, but he insisted on calling on me. I was flattered. I found him to be a charming man, apart from being very knowledgeable. After his retirement, I used to meet him off and on in Kolhapur, during my visits there. When he learnt that I was interested in military science and history, and was reading about the debacle in NEFA, he took out a map of India (in his house), made me sit on the rug beside him, and explained to me the situation in detail. He said that when he was GOC, Eastern Command, he had suggested to the Prime Minister in a forty-page minute, that instead of trying to defend the indefensible border on the MacMahon line, we should maintain a strong defensive line along the Bomdila-Walong axis, if China attacked us. From that position, we could launch a fitting reposte. However, the Prime Minister threw out his note on the ground that the Chinese would never attack India.

In giving these details, it is not my intention to glorify warfare, or suggest that the police or anybody else should adopt an aggressive attitude as a matter of policy. Far from it! I have only suggested that since war is the acid test of men's souls as well as of their bodies, it is incumbent on us to learn some valuable lessons from a study of these aspects of warfare, that willy-nilly affect all of us. And if such a study makes us alert, what is wrong with it? Again, contrary to the common belief, it is not he professional soldiers who want war, or who always direct how it should be conducted. During World War II, on the German side it was not the General Staff that wanted war. In every instance it was Hitler who took the aggressive stance. And it was he who took the fatal decision not to allow the German armies to even withdraw one step, heading to the disaster at Stalingrad and to his ultimate defeat. Churchill was a magnificent war leader, but his interference in the conduct of campaigns was disastrous. Alanbrooke has written that he was a menace in military matters. Even in World War I , we knew of his responsibility for the catastrophe at the Dardanelles.

If then, politicians and the general public know a little about the implications of warfare, it can do them and the country only some good - that is my belief.

With our northwestern neighbours always poised for mischief, and always ready to find a chink in our armour, sending terrorists and making use of our own indigenous variety, killing innocent women and children every day, it behoves us to be alert and wary every moment of our waking lives- at least it is obligatory on those whose duty it is to ensure peace in our time.

The other day I had occasion to pay a brief visit to Satara. On an impulse, I climbed up the old Ajinkya Fort in the afternoon. As I stood on one of the ramparts watching the westering sun, I saw that the scene below me had changed greatly from what it used to be when I had stood there as an ASP some fifty years ago.

Where there had been a forest of trees around me, I saw only bare rock; where green fields dotted the valley on the right of me, now four-storied buildings and factories raised their ugly heads; where bullock carts and an occasional car would wend their way lazily along the road snaking below, I saw long lines of trucks and cars traveling at great speed from both sides.

But in the distance, against the sun, which was now sinking below the hills, I saw the same blue haze around them. So they must have looked to the sentinel who stood on the self-same spot three centuries ago, doing his best to perform his limited and lonely role - that of keeping eternal vigil.

EPILOGUE

Thomas Wolfe has said about the book of Ecclesiastes:

'Ecclesiastes is the greatest single piece of writing I have known, and the wisdom explicit in it is the most lasting and profound.'

In continuation of the line of thought given earlier, the Preacher has further said.

"I returned and saw under the sun that the race is not to the swift, nor the battle to the strong, neither yet bread to the wise, nor riches to the men of understanding, nor favour to the men of skill; but time and chance happeneth to them all....

(Therefore) whatever thy hand findeth to do, do it with all thy might, for there is no work, nor service, nor knowledge, nor wisdom in the grave whither thou goest."

ABBREVIATIONS

ASP	Assistant Superintendent of Police
CP	Commissioner of Police
CID	Criminal Investigation Department
CM	Chief Minister
DM	District Magistrate
DIG	Deputy Inspector General (of Police)
DG	Director General (of Police)
DCP	Deputy Commissioner of Police (same rank as SP)
SP	Superintendent of Police
DSP	Deputy Superintendent of Police
HS	Home Secretary
HM	Home Minister
PM	Prime Minister
PI	Police Inspector
PSI	Police Sub-Inspector
SI	Sub-Inspector (same as PSI)
IG	Inspector General of Police
FIR	First Information Report
DO	Demi official letter
VIP	Very Important Person

GLOSSARY

Bagalbachcha	Stooge. Literally, child in the armpit
Bandobast	Arrangement - whether for the police or the recep tion of a VIP
Bandh or Hartal	Forcibly stoppage of all work
Chavadi	Village office
Chokra	boy
Ghat	Mountain, road through a mountain
Gotha	Stable
Lathi khela	Stick play
Ma baap	Parents
Maalran, Raan	Open undulating ground
Maidan	Open field
Masala	Mixture, ingredients
Ota	Stone or cemented platform
Paan	Betel leaf
Prasad	Food offering to the go
Reader	Sub Inspector. An officer who helped ASP's and DSP's (specially the Europeans) in translating the case papers, which were in the vernacular, into English.
Sant Tukaram	Poet, Saint of Maharashtra, who, according to leg end went up to Vaikunt (heaven) on the Garud (Eagle) lent to him by God Indra
Satyanarayan	Pooja for blessings received or expected
Shikar	Hunt
Sowkar	Merchant
Tamancha	country made pistol
Tapal	Letters/ files received by post or messenger
Vetal	(pronounced Vay-Taal). The demon, according to the legend, who would suddenly jump from a tree on King Vikramaditya's back and offer him gratuitous advice.
Wada	Large old-fashioned house
	Zoppadpatti, Jhuggi Slum, shanty

Index